3/02
.25x
5/02   MIT

954   13 4/98   4/98
MIT   MAY   1996

Michell, George
    The royal palaces of
India.   35"/15

9/97 ⑨

D0889858

720
MIC

THE ROYAL PALACES OF INDIA

The Royal Palaces of India

GEORGE MICHELL

PHOTOGRAPHS BY ANTONIO MARTINELLI

With 250 illustrations, 206 in color

THAMES AND HUDSON

1. Architecture-Islamic
2. Princes-India
3. Palaces
4. Kings and rulers.
5. Mosques

Any copy of this book issued by the publisher as a paperback is sold subject to the condition that it shall not by way of trade or otherwise be lent, resold, hired out or otherwise circulated without the publisher's prior consent in any form of binding or cover other than that in which it is published and without a similar condition including these words being imposed on a subsequent purchaser.

Text © 1994 George Michell
Photographs by Antonio Martinelli © 1994 Antonio Martinelli
Design © 1994 Thames and Hudson Ltd, London

First published in the United States of America in 1994 by
Thames and Hudson Inc., 500 Fifth Avenue,
New York, New York 10110

Library of Congress Catalog Card Number 93-60425

All Rights Reserved. No part of this publication may be reproduced or transmitted in any form or by any means, electronic or mechanical, including photocopy, recording or any other information storage and retrieval system, without prior permission in writing from the publisher.

ISBN 0-500-34127-3

Printed and bound in Singapore

CONTENTS

FRANKLIN TOWNSHIP PUBLIC LIBRARY
485 DEMOTT LANE
SOMERSET, NJ 08873

Inspired partly by British topographical views, the Indian artist of this 19th-century watercolour presents an idealized perspective of the Lal Qila, or Red Fort, headquarters of the Mughals at Delhi. The palace is divided into a number of open spaces arranged according to a strict hierarchy. The symmetrical organization is typical of Mughal royal architecture, which places particular emphasis on formal planning. In a sequence along the central axis, from the most public zone in the background to the private apartments in the foreground, the elements are: the Lahore Darwaza (the principal gateway leading from the city), the

Chhattar Chowk (a covered market), an open court with soldiers and animals, then the Naqqar Khana, or Drum Pavilion, then an open space in front of the Diwan-i Amm, or Hall of Public Audience, filled with courtiers, and finally the Rang Mahal, a sumptuous private apartment with its own enclosed garden. The part-octagonal tower, the Musamman Burj, has been moved by the artist onto the central axis. Among the figures going about their everyday business is the emperor himself: he is making his way across the terrace to the right of the Rang Mahal, accompanied by attendants bearing fly-whisks and standard.

Preface and acknowledgments

Following the example of Marco Polo at the end of the 13th century, a multitude of European traders, entrepreneurs and adventurers made the hazardous voyage to India by land or sea. Some hoped to negotiate profitable commercial agreements directly with the maharajas, while others sought employment as mercenaries, physicians and artists. The reports and chronicles that they published on their return gave Europeans their first glimpse of India. This, however, was hardly an accurate picture. India was portrayed as a land populated with monsters, magicians and maharajas; its rulers were immeasurably powerful potentates enthroned in vast citadels surrounded by every conceivable luxury.

As Asia came increasingly within the orbit of European influence in the 16th and 17th centuries, knowledge about India grew, including its courtly life and royal architecture. Exquisite objects from the courts at Delhi, Ahmadabad and Golconda reached Venice, Amsterdam, Paris and London, accompanied by detailed and often rhapsodic descriptions of the maharajas and their palaces. Simultaneously, Europeans in India found increasing opportunities to make contact with local rulers. Miniature paintings produced in Indian royal workshops at this time record the presence of Portuguese missionaries and British envoys at the public assemblies of the maharajas. In the course of the 18th and 19th centuries, as the British achieved control over most of the subcontinent by subjugating local rulers, Indian courts became the topic of intense scrutiny. Despatches by British soldiers and administrators contain a wealth of descriptive detail about maharajas and palace routines. But Indian courts were not totally accessible to the gaze of these foreign observers, and royal architecture continued to be mysterious and alluring. Indeed, this 'exotic' appeal of Indian palaces has proved to be long-lasting; it has survived the colonial experience and is still a force today, perhaps in compensation for the fact that royalty itself no longer has any role to play in modern India.

Despite the undisputed attractions of India's royal architecture, from both the historical and artistic points of view, scholarly research has only on occasion focused on the palaces themselves. Indian courtly buildings have received little academic attention compared with temple sculpture and miniature painting. Some royal complexes, such as Agra and Fatehpur Sikri in Northern India and Bidar and Vijayanagara in the Deccan plateau, have been the subject of specialized monographs, and certain phases of Indian royal architecture, notably the work of the Mughals and that of the Rajputs, have received special attention. Yet the monumental survey of Indian palaces by Oscar Reuther, published in Berlin in 1925 and long out of print, remains the only attempt at a comprehensive survey of the subject.

The present work, like Reuther's, aims at the discovery of Indian royal architecture within a broad historical perspective. The first part of the volume introduces the different aspects of Indian courtly life, drawing on a wide variety of literary sources, both indigenous and European. The second part examines the major historical and regional traditions of royal architecture, spanning some seven hundred years and encompassing almost all parts of the subcontinent contained within the boundaries of present-day India. Here, the most interesting and best preserved palaces are selected and separately described.

The opening chapter of Part I explores theories of kingship at both Hindu and Muslim courts, concentrating on the divine basis of regal power as expressed in historical and mythological texts. Then comes an examination of the measures taken to provide Indian courts with essential security: royal residences were conceived as fortified citadels, complete with massive walls and defensive gateways, as well as armouries, barracks and stables. The next chapter is devoted to the state business within the palace that was conducted at formal receptions known as *darbars*. These took place in spacious audience halls reserved for the ruler and his most important ministers and nobles; in front were the courtyards where additional visitors and troops could assemble. We then look at the place of religion: temples and mosques within royal precincts were for the exclusive used of kings, courtiers and female members of the royal family; they were also settings for courtly celebrations at festival times. A further chapter reviews the arrangements for accommodating the monarch himself, his entourage and the women of his household in strongly guarded private apartments, terraces and interior courtyards, and the provision of gardens and pleasure pavilions. The last chapter in this section considers service arrangements, including markets, workshops, kitchens and bathhouses, and sophisticated hydraulic systems to guarantee regular supplies of water.

Part II looks in detail at the buildings themselves, after examining the evidence for royal architecture prior to the arrival of the Muslims at the end of the 12th century. The earliest courtly buildings that still stand in India are those erected by the Muslim conquerors at their newly established capital of Delhi in the 13th and 14th centuries; their successors were the Muslim rulers of the 15th and 16th centuries. Many of the citadels of these monarchs survive, as at Mandu in Central India and at Daulatabad, Bidar and Bijapur in the Deccan. The imperial complexes of the Mughals, whose empire incorporated a large proportion of the subcontinent in the 16th and 17th centuries, are the largest and most finely appointed in Northern India, as can be seen in the fortified palaces at Fatehpur Sikri, Agra and Delhi. The Hindu Rajput rulers of Central and Western India were contemporaries of both the early Muslim rulers and the Mughals. Their citadels are comparatively well preserved, partly because many Rajput families survived into the modern era to look after them, as at Gwalior, Udaipur, Amber and Jodhpur. Southern India between the 14th and 17th centuries was largely under the control of Vijayanagara, the Hindu empire that fragmented into a number of smaller realms by the beginning of the 17th century. The palaces that still stand at the Vijayanagara capital, at Chandragiri, Padmanabhapuram and elsewhere display distinctive shapes that are unique to the region. During the era of British domination, from the middle of the 18th century until 1947, when the country achieved independence, Indian rulers were gradually relegated to the status of 'princes'. Even so, they built lavishly in a variety of European-derived styles, as can be seen in their ambitious residences, such as those at Hyderabad, Mysore, Kapurthala and Jodhpur. The volume concludes with an epilogue reviewing the present condition of palaces in India and the varied purposes which they now serve.

The trips to India and travel around the country which were essential for the realization of this book were only possible with the generous assistance of B. K. Goswami, Director General of Tourism, and M. K. Lakhampal, Director of Hospitality, Ministry of Tourism, Government of India, New Delhi; M. K. Kanjilal, Director, Government of India Tourist Offices, Paris; and F. Kapadia, Publicity and P.R. Manager, Air India, London.

In India, both author and photographer were graciously welcomed by H. H. Sharji Arvind Singh Mewar, Maharana of Udaipur. The photographer also received generous hospitality from H. H. Jamsheb, Maharaja of Jamnagar; H. H. Brigadier Sukhjit Singh MVC, Maharaja of Kapurthala; H. H. M. K. Brijraj Singh, Maharajkumar of Kota; Maharani Vijay Kunwerba Saheb, Princess Purna and Garech Browne, and Princess Uma of Morvi; H. H. Iqbal Mohamed Khan, Nawab of Palampur; and H. H. Ranjitsingh, Maharaja of Wankaner. Mrs Qumar Ahmad and R. Anand of Bombay provided logistical support.

Others who facilitated access to the palaces were: Junius and Shashi Sen, and D. K. Bhattacharjee, Director of Information Cultural Activity, Agartala; H. H. Sawai Taj Singh, Maharaja of Alwar; H. H. Ranjit Singh Gaekwad, Maharaja of Baroda; Shariq Nawab, Welcome Group Hotel, Baroda, and J. K. D. Badal, Railway Staff College, Baroda; H. H. Ranjit Singh, Maharaja of Bundi, and Balbhadra Singh, Bundi; H. H. Maharaj Kumar Pranayachand Mahtab, Rani Saheb Nandini Devi Mahtab, and Kumari Usha Devi Rathore of Burdwan; H. H. Madhavrao Sindia, Maharaja of Gwalior, D. S. Sharma, Administrator, Gwalior, and Lal Bahadur Singh, Curator, Central Archaeological Museum, Gwalior; S. H. Javeri, Chairman of H. H. Nizam's private estate, and S. Hashim Ali, and V. V. Krishna Sastry, Director, and Mohammed Abdul Qaiyum, Department of Archaeology and Museums, Government of Andhra Pradesh, Hyderabad; Govind Singh P. Rathod Limdi, Indore; P. L. Chakravarty, Director, Archaeology and Monuments, Government of Rajasthan, Jaipur, Ajit Cheema, Rambagh Palace Hotel, Jaipur; H. H. Shri Gaj Singhji II, Maharaja of Jodhpur; Board and Principal of Sainik School, Kapurthala; H. H. Wadiyar, Maharaja of Mysore, D. V. Devraj, Director, and T. S. Gangadhar, Department of Archaeology and Museums, Government of Karnataka, Mysore, and Anil Malik, ITDC Lalitha Mahal Hotel, Mysore; M. C. Joshi, Director General, and C. Margabandhu, Director of Monuments, Archaeological Survey of India, New Delhi, and Deepak Brara, Indian Airlines, New Delhi; H. H. Maharani Dibbu Kumari Debi and H. H. Maharaja Kirit Bahadur Bikram, Tripura; T. Sathyamurthi, Director, Department of Archaeology, Government of Kerala, Trivandrum; Sally Worsley, Udaipur; and Balasubramanyam, State Archaeology Camp, Government of Karnataka, Vijayanagara.

Useful information, advice and editorial suggestions were given by Naheed Ahmad, Charles Allen, Norman Braden, John Burton-Page, John Copland, Simon Digby, Rathim Gohari, Momin Latif, Rosie Llewellyn-Jones, Christopher London, Eleanor Schwartz, Snehal Shah, Robert Skelton, Andrew Topsfield and Mark Zebrowski. Among the personal friends who proved ideal travelling companions on our tours in India were Corinne Bunzl, Anna Dallapiccola, John M. Fritz, Dalu Jones, Sebastian Loew, Shyam Mitra, Attilio Petruccioli, Alexandre and Helen Philon, Jayaram Poduval, Filippo Salviati, Christopher Tadgell and S. N. Tripathi. Giles De La Mare and Massimo Giacometti must be especially thanked for their personal interest which first inspired the author and photographer. They have also benefited from the expert editorial and design skills of Thames and Hudson.

George Michell *London*
Antonio Martinelli *Paris*

The private apartments in the Mughal palace at Agra were sumptuously decorated. The interior chamber of the Musamman Burj (see plate 57) has marble panels with carved flowers surrounded by inlays of semi-precious stones. The niches above were for storage and for lamps.

I · Courtly Life and Architecture

Divine power of kings

INDIAN HISTORY presents a bewildering succession of royal dynasties. Some ruled over vast empires, like the Mauryas in the east in the 4th and 3rd centuries BC, the Cholas in the south in the 10th and 11th centuries AD, and the Mughals in the north in the 16th and 17th centuries. Others governed only limited territories and were constantly engaged in battles for control of the different regions, thereby effectively restraining one another. Whether great or small, Indian monarchs never hesitated to style themselves as *maharajas*, or 'great kings', in the belief that their powers were cosmic rather than worldly. They were 'great kings' in terms of royal rituals and ceremonies, if not always in authority and influence.

Indian empires, kingdoms and smaller states encompassed striking variations in topography and climate, from the desert wastes of Rajasthan in the west to the tropical coastal belt of Kerala in the south, and from the fertile plains of the Ganges (Ganga) and Jumna (Yamuna) rivers in the central and eastern zones to the rocky expanses of the Deccan plateau at the heart of the peninsula. Each region had its own distinctive language and culture which influenced royal life, even for those rulers who arrived as conquerors from outside the subcontinent. From the end of the 12th century onwards, for example, waves of warriors from Afghanistan and Central Asia swept over the northern plains to become India's first Muslim rulers, or sultans. Despite the foreign background of these invaders, within two or three generations they had successfully fused with local society and culture to become genuinely Indian monarchs.

Diversity of religious beliefs was an intrinsic feature of Indian royal life: the Mauryas were converted Buddhists, the Cholas patronized Hindu cults, and the Mughals were staunch upholders of Islam. Hinduism, the indigenous religion of India, was always a loose amalgam of multiple cults: different gods and goddesses simultaneously received worship within palace temples and shrines. On being introduced into the subcontinent, Islam came into contact with Hindu practices and, in time, came to be infused with indigenous practices.

Theories of kingship

Despite this plurality of regional and religious traditions, Indian royal life was in all essential respects governed by a body of common beliefs. These were based on theories of kingship set down in particular works of literature. Princes, whether Buddhist, Hindu or Muslim, were educated by teachers, holy men and poets familiar with epic stories, myths and legends; expert courtiers used treatises to instruct young rulers in law, statecraft and war. Among the best-known of these works are the *Ramayana* and *Mahabharata*, two mythological epics dating back some two thousand years, and the *Arthashastra*, a textbook on statecraft, of similar antiquity. According to the theories embedded in these works, sovereigns were exalted above ordinary mortals because of the magical power of royal ceremonies. The consecration was the most important of these since it infused the king with cosmic force. In the central rite, the *abhisheka*, or ceremonial bath, the sovereign was identified with a divinity such as Indra, king of the gods. The ruler's magical power was annually renewed and strengthened through the ceremonies that commemorated this consecration. Another important ceremony was the horse-sacrifice, the *ashvamedha*. On this occasion, one of the horses from the royal stables was set free to roam throughout the kingdom for a period of one year. Lesser chiefs were compelled to pay homage to this animal, since it represented the might of the ruler. At the end of the year the horse was ritually killed.

If few Indian monarchs actually performed the horse sacrifice, at least in recent centuries, the coronation ceremony remained a significant moment since it proclaimed the king's divine inheritance. Implying as it did a renewal of the beneficial powers of the universe, such as the passage of the seasons and success of the monsoon rains, the ceremony affirmed the ruler's power as the ultimate source of strength for the kingdom and its inhabitants. Nor was this rite restricted to the Hindu courts. For the Mughals, the anniversary of the emperor's coronation was a spectacular occasion during which the regal figure sat in state on his throne, displaying weapons, standards and other insignia, and receiving gifts from his nobles. Military parades and fireworks took place in the streets of the city, while the monarch's name was proclaimed in the Friday sermons recited in the chief mosques.

✳ ✳ ✳

Cosmic symbols and diagrams

All aspects of royal life in India were infused with cosmic symbols. In the *abhisheka* ceremony the ruler was bathed in water brought in golden vessels from the different oceans as well as from the Ganges and the other holy rivers of the country; he was showered with gold and precious gems. Such rites demonstrated regal command over the elements of water and earth. Resplendent with heavenly motifs such as the globe of the sun, the king's throne was sumptuously ornamented with gold, silver, rubies and diamonds, the treasures of the earth. Sun motifs appeared on the walls and ceilings of palaces, suggesting the beneficial influence of the heavens. Some ruling families, such as the 16th-century Sisodias of Mewar in Western India, even adopted a gleaming sun with radiating spokes as a dynastic emblem. The royal throne was adorned with animals and birds representing the forces of nature. Lions and mythical beasts were particularly popular; so too were peacocks, such as those that adorned the jewelled canopy over the throne of Shah Jahan, the 17th-century Mughal emperor, in his palace at Delhi. Gem-encrusted *chhatris*, or umbrellas, were held over the king as he sat on his throne. The chhatri was a common device indicating celestial power; its multiple tiers indicated the ascending realms of the heavens.

That the king's throne was intended as an *axis mundi*, or cosmic pillar, is demonstrated in the late 16th century at Fatehpur Sikri where a massive monolithic column inside one of the royal pavilions supports a seat used by the Mughal emperor Akbar for private acts of meditation. The importance of free-standing columns dates back to the early Indian kings who used them as emblems of power and as appropriate vehicles for regal proclamations. The principal documents remaining from the 3rd-century BC reign of Ashoka, the most famous emperor of the Maurya dynasty, are the edicts incised on the polished shafts of lofty sandstone pillars. The importance of royal

p. 35

103, 104

1

45

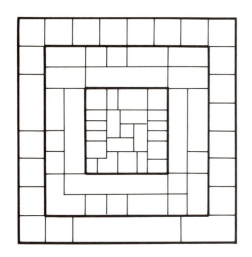

pillars for later Muslim sultans is illustrated in the mid-14th-century citadel of Firuzabad at Delhi, where a ceremonial pyramid was constructed for one of Ashoka's columns. Brought with considerable difficulty from a site almost 200 kilometres (125 miles) away, it was set up by the ruler Firuz Shah as a mark of his own imperial might.

26

Indian kings also viewed themselves as *chakravartins*, universal emperors wielding the *chakra*, or wheel, an emblem that represented the universe. This meant that all of their daily activities, including public ceremonies, had to be in harmony with the heavens, and that the correct time had to be fixed for each event. Astrologers were hired to regulate actions within the palace and, by extension, within the entire kingdom. Astronomy was closely related to astrology, and some kings were themselves astronomers, intent upon observing the movements of the planets on which the fortunes of their realm depended. Sawai Jai Singh, founder of Jaipur in the first half of the 18th century, was the most famous of India's regal astronomers. He stated that 'the very important affairs concerning both religion and administration of the empire depend upon the calculation of the places of the stars.' The observatory that he erected inside his palace testifies to the dependency of royal life upon the heavens.

127

Another expression of the king's divine powers was the belief that both the capital and the palace were microcosmic reconstructions of the universe. According to Indian manuals on architecture and town planning, the *Vastushastras*, some of which are more than fifteen hundred years old, the royal city had to function as a mandala, or sacred diagram. Mandalas were governed by precise dimensions and proportions, repeating in miniature form the mathematical scheme of the cosmos. They were mostly laid out in concentric squares to create complicated geometrical patterns. Zones within the mandala represented the different levels of the universe and were identified with particular divinities; the most powerful point was the central square, the seat of the most prominent deity. One of the favourite mandalas advocated in these texts had nine squares, and exactly such a cosmological scheme appears to have been followed by Sawai Jai Singh. Jaipur's plan is regulated by a nine-square design which situates the royal palace in the middle. The mathematical quality of the scheme is emphasized by broad streets of regular width, standardized building plots, and axial alignments of gateways and temples. Few surviving palaces appear to conform to the strict geometry of mandala layouts, perhaps because their original designs were substantially extended over the centuries, with unforeseen renovations and additions. An exception is the residence of Bir Singh Deo, the early 17th-century ruler of one of the Rajput states of Central India. The plan of the Govind Mahal at Datia is dictated by a twenty-five-square mandala, the central block being occupied by a tower containing the king's audience hall and private sleeping chamber.

p. 156

Mandala plans were advocated for palace layouts, as in that from the Mayamata *(above), one of India's ancient* Vastushastras. *The royal city of Jaipur was laid out on a nine-square mandala plan (below), the palace being situated in the central square.*

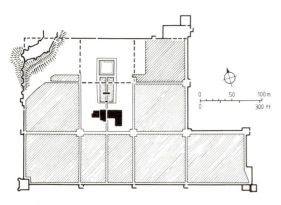

Prowess, law and charity

Indian textbooks invariably describe the royal figure as the pivot of the universe, the embodiment of cosmic force and influence. On a more human level, the heavenly powers of the monarch are expressed in terms of his relationship with his subjects. The ideal ruler was the head of the state, directly responsible for the happiness and wellbeing of his subjects, whom he had to protect from all evil and aggression; for this reason he was the head of the army and first in battle. Many of India's Hindu kings belonged to the Kshatriya or warrior caste, while Muslim rulers were often military leaders. The manuals encourage sovereigns to extend their sphere of influence by notions of 'righteous conduct' that justify their ambitions to extend their territories. In India, as elsewhere, war was the sport of kings, a pastime both potentially profitable and dangerous, consuming considerable resources and funds. Most textbooks on statecraft include lengthy digressions on the art of war, providing details on how to organize armies, military camps, battle strategies, sieges, and an effective network of espionage.

War was intended not merely for the gain of power and territory but also for sheer glory. As soon as the monarch was crowned, he was encouraged to attack his neighbours in order to establish supremacy at the outset. But rulers were warned that such attacks had to be undertaken in the spirit of honour and chivalry, in order to uphold the elaborate codes of conduct prescribed in the textbooks. According to the rules of battle, the rightful fruits of victory were homage and annexation, not slaughter, imprisonment and humiliation. In reality, of course, few kings obeyed these codes in all their rigour, even though many claimed to have attained the ideals of military honour.

That the king's military prowess was dependent upon the powers of the gods is demonstrated in the rites of certain religious festivals. The most important of these at the Hindu courts was Dasara, also known as Mahanavami, a festival developed by the *142, 143* Vijayanagara kings of Southern India in the 15th and 16th centuries into a major religious–political occasion. It thereafter became an integral part of royal ceremonial life throughout the country. At Dasara, the ruler assumed the role of the hero-god Rama by propitiating the goddess Durga. (According to the *Ramayana* legend, Rama sought Durga's aid before setting out to do battle against Ravana, the multi-headed demon who had abducted Rama's wife, Sita.) The monarch offered his weapons and regalia to the goddess for her to infuse with cosmic power; he displayed his elephants, horses and troops in military formations, and received oaths of allegiance and tributes from lesser chiefs and governors. Mock battles, wrestling matches, fireworks and performances of music and dance accompanied these ceremonies. Dasara also signified the beginning of a new season since it occurred annually in September–October, at the end of the monsoon. Only after the rains were over, and with his weapons newly sanctified, could the ruler embark upon warring campaigns.

The symbolic connection between the king's power and seasonal renewal was also enacted in various other holidays, such as the spring festival of Holi, observed by both Hindu and Muslim monarchs. Another splendid occasion at the Muslim courts was Nawruz, the celebration of New Year. Like Dasara, Nawruz was marked by parades of animals and soldiers, offerings of gifts by nobles and governors to the sultan, and spectacular entertainments.

Other than safeguarding the kingdom by the force of his army, the ideal ruler was responsible for maintaining life, property and custom, and for preserving the traditional divisions of class and caste. He protected the family system by punishing adultery and ensuring fair inheritance; he cared for widows and orphans by making them his wards; and he shielded the poor from extortion and oppression. Naturally, such measures required extensive legal power, and for this reason Indian theories of kingship stressed the role of the sovereign as the supreme law giver. Among the principal royal duties was the settling of disputes between subjects and the enforcement of criminal codes. While judges and superintendents of law courts were employed throughout the kingdom, the sovereign remained the highest court of appeal, the 'fountain of justice', as some kings were known. Scales of justice were on occasion used as regal emblems, for instance in the Khass Mahal of Shah Jahan's palace at Delhi, where a semi-circular panel depicting scales is surrounded by planetary motifs.

62

As the source of the kingdom's prosperity, the monarch had to embark upon programmes of public works to safeguard the welfare of his people. Most large-scale irrigation projects, in fact, could only be carried out with funds from the royal treasury. Granaries and other food stores were built with royal aid as a safeguard against famine; great reservoirs to trap rainwater were financed by the imperial treasuries. Kings generally undertook to help charitable institutions and made regular gifts to the poor and deserving. Royal benefaction extended to institutions of higher learning, such as Hindu *mathas* (monasteries) or Muslim *madrasas* (religious colleges), where the daily prayers of teachers and students were interspersed with praises of their royal benefactors.

147

Religious support

Hindu dynasties had protective gods and goddesses who normally received worship inside the palace, and who were honoured in magnificent public festivals. Kings paid for the upkeep of shrines and for the performance of suitable rites of devotion. Emblems of gods and goddesses were frequently incorporated into royal thrones, banners, coins and seals, and rulers acknowledged the support of these deities in their official decrees and edicts. A verse engraved on the rim of the umbrella sheltering the throne of the Wodeyar rulers of Mysore in Southern India proclaims the king as 'Lord of the Earth, resplendent with the blessings of the goddess Chamundeshvari'.

3, 13

But monarchs were not merely enhanced by divinities: they were ritually empowered by gods and goddesses. The usual way for Hindu sovereigns to benefit from divine sponsorship was to patronize a particular cult, especially that of a goddess who was worshipped as a mighty force. A temple honouring the powers of Chamundeshvari was erected by the Wodeyars on the hill that rises above their capital at Mysore. Rulers not only built shrines for such forceful deities: they also participated directly in religious rites, thereby earning the right to adopt the names, weapons and characteristic emblems of their protective gods or goddesses. In was in this way that royal personalities came to be imbued with a celestial dimension.

In practice, there was little difference in the rites of respect to gods and kings. Divinities were daily awakened, bathed, dressed, fed, entertained with recitations and performances and, eventually, carried in palanquins to the sleeping chambers of their consorts. They were usually dressed as royal figures, bedecked with crowns and jewels, and attended by guardians bearing regal tokens such as clubs and *chauris*, or fly-whisks. The climactic moments in temple ceremonies occurred when priests or other devotees had direct visual contact with the deity. Known as *darshana*, this visual contact symbolized the meeting of the human and divine worlds, the breakthrough from the terrestrial to the celestial plane. There was a corresponding emphasis on darshana as the central royal rite, in which rulers formally displayed themselves as gods, in full view of their subjects, in order to receive homage.

Kings were generally dependent on specialists versed in religious rituals and prayers to sustain links with the celestial plane. Brahmin priests were indispensable because of their knowledge of the *Vedas*, the oldest and most sacred texts in India. Monarchs relied on them to sanction royal power by providing religious support, a crucial factor for dynasties that had risen from the lower ranks of society. Indian rulers traditionally belonged to non-Brahmin castes and were therefore dependent on priests to address prayers to gods on their behalf. Sultans also derived their authority from a divine source, but this tended to be expressed in legal terms. The authority appointed and accepted by all Muslims was no less than the Caliph of Baghdad, chief interpreter of the teachings of the Prophet Muhammad, and world-judge. While Indian sultans claimed to represent the Caliph, in practice they behaved as supreme leaders and exponents of Islamic law, defending the territories of Islam and waging holy wars. The names of the sultan were regularly recited in the weekly sermons held in the *jami* – congregational, or Friday – mosques of the capital where the royal figure worshipped with the faithful on all important occasions.

Sultans often required the backing of *imams*, or influential religious leaders, as well as *shaykhs*, or saintly figures associated with the different Muslim holy orders. Akbar was attracted to those of the Chishti order, situating his palace city of Fatehpur Sikri next to the refuge of Shaykh Salim Chishti. Sultans paid repeated visits to shaykhs to seek advice on specific spiritual and secular matters, and to gain authority in the eyes of their subjects. They also went on pilgrimages to the tombs of holy men so as to benefit from the spiritual powers which were believed to be manifested there. Not unlike Hindu monarchs who worshipped at temples of their protective divinities, Muslim rulers prayed at the tombs of their protective saints.

In time, Muslim rulers came to be influenced by indigenous theories of kingship, and behaved in many respects like their Hindu counterparts. In the daily formalities of p. 35 audiences that took place in the court of Shah Jahan, for example, the emperor prominently showed himself so that his subjects could benefit from an auspicious glimpse of the imperial figure. This rite precisely resembled that of darshana as practised by Hindu kings. The honour and respect paid to sultans at their public audiences virtually amounted to worship, since it imitated in all essential respects the rites of devotion that took place within a temple. Muslim rulers generally adopted Indian titles, like 'maharaja', as well as traditional insignia of royalty, such as turbans and fly-whisks.

Forces of nature

As the pivot of the realm and governor of all peoples, the Indian monarch represented all of his subjects. The women of the royal household embodied the unity of the kingdom since they were chosen from all classes of society, including even the lower castes, within the king's domain. Some were brought from territories outside the direct control of the king, their presence within the palace symbolizing the ruler's ambition to be universal emperor.

But palace women also played a symbolic role, being essential accompaniments to the royal figure in his cosmic personality. Since kings were directly involved with the welfare of the realm, the coming of the rains, the fertility of the soil and the success of the crops, they were imbued with an innate ability to command the forces of nature. Indian theories of kingship linked rejuvenation in nature with royal sexuality, broadly interpreting this quality as an earthly expression of universal power. Indian epics, dramas and poems describe the king as divine lover: women succumb instantly to his merest glance or lightest touch. Animated royal seduction scenes occur throughout Indian literature, and are a constant theme in sculptures and paintings. Sexual manuals, of which the *Kamasutra* is today the best-known, instructed princes in a wide range of sensual pleasures. The king was attended by wives, concubines and female servants, together with female musicians, singers and dancers, especially on formal occasions and during festivals.

143

3

97

Parades of elephants, horses and other animals were further expressions of the king's cosmic potency. Elephants and horses, perhaps more than any other animals in India, were an essential component of royal life, indicating the king's prowess in the martial arts; but they were also visible embodiments of the king's universal power since they represented the forces of nature. Only kings were permitted to own elephants, and only kings could import horses and other exotic beasts. Animals from different parts of the country were displayed in courtly menageries; some specimens came from distant lands, such as giraffes and zebras from Africa. Royal command over the animal kingdom was ritually expressed in the daily inspections of elephants and horses. Animal fights were a popular part of courtly routines, with ferocious elephants, tigers and bears being specially trained for this purpose. Shah Jahan spent an hour every morning overlooking the parade ground below his palace at Agra where animal battles took place. The princes and governors of the realm were warned not to hold their own animal fights because this activity was reserved exclusively for the monarch.

2, 3

63

While Indian kings may have been empowered by the possession of animals, they were at the same time considered tamers of wild beasts in their symbolic role as world-masters. Since royal power was greater than animal power, it was presumed that even the most savage beast could be subdued by the ruler. The story of Solomon vanquishing the wild beasts of the forest was translated into Persian and was familiar to the Mughal emperors. An Italian inlaid plaque representing Orpheus, who, Solomon-like, calmed the animals of the forest with his music, is installed above Shah Jahan's throne at Delhi. Seated beneath this image, Shah Jahan could imagine himself master of the universe, tamer of the forces of nature which he had harnessed for his own benefit and that of his empire.

The ruler's throne was the symbolic centre of the universe. The throne and regalia of Raja Sawai Sursingh, who ruled the state of Marwar from 1595 to 1619, stand now in the 18th-century hall of public audience, the Moti Mahal, in his citadel at Jodhpur [1]. His cosmic importance is signalled by the ceremonial umbrella, representing the heavens. On the wall behind, around a mirror-encrusted recess, are further symbols of the ruler's power: another umbrella, an honorific long-handled fan, two shields and a sword – for the ruler is head of the army and protector of his state – and finally, at the top, a European-style coat of arms.

2

The ruler's world, encircled by protective walls, appears in a mural painting in the Rajput palace at Kota [3], above an ornamental band of figures. On the right is the large parade ground, filled with people; a caged feline signals the king's power. This area is separated from the palace proper by a wall pierced by a Hathi Pol, or gate adorned with elephants. Beyond lie residences, gardens, and a shrine where the raja is seen in devotion.

Another painting at Kota [2], a miniature in the Badah Mahal, shows the ruler seated in an elevated balcony or jharoka supported on tiger and elephant brackets. He is depicted as dominant over people and animals: only kings could own elephants, and a caged tiger increases his prestige.

3

5

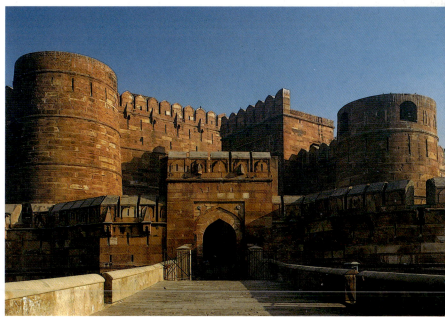

6

Gates controlled admission to and movement within royal citadels. Frequently they formed part of multiple defence systems. The palace-fort of the sultans at Bidar [4] was reached from the town first through the Sharza Darwaza, with decorative lions, then through the Gumbad Darwaza, or Domed Gate. At Agra [6], the 16th-century Mughal ruler Akbar built the high red sandstone walls of the Lal Qila and protected the innermost gate, the Akbari Darwaza [see 50], by another gate at right angles to the walls, the Amar Singh Darwaza; his great-grandson, Aurangzeb, added an outer, lower ring of walls with a further gate a century later.

Within Akbar's city of Fatehpur Sikri, a triple-arched ceremonial gate (*tripolia*) and one with a single arch framed the market square, or Chahar Suq [5]; the bazaar ranges have disappeared.

4

Hunting and owning large numbers of animals were the privilege of kings. Trophies may have been hung on the spikes of the 16th-century Hiran Minar, a lookout tower at Fatehpur Sikri [7]; the Shikar Burj or Hunting Tower at Bundi in Rajasthan [10] was built specifically for sport. The stables for the Mughal emperor's horses at Fatehpur [9] surrounded three sides of a square. Even more grandiose are the elephant stables at Vijayanagara in Southern India [8], which also date from the 16th century; a rooftop structure in the middle probably served for drummers and musicians.

7

8

9

10

Defence and security

Few Indian kings were free of anxiety about political and personal security. If it was not the threat of war, siege and invasion from aggressive neighbours, it was the constant fear of intrigue that might lead to assassination and military coup. The kingdom of Delhi, for example, experienced almost continuous instability from its inception at the end of the 12th century until the coming of the Mughals in the early 16th century. This was due to a succession of military takeovers that repeatedly substituted one ruling dynasty for another. Nor was the situation in the Hindu kingdoms substantially different: three lines of rulers were ousted by military coups at Vijayanagara in the 15th and 16th centuries. Even the most powerful and long-lived of India's royal families experienced internal dynastic conflict. Only after defeating his brother and imprisoning his father was Aurangzeb, the last of the great Mughal emperors, able to seize the Delhi throne in 1658.

✻ ✻ ✻

Strongholds and citadels

Under such circumstances it is hardly any wonder that Indian palaces were intended primarily as fortresses, providing the ruler, his family and immediate entourage with essential protection. That defence requirements were paramount is evidenced by the substantial construction of surrounding walls and gateways. The earliest expression of regal power in India is the royal citadel occupying a strategically advantageous position at the top of a rocky ridge or on an island in a lake or river. Many royal residences were simply forts where rulers could retreat in safety to plot their military campaigns. The inner areas of such strongholds had to be amply provided with residences, reception halls, water and, of course, quarters for troops and animals. Mandu, the 15th-century capital of the Malwa sultans in Central India, occupies a remote and forested site completely surrounded by steep escarpments. Royal, military and religious buildings within the walls benefit from the natural defences. Similarly, the fortified Rajput sites at Chittor and Gwalior, both of which date back to the 11th and 12th centuries, if not earlier, stand on rocky ridges that rise dramatically from the plains of Western and Central India. Walls ring the ridges at both sites, shielding the palaces and temples that dot the level tops; access roads are protected by lines of gateways. Other Rajput citadels, such as Jodhpur, begun in the 15th century, are simply fortified palaces clinging to rocky summits. The 17th-century complex at Amber occupies a steep hillside overlooking the strategic pass that gave entry to the kingdom of the Kacchwaha maharajas from the Mughal territories to the north.

Rocky outcrops in the Deccan offered ideal opportunities for local sultans to construct fortified citadels. Originally a Hindu stronghold, Daulatabad was taken and extended by the Delhi sultans at the end of the 13th century. It is dominated by a great conical hill whose sides were trimmed to create vertical escarpments; the summit is accessible only after crossing a drawbridge that spans the moat and passing through labyrinthine rock-cut passages. The site is further shielded by outer walls that surround

27–31

90

136

118

32

At Bundi in Rajasthan [*11*] the hilltop citadel of Taragarh offered the first stronghold when the state was founded in the 14th century. Later the main palace was built below, with its own massive walls.

the hill in concentric rings. Vijayanagara is another citadel with concentric fortifications. Its irregular plan was determined by the natural defences of the granite wilderness in which the city was set. Walls run along rocky ridges and across the shortest possible distances in between to create an irregularly shaped ellipse. Gingee, one of the most *146* important strongholds of the nayakas of Southern India in the 16th and 17th centuries, has walls running between high granite hills to enclose a vast triangular fort.

Other palaces served as royal capitals and were, accordingly, inseparable from the cities which they governed. The locations of such palaces were often determined by trade routes. This was particularly true of the Mughal capitals of Agra and Delhi, both of which were situated on the great trunk road that followed the west bank of the Jumna. But ease of access for peoples and goods was potentially dangerous, since it could also facilitate the approach of the enemy. In consequence, capital cities were strengthened with walls and gateways that replicated those of the palace itself. In many urban strongholds, royal complexes abutted the external walls of the city so that the monarch's own residence could benefit from the protection of the outer ramparts. In 14th-century Tughluqabad, the third capital of the Delhi sultans, the palace zone was located against the south wall of the city. Ahmad Shah's palace at Ahmadabad, founded in 1411 as the seat of the Gujarat sultans, rose above the east bank of the Sabarmati River. Its fortifications defined a quadrilateral royal zone, the Bhadra citadel (now demolished), with the city extending outwards on three sides. Shahjahanabad, the new Mughal capital at Delhi, followed a similar pattern. The rectangular palace citadel looks eastwards across the Jumna, the urban quarters fanning westwards in part-circular formation.

Yet other variations in this relationship between royal and urban zones were developed in the 15th- and 16th-century cities of the Deccan. Bijapur's citadel is situated in the middle of the city, surrounded on all sides by streets and houses. The royal zone is circular in shape, as is the town itself, the fortifications creating two concentric rings with connecting gateways. Bidar presents an alternative scheme, with a *4* royal fort and city of approximately equal size being situated adjacent to each other to create double circles of defences.

Walls

The protective walls of Indian palaces, as well as those of cities, had to be impregnable and for this reason were usually the most solidly built parts of the royal complex. Both before and after the introduction of gunpowder, in the early 16th century, fortifications were many metres thick and faced with stone both inside and out. Little wonder, then, that such citadel walls have survived, even if the palaces that they once shielded have long ago fallen into ruin. The walls of Tughluqabad are immensely solid, with sloping sides and projecting cylindrical towers, in dramatic contrast to the disintegrated structures within. The fortifications at Gulbarga, the Bahmani capital of the Deccan in the 14th century, are built entirely of tightly fitting basalt blocks. Overgrown rubble piles inside are the only visible indications of any courtly buildings. The ramparts of the Agra and Delhi citadels are magnificent constructions of finely finished red sandstone slabs; accordingly, each came to be known as Lal Qila, or Red Fort. They have regularly spaced, hooded slit-holes for guns, and crowning battlements; sloping-sided round towers project outwards at the corners and flank the gateways.

The forts of the Rajputs had walls built up against the steeply cut sides of natural prominences, reinforced with prominent bastions and battlements. Fortifications were ringed with moats which filled up only during the monsoon rains; where citadels were built on river banks, water was more readily available. Some walls were built directly on bedrock and the encircling moats had therefore to be partly excavated, as at Bidar, where there are triple rock-cut trenches.

Gateways

Access to Indian palaces was constantly patrolled by guards, and the king was personally informed about the arrival of all visitors, animals and goods; gateways were the principal control points and for this reason were usually prominent constructions. The simplest gateways consisted of passages through the walls, closed off by great wooden doors with iron hinges and spikes. Entrance chambers sometimes had lofty vaults and domes that rose higher than the flanking walls. Sequences of gateways with changes of direction, particularly in the Mughal and Deccan forts, created complex patterns of entry intended to prevent unwanted visitors from riding straight through. Where palaces were sited on hilltops, as at Chittor and Gwalior, gateways were aligned along ascending paved roads and ramps. Changes of direction could also be incorporated into individual gates with multiple interior chambers and sequences of inner doors. Small rooms flanking interior passageways accommodated guards who collected tolls and recorded the passage of people and goods.

Gateways leading into the palace precinct itself were invariably positioned between wall bastions guarding the approaches, which were sometimes treated as towers, complete with capping pavilions or turrets. In Rajput and Mughal palaces these pavilions were vaulted or domed and were generally known as *chhatris*, after the royal umbrellas which they resembled. Cylindrical and polygonal towers flanking gateways were sometimes ornately decorated, thereby proclaiming the importance of the entrance. Those of the 15th-century Ram Pol at Chittor are carved with friezes of military and courtly figures, while animals and birds adorn the towers on either side of the Hathi Pol at Agra. Gateways were sometimes provided with additional security by projecting enclosures or barbicans with their own walls and entrance gateways. The principal entrance to the citadel of Bijapur in the Deccan is sheltered by a curved curtain wall.

Gateways to the Rajput forts were generally roofed with lintels supported on carved brackets, rows of which were visible from inside the passageway, which incorporated stylized lotus ornament and sometimes also animals, birds and mythical beasts. Similar brackets supported projecting balconies for guards, or niches housing images of protective divinities. Another method of roofing gateway passages was with a pointed tunnel vault, constructed either like a true arch, with radiating blocks of stone, or made in the traditional Indian manner, with corbelled horizontal slabs cut into arch-like profiles. Large battlements with rows of merlons and even lines of small chhatris run across the openings, creating complicated skylines, as at Delhi. Machicolations, with holes though which to pour burning oil, projected over the entrances. These often had concealed chambers from which to fire arrows or shoot guns.

Gateways were also visible statements of regal might, often being independent architectural compositions of impressive proportions, embellished with animal and geometric emblems that communicated the power and authority of the king. Elephants had particular royal associations, and *hathi pols*, or elephant gates, were a characteristic feature of Mughal and Rajput citadels. At Fatehpur Sikri, the principal entrance to the royal complex from the reservoir that lay to the north has carved stone elephants positioned at either side. The trunks of the animals originally rose up to meet in an arch over the opening. Identical motifs are utilized in the main gates of the 17th-century

107   palaces at Bundi and Kota in Rajasthan. Elephants sculptured in the round, with trunks hanging down and with riders, once stood before the Hathi Pol at Agra. Lions are carved

4   on the spandrels above the archway of the first gate of Bidar's citadel, the Sharza Darwaza, and modelled in plasterwork on the spandrels of Golconda's Bala Hisar Darwaza. Polychrome tilework was occasionally used with splendid effect to create brilliantly coloured friezes. The outer walls and gateways of the early 16th-century

76   palace of Man Singh at Gwalior are cloaked with ceramic designs incorporating geese and *makaras* (aquatic monsters with long snouts). Coloured tile mosaic depicting tigers and royal sun motifs is reserved for the principal portal of the Takht Mahal enclosure of the palace at Bidar.

Geometric designs were ubiquitous, some acquiring particular significance. The six-pointed star, for example, was used as a royal motif by the 16th-century Mughal emperor Humayun: it appears in the spandrels of his gateway additions to the Purana Qila at Delhi. Lotus buds were a perennial theme, deriving from a long-standing tradition in India. Fringes of stone buds, almost completely undercut, decorate the

77   arches of the main gateways at Gwalior and Fatehpur Sikri. Sun-like disc emblems lent their name to the *suraj pols*, or sun gates, which protected the eastern entrances to Rajput citadels, as at Udaipur in the 17th century.

Not all gateways were intended to form part of the defence system of the palace: some functioned as ceremonial portals. A common scheme was the *tripolia*, with its characteristic trio of arched entrances, the central one sometimes being enlarged. A

5   tripolia marks the beginning of the main bazaar street that leads to the palace complex at Fatehpur Sikri; a similar tripolia commands the entrance from the town to the outermost court at Udaipur. Upper chambers roofed with small domes or vaults in the

67   manner of a chhatri sometimes accommodated kettle-drums, or *naqqar*, and were known accordingly as *naqqar khanas*, especially in the palaces of the sultans. The instruments were beaten to announce the different hours of the day as well as the arrival of important visitors. Other musicians such as trumpeters and oboists also assembled here on special occasions.

Towers, doorways and passageways

Lookout stations played an important role in the security of the palace and were often sited at the summits of towers, projecting outwards from the citadel walls. Guard posts frequently took the form of a chhatri, with slender columns supporting a small dome and overhanging eaves. Lines of these chhatris at different levels embellished the outer walls of Rajput fortresses, creating delicate skylines that contrasted with the massive masonry of the walls beneath. Chhatris often had balconies with seating carried on cantilevering brackets where sentries could survey the approaches to the palace, reporting on the movement of all traffic. Corner chhatris and those positioned above the middle of the walls were often larger, or expanded into multiple chambers with clusters of domes and vaults. Chhatris in combination with projecting balconies provide the main interest in *81,89* the otherwise austere façades of the Rajput palaces at Orchha and Datia.

7 Some royal complexes had purpose-built watchtowers standing free of the citadel walls. The Hiran Minar at Fatehpur Sikri served principally as a lookout tower, with a staircase ascending to the topmost chamber; at night, lamps transformed it into a *minar*, or marker for roads leading to the citadel. The royal enclosures at Vijayanagara are *140* overlooked by towers with open pavilions at the top. Despite their imaginative designs, the true purpose of these towers was to guard the approaches to the palace. Palace *148, 149* complexes at Gingee and Tanjore are dominated by square staircase towers with tiers of open arcades; the Gingee example has a pavilion at the summit crowned with a pyramidal roof.

3 Palace precincts were generally divided by high walls into separate courts and enclosures that tended to be arranged in a definite progression, leading from the outermost public zones to the innermost private zones. While internal partition walls were never as massive as those on the periphery, they nevertheless rose to considerable heights to ensure privacy for the king and the women of the royal household. Internal enclosure walls were sometimes punctuated by monumental gateways arranged in a ceremonial hierarchy. Sequences of arched portals at Agra and Delhi proceed from the bazaars of the outer enclosures to the formal reception courts within; beyond, in the more private parts of the palace, communication is through small unadorned doorways, intended only for the king, his family members and private guards.

Some doorways were discreetly hidden so that the king and his entourage could slip in and out of view without being observed, a precaution against plots and assassinations. Secret passageways were expedient, particularly those which connected the king's quarters with the residences of his queens, or which provided escape routes from public reception halls. A corridor within the ramparts of the Gwalior palace leads to the adjacent servants' quarters. At Amber, communication with the innermost court is possible only through a labyrinth of passageways, steps and ramps. Certain suites of apartments in the residential zones at Gwalior and Agra are surrounded by narrow passageways with concealed openings through which meetings could be observed.

Access to the women's quarters of the palace was closely guarded, with lines of gateways and doors watched by soldiers, eunuchs and female attendants. A substantial proportion of the space within the private zone was given over to guard rooms, intermediate courts and access corridors, thereby reflecting the importance accorded to the safety and privacy of the occupants. Buildings situated at the outer edge of the royal complex, approached from one direction only, were often considered the best place for the king to conduct confidential meetings with his most trusted officers. At the end of each morning and again in the evening, Shah Jahan summoned his chief minister and palace guards for councils in the Shah Burj, the isolated tower in the inner garden court at Delhi.

Barracks, armouries and stables

Throughout their daily routines, Indian kings were constantly accompanied by private guards. The Mughal emperors were attended by specially trained soldiers, with different divisions for each month. Every evening in both the Agra and Delhi palaces, the royal arms, standards and insignia were brought out and displayed before the contingents on duty; Shah Jahan personally inspected the guards and took their salutes. The Mughal household also maintained armed personnel to accompany the royal insignia and arms, and to act as a royal bodyguard in all public audiences and processions. These sentinels were beside the emperor throughout the day, and were even on duty while he ate and slept.

Quarters for the palace guards, if actual buildings at all, tended to be unpretentious structures divided into small chambers. The dilapidated arcades that line the main axis of the Golconda palace are a typical example. It was commoner for guards to be accommodated in temporary quarters, usually in tents pitched inside palace courtyards or in the vast open spaces immediately outside the citadel walls.

Arsenals and armouries, known as *shila khanas* in the palaces of the sultans, were a necessary feature, but they were not normally distinguished architecturally. Most were plain structures, with only single entrances and no openings other than small ventilation holes. The armoury in the Golconda fort is a three-storeyed arcaded building situated in the outermost court. Some armouries had vaulted halls, such as the rectangular gabled structure at Vijayanagara, where arms, gunpowder and perhaps even cannon may have been stored.

Among the other buildings connected with palace security were the stables for the royal animals used on state occasions and in military campaigns. Stables invariably faced on to open courts which served as parade grounds for both animals and troops. These courts were generally overlooked by halls or pavilions from where the king could inspect his forces and receive salutes. The stables themselves were typically long colonnaded structures divided into separate bays for each animal, as in the outer court of the palace of the 15th-century ruler Rana Kumbha at Chittor. The colonnaded stables at Fatehpur Sikri are arranged in U-formation, with simple stalls on three sides of a long court. They are in view of Birbal's House, an elaborate courtly residence perhaps used by the Emperor Akbar himself or his military commander. Horse stables erected in the court adjacent to the Delhi Darwaza in the Agra palace are said to have had screens of bamboo woven with twisted silk representing flowers to keep out the flies. Grooms attended the animals, sometimes fanning them to keep them comfortable. At Gingee, long lines of arcades with small chambers for horses and grooms linked the ruler's residence with a pleasure pavilion. The stables at Vijayanagara were intended only for elephants. The most impressive in India, they consist of long line of chambers roofed with domes and twelve-sided vaults. A raised chamber in the middle probably accommodated drummers and musicians.

Formal reception

BY FAR the most important of all courtly activities in India were the formal receptions known from the 16th century on by the Persian term *darbar*. Royal audiences were central to the administration of the kingdom, since on these occasions the monarch and his staff transacted the everyday business of government. Some darbars were grand formal occasions, attended by large numbers of princes, religious advisers, military chiefs, visiting dignitaries, armed guards, bearers of royal insignia, and select members of the public. Others were relatively private affairs in which the ruler conferred only with his closest family members and the most important of his advisers, ministers and commanders. Royal audiences were ideal opportunities to display regal pomp and ceremony so as to emphasize the power of the sovereign and the awe in which he was held. Ceremonial darbars held on religious festivals and on royal anniversaries or birthdays were the most spectacular events in the life of the palace.

Darbars of early Hindu rulers

While scenes of grandiose receptions in spacious audience chambers are commonplace in ancient epics and poems, there is a dearth of precise information about the formal procedures of early Hindu courts; not until Vijayanagara in the 14th century is historical and architectural evidence available. The descriptions of Vijayanagara by foreign visitors, combined with the architectural remains of courtly structures in the royal centre of the capital, give the best possible idea of indigenous traditions at the Hindu courts.

The daily routine of Krishnadevaraya, the 16th-century Vijayanagara emperor, was observed by Portuguese horse-traders who regularly made the journey to the Hindu capital from Goa on the Arabian Sea coast. As chronicled by Domingo Paes, Krishnadevaraya's life was a highly ritualized round of meetings, receptions and ceremonies. Each morning he conferred with his chiefs and governors in the great assembly hall of the palace where he was greeted with formal salutes. During the audience he reclined against a cushion placed on a low seat or mat where he was surrounded by a retinue of officers, servants and guards that constituted his personal staff, and who held umbrellas, banners, standards, fly-whisks and fans. He listened to petitions, settled disputes and legal cases, instructed commanders and officers, received visitors, and bestowed favours and gifts.

All these activities took place in the royal centre of the capital, a zone marked by excavated foundations of courtly buildings. They include the remains of a spacious hall, open on four sides, with exactly one hundred regularly spaced columns. Only stone footing blocks are visible; the columns themselves, presumably of massive timbers, possibly carved and coated with sheets of precious metal, have vanished. If this is the same hundred-columned hall noted by an earlier visitor to Vijayanagara, the 15th-century Persian envoy Abdul Razzaq, then it is the earliest example of an audience hall to survive in any form in a Hindu palace.

As already noted, the most spectacular royal occasion at Vijayanagara was Dasara, known at the time as Mahanavami. Domingo Paes was present at the celebrations there. He describes a building that he calls the 'House of Victory', renovated to commemorate Krishnadevaraya's successful military campaign in the neighbouring region of Orissa, which was built all of stone with carvings on the sides; at the top was a shrine, presumably for the goddess Durga, where the emperor worshipped, and in front of which animals were sacrificed. Krishnadevaraya was seated on a throne nearby, receiving the governors and chief officers of the realm. From here he reviewed the

143   splendid processions of elephants, horses, armed soldiers and female servants; here, too, he was entertained with performances of music and dance, mock battles, wrestling matches and brilliant displays of fireworks.

One monument standing within the royal enclosures at Vijayanagara corresponds

142   closely to the description of Paes. It is a multi-storeyed square platform with granite sides covered with shallow reliefs showing themes of the Mahanavami. Stairs ascend to the highest level, but there are no traces of a shrine or a royal throne.

❈ ❈ ❈

Darbars of the early sultans

Receptions in the palaces of the early sultans, while deriving much from courtly practice elsewhere in the Islamic world, especially Persia, continued and adapted indigenous traditions. The ceremonies of India's first Muslim kings may be reconstructed from the accounts of Ibn Battuta, the North African traveller who was an eye-witness at the court of Muhammad Tughluq, the mid-14th-century ruler of Delhi. According to Ibn Battuta, the outer gate of Muhammad's palace at Jahanpanah was guarded by soldiers and equipped with a band of musicians. At the second gate was the principal usher, whose headdress was surmounted with peacock feathers; he and his assistants checked all those who entered. At the third gate, which marked the entrance to an immense hall with a thousand wooden pillars, the names of all visitors were recorded. The formalities were under the direction of the chief master of ceremonies, generally of royal blood. Together with other deputies his duties were to marshall those attending the darbar according to precedence and seniority, to present all petitions to the sultan, and to transmit the royal commands to subordinate officials and to any petitioners. One officer had the special task of making an inventory of all the gifts received by the sultan.

Muhammad himself sat on a cushioned seat. The *wazir*, or chief minister, and his secretaries stood before him, followed by various officers and more than a hundred assistants. The attendant appointed to carry the fly-whisk was positioned immediately behind the royal figure and there were specially armed bodyguards at either side. Ranged in order down the darbar hall were the religious leaders and holy men, then the sultan's relations by blood and marriage, and finally the principal *amirs*, or nobles, and their commanders. When all of this assembly was in place, some sixty caparisoned horses of the royal stable and fifty adorned war-elephants were brought in. Approved visitors were permitted to hand over gifts in person, often receiving a ceremonial sash or purse of money in return.

Darbars on feast days were more elaborate, and the audience hall was extended by spreading vast awnings. The sultan sat on a cushioned seat on the large golden throne;

attendants held a jewelled parasol over his head. Those attending the court saluted the king individually, in descending order of precedence; then revenue-holders would bring presents, and all would be entertained to a great banquet, again being served in strict order. A large golden brazier would fill the hall with the smoke of different kinds of incense and fragrant woods, and the assembled throng would be sprinkled with rose-water. Dishes were escorted from the kitchen by ushers, and praises of the sultan would be recited before those present were assigned their places. The serving of *pan* (leaves containing chopped betel nut with lime and a bitter gum) signified the end of the meal.

Tantalizingly little of Muhammad's palace has survived. All that can be seen are the column footings defining an audience hall, presumably roofed with timbers, and a second hall with ruined masonry vaults. These two types of structure – one columned, the other vaulted – represent the two most common architectural forms used for formal receptions in the 15th- and 16th-century palaces of later sultans. One courtly structure at the Central Indian site of Mandu, the Hindola Mahal, is a long and spacious hall roofed with transverse arches. In the royal complex at the Deccan capital of Bidar there were two large walled courts, each with a spacious columned hall on the south side – one for public audiences, the other for private audiences. Again, only regular rows of stone footings are preserved, the timber columns having disappeared. Smaller vaulted apartments, presumably for more private business, open off to the side. Audience halls at Bijapur have lofty double-height porticoes which make use of both columns and arched portals; from here the sultan or his representatives appeared to the public. More unusual is the octagonal darbar chamber at Ahmadnagar, headquarters of yet another line of Deccan sultans. This two-storeyed vaulted building serves as the focus for a royal complex built a short distance outside the walls of the city.

❊ ❊ ❊

Public darbars of the Mughals

With the coming of the Mughals, darbars were held on a more lavish scale and there were certain innovations, such as the practice of *darshana*, or public viewing. The earliest public audience hall of the Mughals is that at Fatehpur Sikri. The outermost court of the complex serves as the setting for public meetings and is known by the Persian term *diwan-i amm*. The pavilion facing into the court from the middle of the west side was used by Akbar himself.

The public audiences of Shah Jahan in his palaces in Agra and Delhi were the most elaborate in 17th-century India, according to Persian historians and European visitors as well as the illustrations in royal biographies. Shah Jahan's routine as observed by Jean-Baptiste Tavernier, jewel-merchant, and François Bernier, physician, both Frenchmen, followed a standard pattern. The emperor's first public appearance each morning was to show himself at a balcony, known as the *jharoka*, overhanging the palace walls. Crowds of expectant people, gathered below on the bank of the Jumna, at once bowed while he returned their salute. He remained at the balcony for almost an hour, during which time members of the public could submit petitions or make their complaints directly. Sometimes a chain was let down from the balcony for petitions to be tied to it, and then drawn up for the immediate attention of the emperor.

After the public salute and admission of complaints, the plain beneath the palace was cleared and Shah Jahan enjoyed elephant fights. Next came the public darbar inside the

35

38

48

Diwan-i Amm. At the beginning of his reign Shah Jahan held court at Agra under canvas awnings stretched on poles set up for the occasion. Later he built a temporary wooden pavilion with gilded and decorated columns, and finally a great structure with *55* white marble pillars supporting broad cusped arches, which is the one that still stands. The hall is open on three sides and closed off on the east by a wall, in the middle of which is an arcaded alcove that marks the site of the imperial throne. The Diwan-i Amm in the *65* Delhi palace is similar, but here from the alcove a free-standing marble throne projects.

Public assemblies of Shah Jahan in the Diwan-i Amm pavilions at Agra and Delhi took place early in the morning and were highly ritualized occasions. On either side of *p. 35* the Emperor's throne were the princes; they took their seats only when commanded to do so. Further away stood those who attended on the emperor's person, including standard-bearers, displaying golden banners and poles with yak-tails affixed. In the space immediately in front stood the courtiers, nobles and chief officers of state, ranked in due order on three sides. When the hall was entirely filled with visitors, the courtyard in front was partly enclosed with wooden railings and gold-embroidered canopies. Here the lesser commanders, royal archers and retainers of the various nobles assembled. Mace-bearers and armed guards in splendid uniforms were positioned beside the railings, excluding those who had no entree to the darbar.

The audience stood ready and expectant when Shah Jahan entered the alcove by the rear door, took his seat, and the business of darbar began. The high *bakhshi*, or paymaster-general, reported to the emperor the petitions of the military officers and immediately received his orders giving promotions to some, new posts to others. Officers who had come to the capital from the provinces were then granted audience, and those who had been newly appointed to some post were presented by the different military chiefs. Royal favours were usually accompanied by a robe of honour, jewels, a horse or arms. Next came the clerks of the royal lands or the emperor's privy purse, who submitted their proposals and got prompt instructions. Then the courtiers presented their dispatches, as well as those of the provincial officers, which were read or heard by his majesty.

When this work was over the controller of religious matters and charitable grants brought to the royal notice cases of needy scholars and pious men, each of whom received grants of money. The work of public charity being over, orders previously passed about land and cash grants were submitted for confirmation. Lastly, a display of horses and elephants from the imperial stables took place in the court in front. With this, the public darbar of Shah Jahan, which lasted about two hours, came to an end.

※ ※ ※

Private darbars of the Mughals

Halls for private audience, known also by a Persian term, *diwan-i khass*, were the setting for smaller and more specialized darbars. At Fatehpur Sikri, the southern court of the royal complex was overlooked by the Daftar Khana where the private business of the court was conducted. This structure has a central chamber with a projecting jharoka for the emperor to show himself publicly.

59 The Diwan-i Khass at Agra is similar to the Diwan-i Amm, being a columned structure open on three sides, but without an alcove in the rear wall. In the middle of the

Royal darbars were the most important activities within the Indian palace. This 17th-century miniature painting depicts, with minute accuracy, an audience within the Mughal court at Lahore in November 1638. The Emperor Shah Jahan is seated on a marble throne, ornately decorated with multi-coloured stone inlays as well as with carvings of symbolic regal themes: the scales of justice, the animals living in harmony. Attendants with fly-whisks are seen behind and below; to the emperor's right are the princes Shuja and Murad Bakhsh, together with their counsellor. Various ministers, advisors and courtiers stand in two formal lines on either side of the throne. Among them is the Persian envoy Ali Mardan Khan (between the columns, touching his turban in salute). His followers (left) bear dishes of precious gifts.

Diwan-i Khass at Delhi stood the Peacock Throne, which was a small jewelled pavilion with a pair of peacocks on the roof studded with the finest rubies, diamonds, emeralds and pearls. Shah Jahan generally used the Diwan-i Khass for the more intimate procedures of government. Here he read or listened to reports from the wazir and the highest officers and provincial governors, and answered the most important letters in his own hand, or himself dictated reports. *Farmans*, or imperial decrees, were drafted by ministers following the emperor's verbal orders, and then sent to the royal harem for the seal bearing the emperor's name, of which the Empress Mumtaz Mahal had sole charge. The highest revenue officers reported important matters of the realm, and the head of the royal charity department brought to the emperor's notice special cases of the needy, many of whom received cash grants. The superintendent of public works, accompanied by expert architects, was sometimes in attendance to seek approval for plans of new buildings and to record his majesty's personal additions and amendments. After some two hours occupied in this way, the business of the day was concluded, and the emperor sometimes enjoyed inspecting leopards and hawks that were brought out of the imperial menagerie.

Wednesday assemblies in the Diwan-i Khass during Shah Jahan's reign were courts of law. On that day the emperor came directly to the private audience hall to sit on the throne of justice. He was there accompanied by wise and experienced god-fearing men to act as judges, as well as law officers, jurists versed in legal decrees, pious scholars, and those nobles who constantly accompanied the emperor's person. The officers of justice presented the plaintiffs one by one, and reported their grievances. His majesty ascertained the facts of inquiry, took the law from the state-supported judges, and accordingly pronounced his decisions.

Anniversaries, birthdays and New Year

More magnificent than these daily and weekly darbars were those that marked the anniversary of the emperor's coronation. On these occasions the Diwan-i Amm was richly embellished to present a spectacle of costly and gorgeous fabrics, some imported from Europe, with coloured awnings spread out on three sides. Nobles erected tents in the court in front, as well as in the other open spaces of the palace. During the course of the darbar, the emperor received gifts from all the visitors and enjoyed performances of music and dance. These were followed by a banquet, a tournament of mail-clad cavaliers and a display of fireworks.

Royal birthdays, celebrated according to both the solar and lunar calendars, were announced by the firing of guns from the ramparts, after which the nobles and state officers, wearing rich apparel and jewels, entered the Diwan-i Amm to present gifts and congratulations to the enthroned emperor. He then retired to the apartment of the queen mother or to a tent outside the harem for the weighing ceremony. Here, in full view of the distinguished gathering, his majesty sat on a scale, firmly placed on the ground, to be balanced against gold, silk, perfumes, pewter, butter, rice and milk. After blessings had been recited, the precious articles were all carefully valued and converted into cash to be set aside for distribution among the needy. The ceremony was concluded with the presentation of artificial fruits made of silver and gold fibres, which the emperor scattered amongst the audience.

Of all festivals at the Mughal court, probably the most spectacular was Nawruz. At Delhi, Shah Jahan ordered illuminations to be arranged on a grand scale, with all of the towers and domes being lit up with tiny oil lamps. Kettle-drums were beaten on the morning of the feast. In the outer court of the palace stood two rows of cavalrymen and elephants, with coloured silk banners attached to poles fixed to the howdahs. Nobles pitched their tents in the inner courts. A triumphal arch, with receptacles and braziers for sweet-smelling perfumes, led to the Diwan-i Amm. Here, the king sat on the royal throne surrounded by carpets of silk and gold, receiving homage from the nobles and courtiers. Among the other festivals that were formally celebrated at the Mughal court was the banquet commemorating the Prophet's birthday, an occasion of solemnity attended by all the religious leaders of the capital.

Darbars of other rulers

As the most powerful and influential rulers, the Mughals had a far-reaching impact. Most maharajas in the 17th and 18th centuries, including the Rajputs who were in the service of the Delhi emperors or related to them by marriage, consciously set out to imitate Mughal courtly practices. Audiences at the later Rajput courts, as observed by British visitors, most notably James Tod at the beginning of the 19th century, preserved many of the formalities of earlier Mughal darbars. Tod describes a royal reception at Udaipur in which the ruler was seated on a cushioned throne with silver columns supporting a velvet canopy. The monarch was accompanied by the prime minister, commander of the forces, keeper of the records and lesser chiefs, princes and officers who sat or stood on three sides of a square, ordered according to a strict hierarchy. Among the gifts presented by the king were a caparisoned elephant and horse, jewelled turbans, shawls and brocades. The audience closed with the customary presentation of rose-essence and *pan*. Hindu holidays were also formally celebrated at the Rajput courts. At Diwali (the festival of lamps), for instance, pieces of gold and sweetmeats consecrated at the temple of Lakshmi, goddess of wealth, were borne in trays to the audience hall and then distributed among the assembly.

Rajput ceremonial architecture was profoundly influenced by that of the Mughals, with the result that columned halls and vaulted pavilions, often with characteristic jharokas, imitating those at Agra and Delhi sprung up all over Western and Central India. The 16th-century columned audience hall at Udaipur is built in the early Mughal style to survey the parade ground of the royal precinct. A 17th-century addition to the citadel at Amber is the free-standing Diwan-i Amm in the second court. At Bundi, the *109* Ratan Daulat is a columned audience hall looking down on to the main entrance court. By the 18th century, audience halls with cusped arches and painted decoration in the later Mughal manner had become widespread throughout much of India. Additions at Kota and Jaipur and in other Rajput palaces have painted and inlaid decoration in the Mughal style covering walls, vaults and domes.

Formal receptions remained the focal activity of courtly life during the British period. Public apartments in princely residences often imitated the great houses of the British and French nobility, with darbar halls completely fitted out with European furniture, chandeliers, mirrors, curtains and carpets. Among the numerous examples surviving from the 19th century and the early part of the present century, the grandest *165, 180* and most opulent are those at Gwalior, Indore and Hyderabad. The Indo-Saracenic style chosen by some rulers for their new palaces resulted in more unusual architectural *182* solutions. The darbar hall at Mysore has rows of broad cusped arches, ornately gilded; *189* the smaller hall for private audience, the Amba Vilasa, is remarkable for its stained glass ceiling.

Royal worship

No matter how demanding the task of governing, both Hindu and Muslim rulers always reserved time for private worship in the temples and mosques of their palaces. The ways in which some emperors integrated devotion into their crowded daily routines are disclosed in the chronicles of European travellers. According to Domingo Paes, the Portuguese trader at Vijayanagara already mentioned, Krishnadevaraya woke before dawn, had himself bathed and dressed, and then visited the royal chapel inside his palace to pay respect to the deity enshrined there. Only after this ritual was concluded did he embark upon a strenuous round of riding and gymnastic exercises. Jean-Baptiste Tavernier, chronicler of Shah Jahan, noted that every morning the Mughal emperor spent time in the palace mosque where he sat with his face toward Mecca, reciting verses of the Quran and meditating on God. State duties were dealt with only after these prayers had been completed. Shah Jahan visited the mosque again at dusk to say his evening prayers, after which he continued to conduct business.

Temples and mosques for royal worship were usually situated within the inner zone of the palace, with convenient access from the ruler's sleeping chamber as well as from the private quarters of the king's household. Used only by the monarch, his immediate family and the closest ministers and courtiers, they were modest though sumptuously appointed structures. Houses of prayer situated at gateways or opening off the outer courts were accessible to visitors to the palace as well as members of the public.

Temples

Elaborate Hindu temples for the use of the king and his queens were incorporated into the earliest citadels of the Rajputs. Since they were entirely built in solid stone, they have survived in better condition than the nearby royal residences, many of which have crumbled away. The 15th-century sandstone shrines in the Gwalior fort are dedicated to both Hindu gods and Jain saviours, testifying to the mixed cult affiliations of the Tomar rulers. The temples of the Chittor citadel are finely finished structures, entirely covered with intricate carvings of divinities and attendants. Curved spires rise above the sanctuaries, while projecting balconies with eaves shelter the entrance porches. One of the two lofty stone towers nearby was erected by the 15th-century ruler Rana Kumbha, as a shrine for the god Vishnu and as a monument to commemorate his victory over the *91* Delhi forces. Known as the Jaya Stambha, or Tower of Victory, it is divided into nine ascending storeys, each with balconies, covered with sculptures of Hindu gods. Below is the spot where the Chittor monarchs and their wives were cremated.

Later Rajput palaces also incorporated small shrines into their complexes, especially at gateways. Beside the steps that lead up to the palace from the outer court at Amber is a small shrine to the protective goddess of the Kacchwaha rulers that opens off an arcaded *13* courtyard. Visitors at Udaipur pay homage to Ganesha before they mount the staircase that leads to the private zones of the palace. A marble image of this deity is set into a niche conspicuously decorated with mirrorwork. Rajput princesses at Akbar's court also required accommodation for private worship. The Palace of Jodh Bai at Fatehpur Sikri has shallow wall recesses which may have housed sculptured images of divinities.

138 For the Hindu kings of Southern India, temple building was an important activity, and many impressive religious structures were erected within the royal precincts. The private shrine of the Vijayanagara emperors, dedicated to Ramachandra (another name for Rama), is situated at the core of the royal enclosures of the capital. It is constructed of finely worked granite and, as in the Rajput sites, is well preserved compared with the ruined courtly buildings that surround it. The royal character of the temple is revealed 143 by the friezes of elephants, horses, soldiers and women that cover its outer walls; in contrast, the shrine inside is adorned with mythological reliefs of the *Ramayana* that relate the story of the god himself.

Since not all shrines could be integrated into royal complexes, the residences of some monarchs were spatially coordinated with places of worship that stood outside the walls 81 of the citadel. The Raja Mahal on the island in the Betwa River at Orchha is precisely on axis with the monumental Chaturbhuja Mandir. Larger than any of the royal residences and more imposing in appearance, this temple faces east, directly towards the palace. Another coordinated scheme is seen at Jaipur. The principal wing of the royal residence, the Chandra Mahal, looks out upon a long garden with a central waterway. In the middle of the waterway stands a temple dedicated to Govind Deo, the personal deity of Sawai Jai Singh, who had the shrine built in 1735. Another smaller Ganesha temple crowns the hill beyond, again precisely in line with the palace.

Some temples lay well beyond the frontiers of the king's own domain. Pious kings who made regular visits to far-away holy spots sometimes built palaces at these sites as temporary accommodation for themselves and their retinues. By far the most favoured place of pilgrimage was Benares (Varanasi) on the Ganges, India's most sacred bathing place, where the sins of the past could be washed away and where Vishvanatha, the city's principal god, could be worshipped. Many Rajput royal visitors to Benares found it convenient to erect residences there, some of which were inhabited throughout the year by pious courtiers and royal women. The palaces are located above the steep west bank of the river, within easy access of the bathing ghats and the narrow lanes that lead to the city's most important temples. Upper apartments with projecting balconies take advantage of the river view.

Hindu themes

Sculptures and paintings illustrating religious themes were a constant feature in the palaces of Hindu rulers, and were sometimes introduced discreetly into the residences of Muslim kings. Murals dating from the 17th and 18th centuries depicting Hindu divinities and sacred legends enhanced the walls of shrines in Rajput palaces; scenes from the mythology of Krishna and processions of the Holi festival were particularly popular. Southern Indian palaces were also adorned with large wall-paintings of 157–159 mythological subjects. Courts and pavilions at Padmanabhapuram are overlooked by a tower with a shrine room at the topmost level. The empty bed placed here is for Padmanabha, the reclining aspect of the god Vishnu, after whom the palace was named. The walls are covered with gleaming murals depicting Padmanabha as well as other deities. This chamber can only be reached by a steep flight of narrow steps from the maharaja's own sleeping chamber beneath, and was obviously intended for his exclusive use.

156, 13   But depictions of Hindu themes within Indian palaces were by no means restricted to places of worship. Lakshmi, goddess of wealth, and Ganesha, the god who removes all obstacles, were constant motifs wherever divine protection was deemed necessary. The *122*   Ganesh Pol in the Amber palace has a seated figure of the elephant-headed deity painted over the arched entrance. Divinities associated with particular ruling houses were often incorporated into the decoration of formal reception rooms and royal sleeping chambers. Paintings of Chamundeshvari, together with companion female divinities, cover the rear wall of the Darbar Hall of the palace at Mysore.

Sacred stories also appear, especially those that include scenes of courtly receptions or erotic tales, such as that of the youthful god Krishna. Here there was no obvious distinction between mythological and royal themes, the paintings effectively bridging *12*   the gap between the world of gods and that of kings. Murals in the Raja Mahal at Orchha combine Krishna subjects with the coronation of Rama and the various incarnations of Vishnu. Paintings in the Chitra Shala of the Bundi palace show Krishna sporting with his favourite consort, Radha. The 18th-century palace of the Sethupati rulers at Ramnad in Southern India, though of little architectural interest, is endowed with a remarkable cycle of murals. They depict the stories of Rama and Krishna, in addition to *163*   courtly receptions and battles. Mythological tableaux and depictions of the gods are also the most interesting feature of the palace of the Cochin rulers. Here there is a complete cycle of *Ramayana* scenes, in addition to compositions showing Krishna reclining or holding up Mount Govardhana; processions of male and female courtiers are interpreted as witnesses of the celestial marriage of Shiva and Parvati.

Sets of pilgrimage shrines, shown in simplified form, are another topic that occurs in *114*   palace paintings. Representations of major temples were contemplated by the ruler in memory of the pilgrimages that he had already completed or that he intended to undertake. At Amber, the walls of the dining hall, known as the Bhojana Shala, are covered with murals of the principal temples in the Marwar kingdom. Paintings in the main reception hall of the Ramnad palace include all of the Vishnu temples in the territories of the Sethupatis. Such shrines are invariably shown schematically; the identification relies on labels and on iconographic details of individual deities.

Religious themes – the coronation of Rama and the incarnations of Vishnu – were painted in the 18th century in this vaulted room in the Raja Mahal at Orchha in Rajasthan, built two centuries earlier [*12*].

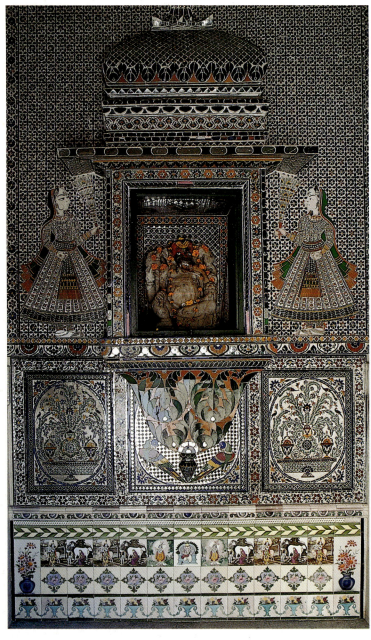

13

The fairytale world of the Indian palace is best seen today in Rajasthan. At Udaipur, before entering the private zones of the palace, the visitor pays homage to an image of the elephant-headed guardian of thresholds, Ganesha [*13*], set in a niche glittering with mirrorwork and coloured glass. The same materials, with the addition of paintings, create magic spaces in the Badi Mahal [*14*].

Overleaf: a brass door surrounded by tilework in the third inner court at Jaipur [*15*], a pierced stone screen at Datia [*16*], and the façade of the Hawa Mahal or Palace of the Breezes at Jaipur [*17*], a set of screened 'boxes' from which the ladies of the court, in purdah, could view the world outside.

14

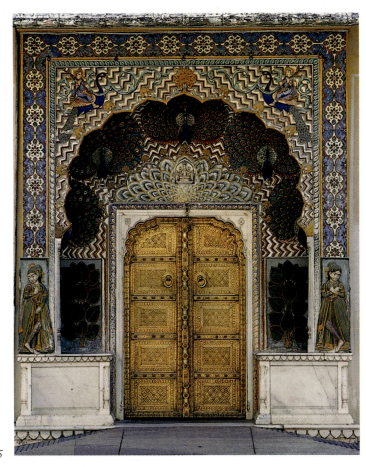

15

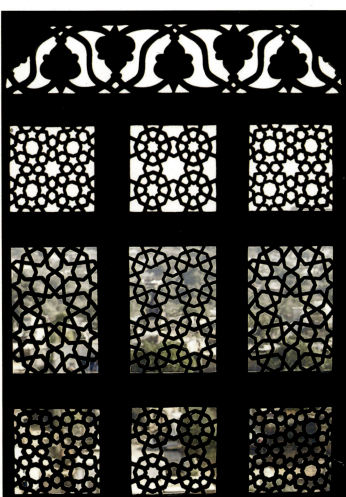

16

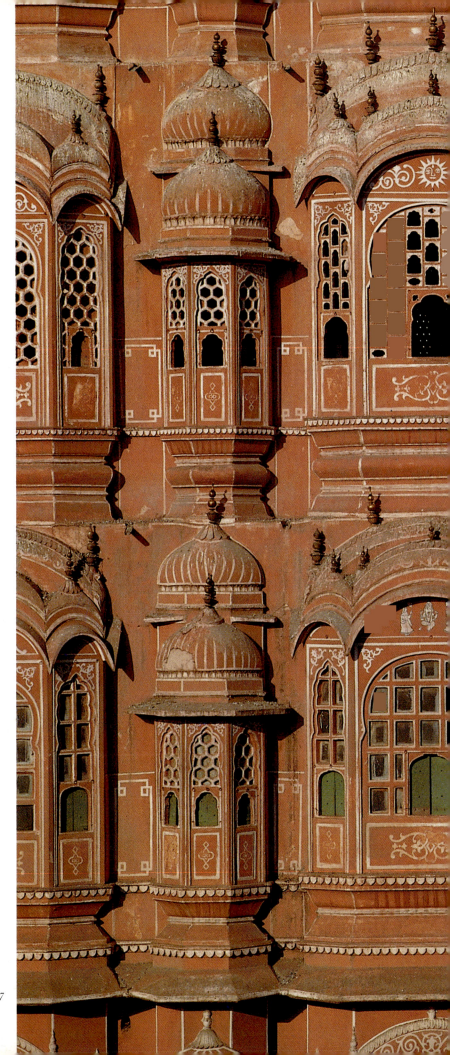

17

Both continuity and novelty are manifest in the palaces that rulers built in the 19th and 20th centuries, often to the designs of Western architects. The Neer Mahal [*18*], on Lake Sonamura in Tripura State in north-eastern India, carries on the tradition of waterside pavilions. Also in Tripura, the turn-of-the-century Ujjayanta Palace at Agartala [*19*] is by contrast wholly European in its elements: the temple [*20*] even looks like a little domed church. An alternative to such wholesale Westernization was the 'Indo-Saracenic' style, of which the early 20th-century Pratap Vilas at Jamnagar [*21*] is a late example.

18

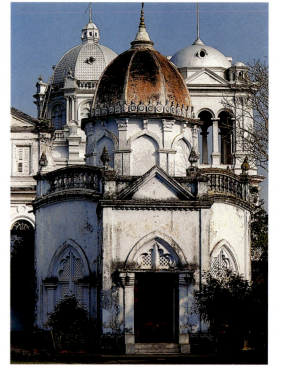

20

19

Inside too, the palaces of the princes show a mixture of traditional and imported elements: the decoration of the Amba Vilasa at Mysore [see *189*] incorporates a traditional Hindu image of Lakshmi [*22*; cf. *156*]; in the banqueting hall of the Jai Vilas at Gwalior [*23*] a silver train, rather than a host of servants, delivered drinks and cigars; and in the Shiv Nivas at Udaipur [*24*] Western forms were transfigured in response to the Rajput love of mirror and glass [cf. *13*, *14*].

Mosques

Just as Hindu rulers had their palace shrines, so did Muslim kings have their palace mosques. These private places of worship generally reproduced at a smaller scale the features of the larger, more public mosques of the city. A notable example is the late 14th-century structure that stands inside the citadel at Gulbarga, originally intended for the Bahmani sultan, his courtiers and commanders. Unlike almost every other example in India, the Gulbarga mosque is entirely roofed with vaults and domes, without any open court at all; the interior presents continuous perspectives of low arcades. Royal residences once surrounded it, but these are no longer preserved. Similarly, no buildings survive in Delhi's Purana Qila other than the royal mosque erected in the mid-16th century for Sher Shah. It is a modest structure with a simple five-bay prayer chamber capped with a central dome; the inlaid stone and tile decoration, however, is sumptuous. The royal mosque and palaces at Bidar are coordinated in an architectural ensemble that constitutes the focus of the citadel. The Solah Khamba Masjid faces eastwards onto a formal garden in which there is a long water channel connecting the residential apartments with a bath-house for courtiers.

35

Mughal palaces always integrated mosques into the overall architectural schemes. In the Agra and Delhi citadels, the most important of these royal mosques is the Moti Masjid, or Pearl Mosque – so called because of the finely worked white marble that cloaks its walls and domes – situated between the public and private zones. The example at Agra, which has a triple-domed prayer chamber opening off its own courtyard, was frequented by Shah Jahan and the male members of the royal family. Royal women had their own place of worship, the smaller but similarly appointed Nagina Masjid nearby, reached through a narrow passage from one of the inner courts of the palace. Another example of a palace mosque intended only for courtly women stands inside the citadel at Bijapur. Known as the Mecca Masjid, it is surrounded by high walls that completely conceal it from view; access is through a inconspicuous gateway on the north.

55

73, 74

36

An essential part of the religious life of the sultans was participation in the prayers at the Jami Masjid. These public mosques required spacious courts and prayer chambers to accommodate the large numbers of commanders, soldiers, merchants and other male inhabitants of the capital that assembled there every Friday. That Jami Masjids were also conceived as royal places of worship is indicated by the *maqsura* with which many of them were provided. This special feature was characteristically a raised gallery inside the prayer chamber, surrounded by pierced stone screens and reached by a separate flight of stairs. Reserved for the sultan and his retinue, with access through an entrance on the side nearest to the palace, it ensured the ruler's privacy and safety.

Because they were usually so finely built, Jami Masjids still stand in the capitals of almost all of India's Muslim rulers, even when the citadel walls and royal residences have fallen into ruin. One of the first actions of Qutbuddin Aibak after he established his headquarters at Delhi in 1198 was to build a vast court for public prayers as the centrepiece of his new capital. The adjacent Qutb Minar, a tower more than 70 metres (over 230 feet) high, served as a visible symbol of Muslim domination. To commemorate their conquest of the Deccan in the early 14th century, the Delhi sultans commissioned a large Jami Masjid at Daulatabad, near to which rose a minaret, the highest in the region, which still stands complete. Impressive congregational mosques were erected immediately outside the palace walls, sometimes even next to the main gate of the

Piety and pleasure: the living and the dead come together in harmony on the banks of Man Sagar outside Jaipur [25], as the Jai Mahal, an island palace built about 1735, is watched over by a cluster of chhattris that commemorate the city's rulers.

citadel, as at Champaner, capital of the Gujarat sultans in the 15th century. Akbar's residence at Fatehpur Sikri shared the level top of a sandstone ridge with a Jami Masjid; its monumental entrance, the Buland Darwaza or Victory Gate, dominates the whole site. At Delhi, while the Jami Masjid is nearby, the principal axis of Shah Jahan's palace was extended as a bazaar street, the Chandni Chowk, which culminated in the mosque of Fatehpuri Begum, one of the capital's principal places of worship, named after the emperor's third wife.

Other royal religious buildings coordinated with the residences of the sultans were the *imambaras* which accommodated the rites of the Muharram festival celebrated by Shia Muslims. In the late 18th century the nawabs of Lucknow erected a monumental Imambara adjacent to the Macchi Bhavan palace. Still under veneration, it enshrines the green glass *tazia* that represents the tomb of the martyr Imam Husain, surrounded by lamps and costly mirrors identical to those that once adorned the reception rooms in the nearby royal quarters.

Tombs and memorials

Tombs were sometimes also coordinated with palace layouts, rather than being situated far outside the city which was the usual practice. The coordination of palaces and mausolea implies a desire on the part of certain sultans to forge symbolic links between their terrestrial home and their future heavenly abode. In this respect, Indian rulers seem to have acted in the belief that worldly power was enhanced if their own tombs stood within sight of their palaces. An outstanding example of this correlation was created at Tughluqabad: here a causeway crossing the water of a vast reservoir connects the main gate of the citadel with a second, smaller citadel where Ghiyathuddin, the early 14th-century sultan of Delhi, erected his own tomb.

Elsewhere, Jami Masjids and royal tombs were built close together to create coordinated mosque-tomb complexes. Ahmad Shah understood well the relationship between royal power and city planning. Having completed his residence in the Bhadra citadel at Ahmadabad, he ordered a vast parade ground, the Maidan-i Shah, to be cleared outside the main gate of the palace. A monumental triple-arched gateway, the Tin Darwaza, on the east side of the maidan, marks the beginning of a broad processional way that runs eastward to the Jami Masjid and two tombs, one for the sultan himself, the other for his queens. Parade ground, gateway, mosque and tombs were all coordinated on a strict west-to-east axis. Hoshang Shah, ruler of Mandu in the first part of the 15th century, was responsible for another coordinated royal complex. The Jami Masjid in the citadel stands next to the sultan's own mausoleum; both are entered through monumental doorways on the north.

The tombs of the Mughal emperors served as focal points in grandiose formal gardens established on the outskirts of their capitals. Several of the private apartments in the Agra palace look out over a bend in the Jumna toward the distant prospect of the incomparable Taj Mahal, where Shah Jahan and his wife Mumtaz Mahal are buried. Tombs of non-royal figures were also associated with palaces. For the site of his palace-city Akbar chose Sikri, near to the refuge of Shaykh Salim Chishti, thereby fulfilling a vow that he had made in the presence of the saint. Akbar's descendant, Shah Jahan,

59

erected a white marble tomb for this holy man in the courtyard of the Jami Masjid. Exquisitely carved screens enclose a passageway used by worshippers as they circumambulate the grave.

Hindu rulers were always cremated, so there was among them no tradition of tomb architecture. Under the influence of Muslim practice from the 17th century onwards, however, Hindu monarchs, especially the Rajputs, began to erect structures which, although they did not enshrine ashes or any other actual remains or relics, nonetheless functioned as funerary monuments. They generally took the form of domed pavilions that imitated the chhatris used above gateways and walls of the palaces themselves; in time, the memorials themselves came to be known as chhatris. Not unlike sultans, Rajput rulers constructed memorial chhatris outside the walls of their palace citadels, on the banks of rivers and overlooking artificial reservoirs. Some were even axially coordinated with palaces, thereby establishing spatial and symbolic links between living and dead kings.

Midway between Amber and Jaipur is Man Sagar, a reservoir that provides a picturesque backdrop for an island palace. A cluster of funerary chhatris of the Kacchwaha rulers is built on the bank facing toward the palace. At Mandor, the old capital of the Jodhpur maharajas a short distance north of the capital, stands the 18th-century palace of Ajit Singh. The complex includes a small formal garden and a royal cremation ground with memorial chhatris, each resembling a temple, complete with curved spire and entrance porch. The palace of the Rajput rulers at Alwar backs onto a large rectangular pool, with steps on all sides and twelve ornamental chhatris protruding into the water. A chhatri of the late 18th-century king Bhabhtawar Singh stands on an elevated terrace; it is capped with a fluted dome that rises imposingly above a cluster of curved vaults.

Chhatris were sometimes grouped together into formal arrangements surrounding a large reservoir, to be visited by courtiers as resting places on excursions from the capital. Here, sovereigns and their retinues could offer prayers to the deceased while enjoying the cooling effects of the lake. The chhatris at Kusum Sarovar, just outside Govardhan in Central India, commemorate the 18th-century Jat rulers of the kingdom of Bharatpur. They are elaborate, pavilion-like structures, with platforms suspended invitingly over a large square pool. Steps descend to small waterside chambers that function as hot-weather retreats.

Privacy and pleasure

Wᴴɪʟᴇ Iɴᴅɪᴀɴ palaces had always to satisfy the requirements of government, they were essentially residential in function, housing the king, his immediate family and all those who constituted the royal household. Royal complexes were carefully laid out so that privacy could be achieved at a convenient distance from the more public zones. Nor were the private quarters of the royal family intended merely as accommodation: they were also settings for informal gatherings and pleasurable pursuits.

Royal women

According to long-standing tradition in India as embodied in texts such as the *Arthashastra* (the treatise on statecraft already mentioned, p. 10), the female members of the court had always to be segregated from the public zones of the palace. From the 15th century onwards, their restricted and well-guarded quarters were commonly called 'harems' or 'zenanas', following Persian practice. While these private sectors were generally within easy reach of the king, who visited them regularly, they were clearly distinguished from the ruler's own apartments. Harems in later Indian palaces accommodated considerable numbers of women, from the queen mother and wives of the monarch to various female attendants, maids, servants and slaves. Akbar's household at Agra has been estimated at some five thousand persons, including attendants, guards and eunuchs. Nor were zenanas the exclusive abode of females; younger male members of the court, such as royal princes, also lived there for a time.

Female inhabitants of both Hindu and Muslim courts spent most of their lives confined to the harem, seldom leaving the palace, except perhaps to accompany the king when he went on a visit to relatives or on pilgrimage to some holy place. Access to their quarters was tightly controlled, all visitors being scrutinized by guards and accompanied by attendants. This seclusion of courtly women, widely known in India as *purdah*, was strictly maintained down to the present century.

Indian queens were not formally partners in sovereignty, being neither enthroned nor crowned; their impact on state affairs was purely personal. Even so, some women in the harem wielded considerable influence, taking a keen interest in the political and cultural life of the court. Nur Jahan, wife of the 17th-century emperor Jahangir, actively involved herself in the government of the Mughal empire; she held the king's seal and was responsible for despatching his decrees. Courtly ladies played an important part in settling quarrels amongst members of the royal family, interceding for injured parties and attempting to bring about reconciliations. Other courtiers and even common people sought their protection, petitioning them to plead their cases with the ruler. On the other hand, intrigues and feuds within the harem were common, and courtly women were sometimes responsible for exacerbating disagreements between members of the royal entourage. Competition could be fierce between the different wives and concubines, especially when it came to the future careers of their sons.

Opposite: *Life in the zenana, the more private zone of the palace, was often devoted to pleasure. This miniature painting shows the early 17th-century Mughal Emperor Jahangir conversing with Nur Jahan, his favourite queen; their son Khurram, the future Shah Jahan, is seated to one side. This domestic scene takes place on an outer terrace of a palace, in front of a pavilion hung with rolled-up textiles; but there is no indication as to which Mughal residence is intended. A white cloth is spread over an elaborate carpet woven with fantastic beasts and birds; flowers and trees indicate a garden nearby. Nur Jahan holds a rose-water sprinkler, and there are roses scattered on the cloth; female attendants bear sweets and drinks.*

122

Royal women watched the proceedings of darbars or receptions and took delight in palace festivals, usually following the celebrations from behind screens or curtains. Feasts took place inside the harem, with entertainments being provided by singers, dancers and actors; births or circumcision ceremonies of princes as well as marriages were also celebrated there. On these and other occasions the women of the harem entertained their kinsmen at lavish banquets. The most picturesque feast in the Mughal harem was Khushruz, which functioned both as an entertainment for royal ladies and as an opportunity for presenting petitions to royal women. For five to eight days each year, the wives and daughters of the nobles and other officers opened stalls in the harem, assuming such roles as grocers, goldsmiths and jewellers. The emperor usually played the part of the broker for his ladies, preferring the wittiest and most beautiful sellers. He and his retinue purchased generously, often with fake disputes and haggling.

For marriages at the Mughal courts, the more public parts of the palace, such as the Diwan-i Amm, were converted into a zenana, by being thrown open to the ladies of the imperial household; purdah was assured by erecting temporary screens and curtains. Special arrangements were also made when female members of the court were married. The bride, surrounded by ladies-in-waiting, all in purdah, ceremonially received priests or religious leaders, the two fathers and the groom within the confines of the zenana.

Palace women were generally provided with ample means from the royal treasury to lead lives of dignity and luxury. They entertained lavishly out of their own funds; they invited the king to make a formal visit to the harem and made him valuable gifts. Princesses were highly educated and cultured, and some wrote excellent poetry and had their own collections of books. Female courtiers were patrons of the arts, personally commissioning writers, artists and architects. They endowed religious ceremonies and celebrations, and paid regular visits to temples and mosques.

Harems and zenanas

As the most private zone of the Indian court, the harem was invariably located in the innermost enclosure of the royal precinct, at the furthest possible point from the outer gates. High walls concealed the inhabitants and their activities from view; gates were strongly guarded, and had elaborate provisions for security, often with intermediate courts and entries with many changes of direction. Smaller sub-enclosures inside the harem defined a hierarchy of ever-increasing privacy, some enclosures being set aside for individual queens and their retinues.

The headquarters of the early sultans generally situated the harem against the rear wall of the fortified zone. In the 15th-century royal city of Firuzabad in the Deccan (not to be confused with Firuzabad at Delhi) separate enclosures were reserved for different queens and their female attendants. Residential apartments for the royal women at Bidar, such as the Rangin Mahal, have symmetrically arranged chambers opening off small inner courts. The zenana at Golconda is positioned in one corner of the fortified zone, where it can only be reached through a long succession of courts, intermediate halls and doorways. pp. 116, 119 The private quarters of the imperial Mughals at Agra and Delhi stretch along the rear wall of the fort, looking eastwards over the Jumna. p. 114 Almost the whole of the western half of the palace complex at Fatehpur Sikri served as the harem,

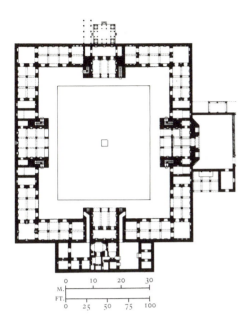

Palace of Jodh Bai at Fatehpur Sikri, with residential apartments arranged symmetrically around a central court on the model of a Rajput mardana.

being separated from the public parts of the palace by a high wall with only small communicating doorways.

Arrangements made by the Rajputs for their royal women were somewhat different, since their residences did not at first provide completely isolated female quarters; as the palaces expanded in the 17th and 18th centuries, however, the older wings were transformed into zenanas. Rajput harems tended to be inward-looking, with apartments on four sides of an open court surrounded by solid external walls. Those in the Amber and Udaipur palaces are located at the end of the royal complexes, with spacious courts occupied by small pavilions for recreation. Residential apartments opening off the courts are laid out on ascending levels, set back so as to create roof-top walkways and terraces. Each suite consists of a pair of chambers connected by a small court; those on the upper level are crowned by gabled roofs and domes. The suitability of this scheme was appreciated by the Mughals, who incorporated Rajput-style zenanas into their own royal complexes. Despite its name, the Palace of Jodh Bai at Fatehpur Sikri was an abode of royal women. It is entered through a well-guarded gateway which leads to a spacious central court on to which the apartments face. pp. 163, 159 47

Harems in Southern Indian palaces were also set apart from the more public sectors. The private enclosures of the royal centre at Vijayanagara are completely surrounded by high tapering walls, the only access being through complicated entries. Many structures inside the enclosures are individual residences, perhaps for different queens, each with one or more sleeping chambers surrounded by columned verandahs. The royal complex at Chandragiri includes a completely separate building for royal women, the Rana Mahal; its upper level has a formal reception room above which rises a central dome. In the Kerala palaces, the private quarters are walled compounds with free-standing structures in the middle. The Thai Kottaram at Padmanabhapuram, the residence of the queen mother, has chambers on two levels arranged around a small square court. 145

Courtly women continued to be segregated in India during the 19th and early 20th centuries, and zenana wings were a necessary part of palace design. The Falaknama at Hyderabad was built in a European, classical style, but the women's apartments are clearly separated. Palaces built in Indo-Saracenic styles, such as the residence of the Gaekwads at Baroda (Vadodara), have a well-defined harem with its own separate entrance portico and internal court.

Private quarters of the ruler

The harem was not the only private zone within Indian palaces: the monarch himself required seclusion from the more public activities of the court. Access to the king's apartments, including his sleeping chamber and the adjacent rooms for his personal use, was strictly guarded; only those summoned could enter. Other parts of the palace were for the sovereign's entertainment, where he could sit surrounded by small groups of male guests smoking the hookah, enjoying readings of poetry or listening to performances of music. 169

Residences of the early sultans included detached structures that functioned both as private quarters and as places of formal reception. The Palace of Rupmati at Mandu has two wings of apartments opening off an audience hall, while stairs ascend to a roof-top 27 terrace with domed viewing pavilions. The private quarters of the Mughal emperors were sometimes coordinated with ceremony and business. The sleeping chamber of

43, 44 Akbar at Fatehpur Sikri, the Khwabgah, or House of Dreams, is built high above the Mardana terrace, precisely aligned with two more public buildings: to the north is the Diwan-i Khass, with its internal column for the meditational seat of the emperor, while to the south is the Daftar Khana, supposedly the hall for private audience. The private

58 apartments of Shah Jahan's palaces are small rectangular pavilions with verandahs on all sides, laid out in formal, linear ensembles that include both public and private darbar

66 halls. The Khass Mahal at Delhi, which functioned as Shah Jahan's private quarters, gives a good idea of one of these pavilions. It has a sleeping chamber for the emperor and a small retreat for his private prayers opening off a central hall. The luxurious

62 ornamentation includes pierced marble screens, inlays of semi-precious stones, and designs painted in gold and silver.

Rajput citadels included assemblages of residential apartments for the king and the

90, 92 male members of the court. The Palace of Rana Kumbha at Chittor is composed of a number of such units, each with a central court flanked by multi-storeyed apartments.

88 At Datia, the royal apartments form part of the central tower that soars above the inner

85 court. The royal sleeping chamber, distinguished by a shallow petalled dome, is situated on the topmost level, immediately above the darbar hall. Suites of apartments used by the ruler himself often overlooked the inner courts of the palaces; better still, they

122 surveyed the pleasure gardens. The Chitra Shala at Bundi, so called because of the paintings (*chitra*) of processions and mythological subjects on the walls, opens off a private garden. Southern Indian palaces also had royal suites which functioned as both private residences and places of formal reception. Among the courtly structures at Vijayanagara which probably operated in this dual way are the nine-domed audience

141 hall and the two-storeyed pavilion with a fanciful cluster of domes known as the Lotus Mahal. The interior of the Raja Mahal at Chandragiri combines a double-height reception room with vaulted apartments intended for private use. A similar juxtaposition of public and private chambers is achieved in the tower of the 18th-

157, 158 century ruler of Kerala, Martanda Varma, in his residence at Padmanabhapuram. Here, successive storeys serve as the state treasury, the sleeping chamber of the king, and a royal meditation room.

❊ ❊ ❊

Pleasure pavilions

Royal architecture had to provide suitable settings for private pleasures where monarchs could meet with their queens and concubines. Miniature paintings executed at the Mughal and Rajput courts give a good idea of the erotic life of the court. An often repeated scene shows the royal figure at night accompanied by one or more female consorts seated in an upper pavilion of the palace, or lying on a terrace beneath an awning. Cushions are spread out and there are cups for wine and other intoxicating drinks, as well as trays filled with fruits and sweetmeats. Female attendants, discreetly posed to one side, are present even at the most intimate moments. Storm clouds with lightning and distant views of forests with flying birds enhance the erotic aspects of the scene.

31 One structure at Mandu obviously devoted to pleasurable diversions is the Jahaz Mahal, or Ship Palace, which owes its name to the floating effect of the building when reflected in the waters of the two lakes between which it is built. On one of his visits to Mandu, Jahangir wrote about an entertainment in the Jahaz Mahal: 'In the beginning of the evening they lighted lanterns and lamps all round the lake. [These] . . . cast their reflection on the water and it appeared as if the whole surface of the water was a plain of fire. A grand entertainment took place and the drunkards indulged themselves to

29 excess.' The Jahaz Mahal has residential apartments below and a terrace above where cooling breezes could be enjoyed by courtiers. The Sat Manzil at Bijapur is a pleasure pavilion that rises above the outer walls of the palace. Water cisterns for bathing are provided in some chambers, and paintings of courtiers with dancing girls, now faded, adorn the walls.

The luxurious and refined tastes of the Mughals found expression in the inventive pleasure pavilions with which they furnished their palaces. The Mardana at Fatehpur

42 Sikri is overlooked by the Panch Mahal, with ascending terraces arranged in a fanciful pyramidal design. The pavement in the middle of the Mardana is laid out as a vast *pachisi* board, on which human beings served as pieces, all to be viewed from above by the imperial players. To the south is the Anup Talao, a square pool with a central platform reached by four bridges; the raised seat in the middle may have been used by the emperor himself. An ornately decorated pavilion at one corner of the pool has no purpose other than diversion.

The most sumptuous part of the Delhi palace was the Rang Mahal, or Golden Pavilion, originally surrounded by zenana apartments. The main hall has apartments at the ends, each decorated with mirrored vaults and ceilings. A marble fountain set into

69 the floor is shaped like a large lotus flower, surrounded by inlays of semi-precious stones. That sensual gratification was the overriding intention is implied by a verse from

71 Khusraw, the famous Persian poet, inscribed on the corner arches of the nearby Diwan-i Khass: 'If there be paradise on earth, it is here, it is here, it is here.'

Rajput palaces, though less formally organized than those of the Mughals, were abundantly provided with pavilions, balconies and terraces, especially at the upper levels, to serve as retreats for members of the court. Picturesque arrangements of roof-top chhatris and jharokas provided ideal settings for entertainment and leisure, with fine

101 views of the surrounding landscape. Almost all Rajput palaces included apartments
123 known as *shish mahals*, or mirror pavilions, intended for visual delight – their walls,
13, 14 vaults and domes entirely covered with mirrors, and their niches and windows inset with
16 pieces of coloured glass. Pierced stone screens known as *jalis* were also used, especially in the upper balconies from where courtiers and royal women could gaze into the inner courts. The Jhanki Mahal, or Glimpse Pavilion, in the zenana of the Jodhpur palace derives its name from the breathtaking panoramas that are visible through the geometric jalis.

Southern Indian palaces, too, were partly devoted to pleasurable diversions. The complex of the nayakas at Gingee has apartments arranged symmetrically around a square pool where courtly entertainments took place. The Madurai palace preserves an

151 impressive dance hall with a stage at one end for musicians and performers. The hall is roofed with a lofty vault carried on transverse cusped arches. A dance hall also forms

part of the Padmanabhapuram residence, its polished plaster floor and aisles separated by stone columns providing an ideal setting for evening concerts. The upper walkway with wooden screens allowed courtly women to enjoy the dancers and instrumentalists without being observed. *162*

Royal architecture in the 19th and 20th centuries gave particular emphasis to the pursuit of pleasure and comfort. Guest houses for European visitors were none other than pleasure pavilions, designed purposely for recreation and pleasure, with facilities for sports and games, including tennis courts, billiard rooms, card rooms and swimming *198,* pools. Large reception halls were more often used for parties and concerts than for state *201* receptions.

Gardens

Indian rulers and their courtiers relaxed in palace gardens where they could enjoy *117* verdant and refreshing surroundings as well as a certain degree of privacy. Planting was defined by geometric formations of pools, channels, fountains and water chutes, the most popular arrangement being that of four plots, known by the Persian term *charbagh*. Certain courtly celebrations took place in gardens: at Holi, for example, courtiers squirted each other with vividly coloured water. Gardens were also the setting for feasts and entertainments; miniature paintings show courtiers eating and drinking, listening to music and enjoying displays of fireworks.

Elaborate arrangements intended to delight the court were made at Delhi where a *p. 119* long waterway, the Nahr-i Bihisht, or Stream of Paradise, flowed continuously through *66,* the private apartments. Water issued from a pavilion at the extreme north-east of the *69,* royal complex from where it proceeded to the Hayat Bakhsh Bagh, or Life-bestowing *71* Garden. In its original form, this was a symmetrical arrangements of sixteen plots with a central pool; the end pavilions have chutes with cascades.

The palace at Amber is well endowed with courtly gardens. The small private *p. 162* garden in the third court has a central star-shaped pool surrounded by geometric flower beds. Below the citadel is an artificial lake with a formal garden protruding into it from *119* one side. Its uppermost terrace has a large octagonal pool; geometric flower beds cover the other terraces. Because of its matchless setting overlooking Lake Pichola, the City Palace at Udaipur illustrates to perfection the Rajput ideal of courtly delight. The *96* climax of its interior is the Amar Vilas at the topmost level, an elevated garden with trees and plants growing around a square pool. A hall on the north side, the Badi Mahal, has a *98* square marble bath for the enjoyment of the ruler and his women. Further diversions for the Udaipur court were boating trips to garden palaces on islands in the lake. The complex on Jag Mandir includes a small garden with three towered pavilions arranged *95* around a pool with fancifully shaped sides.

That some royal complexes were actually conceived as garden residences is best demonstrated by the 18th-century palace of the Jats at Dig, where pleasure pavilions are *p. 166,* disposed on four sides of a formal water garden, complete with axial channels, pools and *128–* fountains. Artificial lakes at either end of the garden are treated as reflecting pools, *132* overhung by courtly balconies. That this garden was intended to evoke the monsoon season is shown by the names of two pavilions, which are those of the monsoon months,

Opposite: *Many parts of the palace were intended simply for enjoyment, such as the terraces from which to view the fountains and formally planted flower beds, and to experience the cooling breezes of the evening. In this miniature painting, Muhammad Reza Khan, an 18th-century deputy nawab of Bengal, has put aside his sword and shield. He sits on a carpet smoking a hookah, undisturbed by the two fan-bearers and the valet who holds out his turban. Other than two guards on a distant terrace, the palace is empty and tranquil.*

and by the system of pipes, water and large loose stones that creates thunder-like noises inside another pavilion.

Resorts and lodges

Recreation in itself was sufficient reason for constructing a palace, and many courtly buildings were located outside the capitals. Indian pleasure resorts were usually set in spacious parks with lakes, well stocked with animals, birds and fish, where hunting expeditions and picnics could take place. Small lodges were expressly built for rulers and their retinues to rest in during the heat of the day or to camp in overnight. Among the earliest remains of this type of architecture are the hunting lodges erected by Firuz Shah in what was once the wooded hinterland of Delhi. Designed as temporary places of relaxation, these small buildings have vaulted chambers with terraces above. Another example of a purpose-built pleasure resort is at Kumatgi, a short distance from Bijapur, on the bank of a large reservoir. One pavilion with an octagonal tower is surrounded by water; another is decorated with paintings showing royal courtiers hunting, eating and dallying with their lovers.

The Mughals never lost their taste for nomadic life and always loved camping expeditions. The palace established by the first emperor, Babur, in the early 16th century at Dholpur in Central India is, in fact, little more than a garden setting for the imperial camp; almost the only permanent features are the pools and water channels cut into the bedrock. Pleasure gardens once lined the Jumna, on the bank opposite the imperial citadels. One of these, the Ram Bagh at Agra, established by Jahangir's wife Nur Jahan, has a small terrace with a central pool and two pavilions at the south-western corner. But by far the most spectacular Mughal pleasure resorts are the gardens laid out along the shores of Lake Dal in Kashmir's Srinagar Valley. Many of these are associated with Jahangir, who made frequent trips to Kashmir. The luxuriantly planted and well-watered terraces of these resorts bore poetical names like Shalimar Bagh ('Garden of Happiness') and Nishat Bagh ('Garden of Gladness'). Having accompanied the emperor on the arduous journey from the plains, the royal party rested in sumptuously appointed tents pitched on the grassy terraces. Permanent pavilions, with tiled pyramidal roofs in the Kashmiri style, were intended for recreation rather than business. The stone seat used by the emperor inside the Diwan-i Amm at Shalimar had water flowing beneath it before descending to the lake below.

With their love of hunting, the Mughals erected shooting lodges on the edges of great estates. Some took the form of towers, such as the Hashtsal Minar at Palam, not far from Delhi, which was erected by Shah Jahan in imitation of the much earlier Qutb Minar. The Rajputs also had the habit of building shooting towers outside the walls of their citadels. Among the hunting lodges that dot the hills around Lake Pichola is the Khas Odi, which even includes a cage for wild animals. The Shikar Burj in the wooded hills above Bundi is a hunting lodge with a central tower distinguished by its large curved roof. The reservoir to the rear is overlooked by balconies from which tigers and other wild animals were once shot.

10

Essential services

INDIAN PALACES demanded constant supplies of provisions and goods for which they depended on markets, workshops and stores. Merchants and artisans were regular visitors at the courts, where they received orders and commissions from the royal officers as well as from members of the royal household. Of all commodities, however, water was the most precious, especially in the dry zones of Northern and Western India and in the Deccan. Residences were equipped with sophisticated hydraulic schemes that guaranteed regular supplies throughout the year; only in this way could the royal kitchens and baths operate, not to mention the channels, pools and fountains of the palace gardens.

Markets and workshops

Not all items required by the palace could be produced by artisans directly employed by the king. Palaces relied on bazaars where goods made all over India, and even imported from foreign countries, were on sale. Such markets were usually located on the outskirts of the citadel, immediately next to the main gate of the palace, and sometimes even inside the fortified zone itself. Here were sold everyday items, together with luxury goods such as woven cloths, silk fabrics, embroidered velvets, gold chains, silver vessels, gilded steel weapons and gem-encrusted jewels. Near to the bazaars were the stables where horses and elephants were housed, as well as bullocks, oxen, asses, camels and other beasts of transport and labour.

8, 9

Bazaars were closely related to workshops, or *karkhanas* as they were called at the Muslim courts, where goods were manufactured exclusively for the palace. They included stores for precious items, such as wines and spices, as well as factories employing large numbers of skilled craftsmen – weavers to make luxury carpets and brocades, scribes to copy religious texts and historical epics, painters to provide illustrations for books, and jewellers to cut precious stones and mount them. Mints, where coins of silver and gold were produced under the watchful eyes of armed guards, were sometimes also associated with the karkhanas.

Not all palaces in India preserve their bazaars and karkhanas, since these buildings were often poorly constructed; even so, limited architectural evidence does exist. At Golconda, the principal east-west road of the town leading up to the main gate of the fortified precinct is lined with arcades for merchants, artisans and troops. Similarly, the main approach road to the royal residence at Fatehpur Sikri from the north-east has shops on both sides for almost its entire length. Excavations show that each shop had a small rectangular chamber with two descending platforms in front; costly wares were probably stored in the back while the platforms were used for everyday business. Pitched wooden roofs sheltered the bazaar from sun and rain. The market opens up into a large square court with entrance portals in the middle of each side; this is the Chahar Suq, where stalls were set up under awnings. Honoured guests were ceremonially received here by the emperor himself.

5

Before arriving at the Diwan-i Amm, the bazaar street of Fatehpur Sikri passes by the imperial karkhana. The workshop consists of a spacious quadrangle surrounded on four sides by double rows of vaulted chambers for different stores and factories. There are also two market streets forming a cross in the town below the citadel, with red sandstone colonnades defining individual shops and stores. North of the royal residence, below the ridge overlooking the great tank, is a large caravanserai for travelling merchants and mercenaries. Lodgings are arranged around a spacious court, with corner suites for special guests.

p. 116 The Mughal citadels at Agra and Delhi integrated bazaars lined with small shops into the overall planning of the royal precincts. The Minar Bazaar of the Agra palace, so called after the *minar*, or lamps, that were lit there on festival occasions, proceeds from the Hathi Pol to the main court between the Diwan-i Amm and the Moti Masjid. The one at Delhi, known as the Chhatta Chowk, still functions as a market for luxury items. p. 119 It leads from the principal entrance of the palace, the Lahore Darwaza, to the Naqqar Khana, a building that marks the beginning of the formal reception area. The Chhatta Chowk is double-storeyed, with arcaded shops on both levels. Masonry vaults roof almost its entire length, except for the octagonal court in the middle which is open to the sky. The main city bazaar, the Chandni Chowk, extends on the same line outside the gate.

Rajput residences never included bazaars within their walls. The market street leading up to the Badi Pol at Udaipur links the commercial quarter of the city with the residence of the ruler. The first interior court of the palace is enclosed on three sides by arcades for stables and guards; additional accommodation for animals and servants is provided in long wings at a lower level to the east. Service quarters and stables are similarly distributed below the walls of the Bundi palace. In contrast to these traditional Rajput schemes, Jaipur provides an exceptional instance of urban planning, with the palace surrounded on three sides by wide streets with ample provision for shops and markets.

Kitchens and dining rooms

Though there are copious references to royal banquets and feasts at Indian courts, and some allusions to the favourite dishes of rulers, almost nothing is recorded about royal kitchens until the Mughal period. The Mughal courts were provided with an imperial kitchen department, the *matbakh*, responsible for all of the drinking water consumed at court, the supply of fresh and dried fruits, the preparation of cooked foods, and the baking of various breads. The kitchen staff and their activities in the Agra palace are described in some detail by Abul Fazl, chief chronicler of Akbar's reign. They included a treasurer and his assistants to keep detailed estimates and accounts, clerks, food-buyers, a large retinue of cooks 'from all countries', food-tasters, and servers. Storekeepers checked on incoming food, stocks of spices and intoxicants, and the collections of precious serving dishes made of gold and silver, as well as the ceramic bowls and dishes imported from China.

Under the expert care of the cooks at Agra, rice from various sources, corn, pulses, sugar, salt and clarified butter were gathered and stored at the beginning of each season;

kitchen gardens provided most of the fresh vegetables. Goats, sheep and fowl were slaughtered outside the palace, and the meat washed and sent to the kitchen in sealed sacks; within the kitchen it was washed again in water taken from sealed vessels before being cooked. After being tasted by the cooks and the masters of the kitchen, the finished dishes were placed in utensils of gold or silver, tinned copper or earthenware, tied up in cloths and sealed with a note of their contents, and then sent to the table. Storekeepers made lists of the vessels used so that none might be replaced on its way to the imperial table. Dishes were carried by masters and cooks accompanied by mace-bearers; a similar procession proceeded from the bakery. As a mark of special favour, some dishes might be sent to the queens and princes; rare fruits were distributed as gifts by the emperor among the courtly ladies. Apart from preparing the meals required for the emperor's own table, the kitchen was also responsible for meals eaten in the zenana. The same department supplied courtiers with wine and drugs such as opium. A subordinate kitchen department, completely separate from that of the royal household, prepared the food that was distributed as charity among the poor.

Cooking tended to take place in open courtyards, under awnings or temporary shelters, always at some distance away from the inhabitants of the royal precinct, which explains the overall lack of architectural evidence for kitchens in most palaces. Even so, some kitchens were built in permanent materials, almost always with holes in the roofs for smoke to escape. Among the service buildings situated below the royal residence at Fatehpur Sikri is a multi-storeyed complex known as the House of Hakim, after the master of the matbakh. It has narrow vaulted chambers and a domed hall, all with ventilation holes and water outlets; a wide passage and a spacious court link the complex to the public parts of the palace.

As Rajput citadels expanded over the centuries they incorporated kitchens and food stores outside the main residential blocks. The Moti Chowk at Udaipur, which gives access to the inner parts of the palace, also leads directly to a kitchen complex with its own small court and a number of vaulted chambers with characteristic ventilation outlets. Food stores in Southern Indian palaces were sometimes separate buildings of some importance. The granaries standing in the royal zone at Gingee, as well as on the summits of the nearby rocky citadels, are monumental structures with lofty interior vaults. One example has four interconnecting chambers, with communicating doorways raised high above the floor which would have been deeply covered with grain.

In contrast to food preparation, dining took place inside the private apartments of the palace; only rarely was a particular room separately designated for this purpose. An exception is the eating chamber in the Gopal Bhawan at Dig where diners sat on the floor, facing a raised bench in the shape of an ellipse. The largest edifice in the Padmanabhapuram complex is the Uttupura, a long dining hall on two levels where many hundreds of Brahmins were fed on festive occasions. Dining areas for members of the royal household are located in the private apartments overlooking one of the palace pools.

By the 19th century, banqueting halls had become an essential feature, partly in imitation of the European habit of public dining on state occasions. Most of the great Western-style palaces of the period, from the Aina Mahal in Murshidabad to the Lalbagh in Indore, are provided with formal banqueting rooms, furnished with

European tables and chairs for both Indian royal guests and British governmental
23 visitors. The impressive dining chamber of the Jai Vilas at Gwalior is almost completely
filled with a U-shaped table; brandy and cigars were circulated among the guests by a
solid silver model railway that runs along the top. In the 20th century, dining rooms in
the latest Modernist styles, as at Indore and Morvi, reflect the triumph of European
eating habits among India's princely families.

※ ※ ※

Water supply

Palace citadels generally made good use of wells and cisterns to capture rain water, but
these always had to be supplemented with artificial reservoirs, known as 'tanks', in
which water was trapped by earthen or stone dam walls. Such tanks sometimes
dominated the overall planning of the royal complex. Tughluqabad is built right up to
the edge of an immense artificial lake with a dam wall extending outwards that protected
the stronghold as well as supplying it with water. Large reservoirs dammed with earthen
31 walls were created on the forested plateau at Mandu, providing a picturesque setting for
many of the pleasure pavilions and residences of the Malwa rulers. Evidence of a
29 comprehensive system of hydraulic works there is seen in the fountains and water
channels set into the floors of numerous courtly structures.

Situated as it was in a particularly arid part of the Deccan, Bijapur was entirely
dependent on an artificially created water collection scheme. The Adil Shahi rulers of
this city created a network of aqueducts and tunnels, the latter with square towers at
regular intervals to control the pressure, conducting water directly into the fortified
royal residence. Terracotta pipes in the walls of the upper apartments of the Sat Manzil
confirm that water was not confined to the ground floor of courtly buildings. Tanks and
channels at Golconda were constructed beside the steps that led to the summit of the
Bala Hisar. Teams of oxen at each level, pulling huge leather buckets by ropes and
pulleys, poured water into the higher cisterns; waste flowed downwards through
earthenware pipes embedded in the walls.

The Mughals took great trouble to invent effective hydraulic systems. Channels and
aqueducts conducted water from many kilometres upstream on the Jumna to the
citadels at both Agra and Delhi; in addition, complicated arrangements of wheels,
pulleys and buckets lifted water directly from the river. The Shah Burj at the north-east
corner of the Delhi fort marks the point where water was transported to the upper level
of the palace to feed the Nahr-i Bihisht channel. The vast reservoir to the north of the
ridge at Fatehpur Sikri provided the major source of water for the gardens and orchards
laid out along its bank, as well as for the animals housed in the stables nearby. An
ingenious line of wells, aqueducts and multiple tiers of pulleys with buckets raised water
up to the ridge, where it was stored in plaster-lined tanks before being conveyed in
channels through the palace courtyards. One element in this elaborate scheme is the
baoli, or step-well, on the edge of the reservoir. It has podiums on the roof for bullocks
and winches for pulleys; staircases descend to a vaulted gallery that runs around a deep
octagonal well. The garden palaces of Kashmir, which are still well maintained today,
take advantage of the hilly terrain to divert streams into artificial canals; water is led
through the gardens in channels, descending as chutes from one terrace to the next
before being discharged into Lake Dal.

Equally comprehensive procedures were developed by the Rajputs to equip their residences with water. Many royal complexes were constructed on the edges of artificial reservoirs from which water was gathered in buckets, hoisted up and then forced through concealed pipes to the inner zones. Only in this way could the royal gardens, pools and fountains be serviced, especially those which, like the Amar Vilas at Udaipur, are situated at the upper levels. The extreme shortage of water in the desert areas of Rajasthan meant that citadels in these regions had to depend on deep step-wells. One of the most ingenious hydraulic systems is still in operation at Dig. Here, a plaster-lined tank for collecting rain has innumerable pipes set into the sides, each hole numbered to indicate the channels and fountains that it feeds. Rags dipped in different pigments are stuffed into the holes to colour the water, resulting in dazzling, multi-tinted sprays.

Southern Indian palaces were also well provided with water, great tanks being situated on their outskirts or excavated into the ground within the royal precincts. Channels drew water off the Tungabhadra River at a higher level some distance from Vijayanagara, and transported it to storage tanks from where it flowed in masonry
137 channels and aqueducts through the royal enclosures, filling ceremonial baths and pleasure pools; other channels were diverted to rice fields and orchards. Gingee has a
148 large rectangular tank partly excavated into the rock where sufficient water could be stored to sustain the occupants of the fort through long sieges.

Baths

Open pools, often with fanciful designs and stepped sides, were a regular feature of palace architecture. There were also purpose-built bath-houses, known in India – as elsewhere in the Islamic world – as *hammams*, where hot water and steam were available. Imported from Persia, they became an essential part of royal life, especially at the Mughal courts, where the emperor and his immediate entourage could retreat for invigorating baths, massages and cures to relieve the discomfort of heat or cold, and where they could relax and enjoy private discussions. Women of the court had their own hammams, strictly segregated from those of the men, for both ritual ablution and luxury bathing.

The earliest hammams in India stand within the royal enclosures of Firuzabad in the Deccan. Now dilapidated, they still show small chambers roofed with domes and vaults provided with holes for escaping steam, a characteristic feature. The hammam at Ahmadnagar has an unusual ventilator tower, or *badgir*, which trapped air currents for drying hair and clothes in the chambers below. The importance of royal hammams appears at Golconda, where a monumental bath is situated immediately inside the main gate of the fort, accessible to nobles, commanders and other important male visitors. It consists of a sequence of chambers with stone-lined pools and ventilated brick vaults.

Hammams were incorporated into all the Mughal palaces. There were no less than twelve inside the citadel at Fatehpur Sikri: those below the Diwan-i Amm, next to the rainwater tanks, were for the emperor and the most important of his courtiers; the bath opening directly off the Palace of Jodh Bai was for the royal women; while the other baths located on the edge of the great reservoir near the orchards and gardens were for visitors. Each has a different combination of interlocking chambers roofed with ventilated domes and vaults, some with fountains set into the floors. Narrow doors and long corridors with multiple changes of direction ensure privacy while warding off the outside air. The need to insulate the inner chambers sometimes results in the doubling of walls and roofs. Pipes are embedded in the walls, and the floors of hot rooms are elevated on short pillars, creating a hollow space below for the hot air. The decoration in some of the bath buildings is elaborate, with ample use of gold paint. Only one hammam is preserved in the palace at Delhi. That this was a structure of some importance is indicated by its position on the main axial waterway of the royal complex, adjacent to the splendidly appointed Diwan-i Khass. Changing and bathing rooms have marble fountains and wall panels decked with inlays of semi-precious stones, some with sunflowers surrounded by petalled stems; communicating windows were once filled with coloured glass. Floor channels in the corridors served to conduct heated water.

The inclusion of modern amenities in the European-style palaces of the present century did nothing to rob bathing of its sense of pleasure and luxury. Elaborate plumbing systems guaranteed water for the increasing number of washbasins, baths and showers with which these palaces were furnished. In the private residential suites at *197, 206* Morvi and Jodhpur, baths and washbasins are fashioned out of marble and onyx to *198, 201* resemble gigantic sea shells and other fanciful designs. Swimming pools – much less novel in India than in Europe – exercised the imagination of designers who sometimes supplied murals with aquatic and zodiacal themes.

Religious themes are common in Indian palaces, since they affirm significant links between kings and gods. The doors opening onto the third inner court in the City Palace at Jaipur have panels of beaten brass showing scenes from the life of Krishna. In these 18th-century compositions the god appears as the youthful guardian of the village cows. In the upper panel he hides in the tree together with the clothes that he has stolen from his female companions who sport in the river beneath; in the lower panel he plays the flute while tenderly embracing his favourite, Radha.

Palaces lost and imagined

DESPITE THE antiquity of Indian civilization and the frequent references to palace architecture in historical literature, almost no royal buildings, standing or in ruins, predate the arrival of the Muslim invaders. That Indian kings began building palaces only after the 13th century is obviously not the case. Archaeological fragments of lost palaces suggest something of a flourishing tradition that made ample use of wood, a material which could not long withstand India's severe monsoonal climate. Wooden palaces *157–* built in more recent centuries, such as that at Padmanabhapuram, *162* represent an indigenous tradition that has virtually disappeared.

Valuable data about India's royal architecture is also available from artistic sources, such as the sculptured reliefs and mural paintings on early religious monuments. Additional information, though of a theoretical nature, is contained in treatises and manuals, such as the *Arthashastra* and the *Vastushastras*; epics in Sanskrit, India's oldest sacred language, present poetic evocations of courtly life and its buildings. In one way or another, these literary descriptions are ideal pictures of an imagined royal architecture rather than a record of any particular palace.

Representation of a palace in a carved relief from the Buddhist monument at Bharhut dating from the 2nd century BC.

Archaeological remains

Scattered remains give tantalizing glimpses of Indian palaces in the pre-Muslim era, indicating an ephemeral tradition of brick, timber, thatch and plaster. For some reason, architects in these early centuries seem to have been reluctant to choose permanent materials for royal buildings, even though stone construction was in widespread use for religious monuments. Despite the attested skills of Indian masons and carvers over some two thousand years and more, royal architecture appears to have been more closely related to domestic practice in terms of materials and techniques, even if it was larger in scale and more elaborate in execution.

The oldest remains in India that can with any certainty be identified as royal in function are at Patna in Eastern India, once Pataliputra, capital of the Mauryas. The city was visited in the 4th century BC by a Greek envoy to India, Megasthenes, who reports that it was a parallelogram, girded by a ditch and a wooden wall, with 570 towers and 64 gates. The Maurya palace was set in gardens and contained a series of open halls with wooden columns decorated in gold and silver, excelling in magnificence the Achaemenid palaces of Persia. This comparison with Achaemenid royal architecture is significant, since there were obvious cultural and artistic contacts between the Mauryas and their Persian predecessors.

Archaeologists working at Kumrahar and Bulandibagh, two sites within modern Patna, have revealed traces of the Maurya palace. Wooden footings and floor planks indicate a columned hall with regularly spaced circular columns, possibly used for receptions and royal audiences; a unique wooden passageway, more than 75 metres (some 250 feet) long, may have formed part of the defence system of the city. Among the stone fragments that were discovered at these sites are column capitals with fluted sides and stylized foliate ornament in typical Achaemenid style. These meagre clues suggest that the Mauryas modelled their palace on Persian practice, with an emphasis on symmetrical and formal arrangements of columned halls, known in ancient Persian as *apadanas*.

Unfortunately, other early cities in India yield even less archaeological evidence about past royal buildings. Investigations at Kausambi and Sravasti in Central India have brought to light levels of occupation that go back to the 6th century BC; architectural traces include earthen ramparts, brick walls, moats and gates. Sisupalgarh in Eastern India is an almost perfectly square fort dating from the 3rd century BC, with similar proof of past occupation. At none of these sites has it been possible to recover the forms of actual courtly buildings, despite the fact that historical sources insist that they were once flourishing royal cities. Modern centres, such as Ayodhya, Kanauj and Ujjain in Central India, which have well-attested past histories, remain largely unexplored; whether the piles of earth and rubble visible on their peripheries conceal the remains of royal buildings has yet to be

Royal architecture in early Indian art: crowds of city dwellers with palaces beyond, on a carved panel of the monument at Sanchi dating from the 1st century BC (above); and a 5th-century AD mural at Ajanta showing courtiers within a pillared verandah (right).

determined. Surveys at Halebid and Gangaikondacholapuram in Southern India, headquarters of the Hoysalas and Cholas in the 11th and 12th centuries, have uncovered stone basements and brick walls; the original forms of these palace buildings, though, are lost forever.

Artistic sources

A more satisfactory picture of India's lost palace architecture emerges from a study of early sculpture and painting. Gateways at the Buddhist sites of Bharhut and Sanchi in Central India, dating from the 2nd century BC to the 1st century AD, have posts with tiers of slightly curved lintels in formations known as *toranas*. Relief carvings on the posts and lintels relate the story of Buddha's life as well as popular folk tales with animal and bird heroes known as *Jatakas*. Many of these lively narratives take place in the busy streets of cities and inside the elaborate halls of courtly complexes.

The Bharhut and Sanchi artists show Indian royal buildings of some two thousand years ago as multi-storeyed constructions. Lower levels have open colonnades, with elaborately carved columns and brackets, or solid masonry walls; upper levels are distinguished by projecting wooden balconies. Curved roofs, covered with thatch, have characteristic horseshoe-shaped gabled ends and rows of pot-like finials on the ridges. Towers are created by placing one storey on top of the other in pyramidal fashion, with miniature dome-like roofs at the summits. Wings meeting at right angles enclose courts on two or three sides. Royal gateways take the form of toranas, with tiers of curved lintels supported on pairs of posts.

A comparable picture of royal architecture emerges from the wall-paintings inside the rock-cut Buddhist shrines and monasteries at Ajanta in the western Deccan. Dating from the late 5th century AD, these remarkable murals again portray the life of the Buddha and *Jataka* legends. Animated compositions showing kings, princes, consorts, courtiers, musicians, dancers and attendants in crowded settings give a vivid impression of courtly life of the era. The attention to detail, unsurpassed in Indian art, suggests that the Ajanta painters directly recorded what they could observe of contemporary architecture.

In the compositions we see courtly figures seated or going about their everyday tasks inside royal halls and galleries. The supporting columns of these structures, which are obviously wooden, are hung with garlands of flowers and appear to be inset with semi-precious stones. Plaster floors are reached by steps flanked by animal balustrades; some structures are multi-storeyed. The roofs sheltering the open pavilions are mostly flat, but the eaves overhanging the columns to provide shade are curved. Thatched roofs are shown with supporting timber beams, brackets and rafters. Rudimentary furniture includes beds on short legs and seats with decorated sides and backs. Outside the palaces are gardens with fruit trees inhabited by birds as well as ponds with ducks and fish. Royal precincts are enclosed within solid masonry walls pierced by prominent gateways.

Literary sources

A complementary view of India's vanished courtly buildings may be had from textbooks, architectural manuals and epic compositions. Several chapters in the *Arthashastra* (see p. 10) concentrate on the layouts of fortified palaces. The most satisfactory royal headquarters, it is suggested, are those constructed on a plain surrounded by low ground, on an island in the middle of a river, or at the top of a hill. The fort is to be surrounded by three ditches with sides built of stones or bricks; water flowing through the ditches is filled with crocodiles and lotus plants. Beyond are the ramparts made of earth trampled by elephants, with brick parapets and towers. The ramparts have multi-storeyed entrance gates and small secret passageways.

One chapter of the *Arthashastra* gives information on the interior of a royal fort. It is divided into nine squares by roads running from east to west and from north to south. The central square is occupied by the king's palace, which faces either north or east, next to the 'apartments of the gods', or temple. The text goes on to give the precise locations of the royal kitchens, elephant stables, stores, treasury, accountant's office, guards' quarters and arsenal. Another chapter describes the private chamber of the king, especially the security arrangements required to ensure safety. Courtly women are segregated in their own self-contained quarters which, like those of the king, are provided with guards.

Palaces are also imagined by the authors of the *Vastushastras* (see p. 12), intended as theoretical guidelines for kings and their builders but perhaps reflecting something of actual building practice. The *Mayamata*, a treatise composed in Southern India at some date between the 9th and 12th centuries, is precise in its delineation of palace architecture. According to this text, the royal headquarters consist of a cluster of buildings arranged in concentric enclosures separated from one another by fortifications protected by moats. The number of enclosures differs according to the status of the ruler, a typical scheme consisting of three concentric zones. The innermost enclosure invariably contains the dwellings of the king and queen placed on either side of a central court. In the middle is an altar for the god Brahma, or a covered area with a hundred columns for formal receptions and the administration of justice; they are coordinated with the east-facing coronation pavilion that is situated nearby. Among the surrounding buildings are a treasury, theatre, bath-house, dining hall and residential quarters for guards and for female retainers. The second enclosure has a formal court where parasols, drums and other royal regalia are displayed. Here, too, are service buildings, such as stores, stables, armoury, kitchen, the commander-in-chief's residence, a home for magicians and conjurers, an alms-house, baths, lodgings for nurses and other female servants, and also pleasure pools and gardens. In the third and outermost enclosure are additional stores and stables (including those for elephants), a wrestlers' house, gardens and reservoirs. Immedi-ately outside the palace are barracks for the royal army and bazaars with houses for merchants; orchards and well-stocked game parks occupy the open land beyond.

Particular features of royal buildings are specified in the *Mayamata*. The king's own residence is multi-storeyed, varying in height according to his power and influence. The council chamber is surrounded by pillars and elevated above a parade ground; the royal throne, adorned with appropriate lion motifs, is installed at the western end so that the king may face east when seated upon it; the seats of the chief ministers and commanders occupy the four corners. The coronation building is a columned hall with a raised platform covered by a canopy in the middle. Another important structure is the pavilion in which the king is ceremonially weighed.

Royal architecture also makes an appearance in the *Ramayana* and *Mahabharata* epics, generally as a setting for the courtly audiences, councils of war and discreet conferences in the harems that recur throughout these narratives. Palace descriptions conform to often repeated formulas that express courtly ideals: the reader is encouraged to imagine the might and moral perfection of the monarch, the pomp and glory of his court, and the prosperity and delight of his subjects, rather than any specific architectural details. The treatment of Rama's palace, though only one of many royal buildings mentioned in the *Ramayana*, may be taken as typical. It is a heavenly mansion, comparable with the celestial homes of the gods, such as that of Indra, lord of the skies. Its terraces and towers gleam like snowy mountain peaks in the monsoon clouds, reflecting the sunshine and glittering with jewels like a rainbow. As if to reinforce this connection with the heavens, certain royal apartments are set aside for different seasons, one for the dry winter months, another for the wet monsoon months, and so on. Rama's residence embodies the teeming energy of nature: the gardens are filled with trees that are forever bearing fruit; swans and ducks frolic among the lotuses of the pools and lakes; tame deer, elephants and birds populate the game parks. The floors are inlaid with gold and silver, the walls inset with precious gems and corals that glisten, and there is a profusion of choice textiles, bouquets of flowers, and sandalwood and aloe scents. The audience chamber is illuminated by glorious lamps and the brilliance of the weapons hung on the walls; fires burn for blessings and good fortune, and the smell of incense mingles with the perfume of colourful war-garlands.

The palace as a fortress is another popular motif in the *Ramayana*. The stronghold of Ravana on the island of Lanka, where the climactic battle of the story takes place, is of heavenly beauty, only temporarily inhabited by demons. Its walls are as bright as sunshine and there are heavy gates facing in the four directions. There is a surrounding moat, and three of the gates are guarded by drawbridges; the principal entrance has an immovable bridge lined with a railing and benches of gold. Catapults, cannon and other war machines are concealed in the walls.

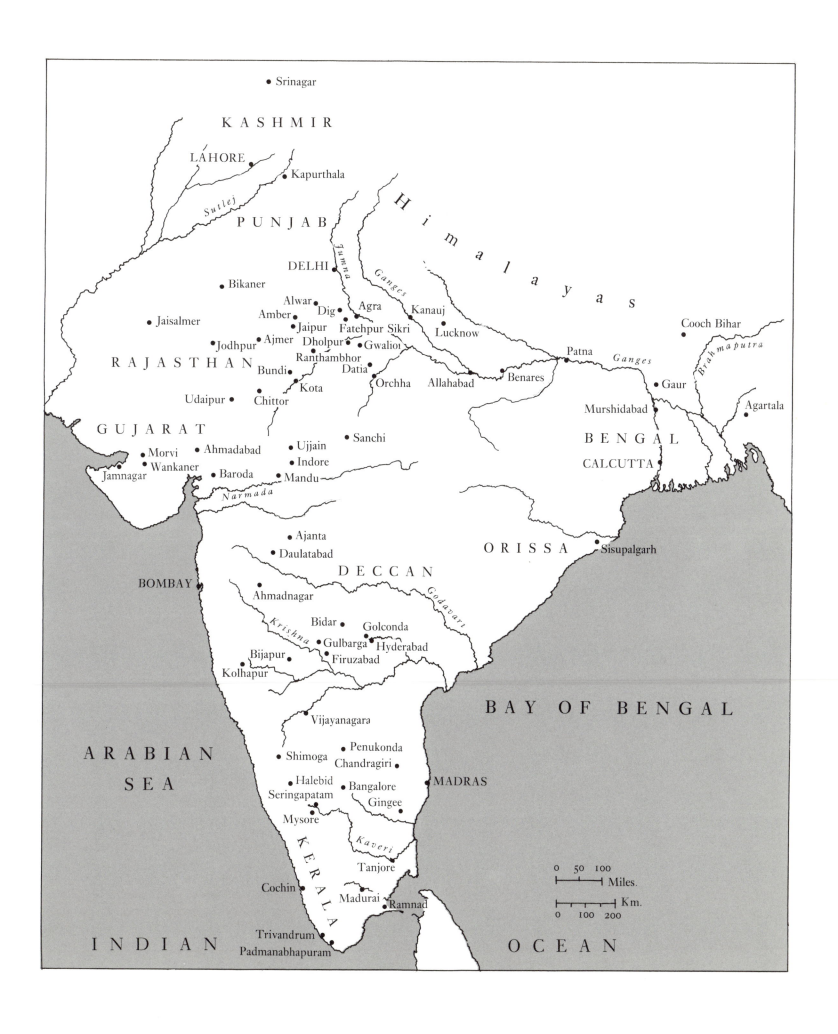

Early Muslim strongholds

Delhi ⚜ Mandu ⚜ Daulatabad ⚜ Bidar

Bijapur ⚜ Golconda

Delhi The first kings to build palaces in stone were the sultans of Northern India. Among the collapsing masonry structures that dot the area in and around Delhi is Kotla Firuz Shah, the citadel of the 14th-century ruler Firuz Shah Tughluq. At the core of his fortified palace complex is an unusual ceremonial pyramid with tiers of arcaded storeys [26]. The sandstone column at the top, erected in the mid-3rd century BC by the Buddhist Emperor Ashoka, was brought from a great distance by Firuz to be re-used as an emblem of royal power.

Mandu

Capital of the sultans of the Malwa region of Central India in the 15th and 16th centuries, this remote hill fort preserves a large group of royal buildings, constructed in a bold style that contrasts sloping massive walls with delicate rooftop pavilions or chhatris. The Palace of Rupmati [27] has a terrace with a pair of chhatris overlooking the ramparts. The Hindola Mahal [28] may have functioned as a formal reception hall.

Water is used effectively: the Palace of Baz Bahadur contains arcades surrounding a basin [30], while the Jahaz Mahal [31] is built on a narrow strip of land between two reservoirs; steps ascend to the upper terrace, where water runs through a spiral channel [29] to a rooftop pleasure pool.

27

28

31

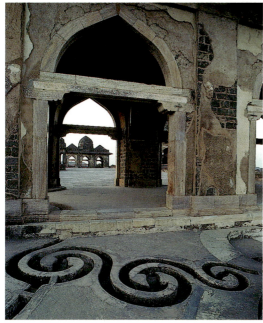

29

30

32

Daulatabad

This site was the first capital of the Bahmanis, rulers of the Deccan plateau in the 14th and 15th centuries. Developed as an impregnable stronghold, Daulatabad consists of a citadel on a steep hill with two fortified complexes of royal buildings at its base [32]. The ramparts are more intact than the courtly structures, which today present a maze of collapsing walls and overgrown courts. The flattish domes and ornate plasterwork are hallmarks of the early Bahmani style.

Bidar

By the middle of the 15th century the Bahmanis were established at Bidar, which for a time commanded much of the Deccan. The relatively complete palace complex inside the fort is dominated by a great mosque, the Solah Khamba Masjid [35]. Its principal dome overlooks many of the royal buildings, including the Diwan-i Amm [35, left], or hall of public audience, where only the stone footings of timber columns survive. The most complete of them, the Rangin Mahal, contains a great hall with delicately carved wooden columns [34]. It and adjacent rooms are ornamented with inlaid mother-of-pearl designs dating from the early 17th century [33], which resemble the patterns of the silver-inlaid gunmetal *bidri* work for which Bidar is famous.

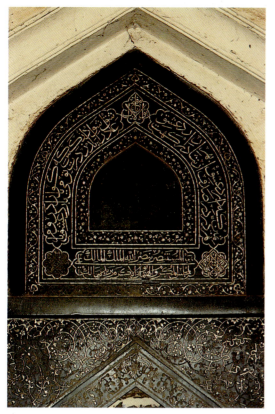

33

34

36

37

Bijapur

The capital of the Adil Shahis enjoyed its heyday from about 1550 to
1650. The royal complex was surrounded by a complete circuit of
walls. The Dad Mahal [38], erected in 1646, is the best-preserved
palace inside: its double-height verandah with lofty timber columns is
backed by vaulted rooms on two levels, some adorned with murals
[37]. Originally intended as a hall of justice, it was later converted into
a relic shrine. The nearby Mecca Masjid [36] is a royal mosque,
possibly intended for courtly women.

38

Golconda

Another Deccan citadel to achieve importance in the 16th and 17th centuries was the capital of the Qutb Shahi rulers. Like Daulatabad [see *32*], it is dominated by a steep fortified hill, the Bala Hisar, with the main palace complex below shielded by massive walls [*39*]. Though most of the buildings have now collapsed, the linear sequence of courts, corridors and halls leading to zones of ever-increasing privacy is still plainly evident. The ruined arches of the Rani Mahal [*40*], once covered with finely worked geometric designs in plaster, face on to a spacious inner court.

40

IN 1198 DELHI became the capital of India's first Muslim kingdom after a successful invasion led by Qutbuddin Aybak, commander of the Ghurid sultan of Afghanistan. Successive dynasties of sultans ruled from Delhi, rapidly extending their influence throughout the subcontinent by conquering Bengal to the east, Malwa to the south-west, Gujarat to the west, the Deccan plateau further south, and even the extreme southernmost tip of the peninsula. Due to the disruptions of military coups and invasions, the Delhi sultans were unable to maintain control over their farflung territories, and by the beginning of the 15th century most of their provinces had broken away to achieve independence.

The capitals of the most important of these newly established kingdoms were Gaur in Bengal, Mandu in Malwa and Ahmadabad in Gujarat; in the Deccan, Daulatabad was the first independent centre, succeeded soon after by Gulbarga. This Deccan kingdom further disintegrated and by the turn of the 16th century was divided into lesser realms, with capitals at Ahmadnagar, Bidar, Bijapur and Golconda. Conflicts between the various sultans meant that no one of these small states was able to establish supremacy. The arrival of the Mughals in the early 16th century marked the end of the Delhi kingdom, and it was not long before Bengal, Malwa and Gujarat were all incorporated into the expanding Mughal empire. Because of their distance from Delhi, the Deccan kingdoms had longer careers, but in the end they too succumbed to the superior Mughal forces.

Stylistic development

India's first sultans came from Afghanistan and Central Asia, regions which had already been converted to Islam, as well as being thoroughly exposed to Persian cultural influence. It was these conquerors who introduced Islam into the subcontinent, together with Persian language, courtly practices and architectural techniques. The first sultans built ambitiously throughout the 13th, 14th and 15th centuries in a style affected by Persian and Central Asian traditions. Rubble and mortar construction, the use of pointed arches for doorways, wall niches and structural supports, and domes and pointed vaults are among the most obvious characteristics. Walls tend to be solid and are sometimes slightly sloping, or battered; they are capped with rows of merlons.

In time, these imported devices came to be blended with indigenous features, since the craftsmen who worked on the palaces would mostly have been local, even if the architects may have been foreign. In traditional Indian architecture the arch is unknown: instead, openings are bridged by setting successive courses of stone further out until they meet at the summit. Other Indian features found in the palaces of the sultans are stone columns with curved brackets; *chhajjas*, or angled eaves that overhang openings and run along the walls as string-courses; and

chhatris, or miniature domed pavilions, that rise above the roof. Surface decoration tends to imitate Persian precedent. Plasterwork is cut into friezes and medallions and filled with stylized arabesque designs, geometric patterns and Persian calligraphy; paint and tilework in similar designs add bright accents of colour. But Indian motifs are also adopted, in particular the lotus flower, which appears in endless variations in bands around the openings and along the walls, as well as in fully modelled form at the summits of domes and vaults.

All of these elements and themes contribute to an austere but rich architectural style that is already apparent in the earliest buildings of the Delhi sultans. The mid-14th-century ceremonial pyramid of Firuz Shah, for instance, is a powerfully conceived building with superimposed arcades. Regional variations of this somewhat stern style are developed in the 15th century, especially at Mandu and Chanderi, twin capitals of Malwa. Palaces at the remote wooded citadel of Mandu have characteristically long low elevations, broken only by rows of arched openings with distinctive angled profiles. The upper portions of the buildings are provided with pyramidal vaults and flattish domes, the latter raised on high drums decorated with merlon motifs. Inventive combinations of arched openings and roof elements are responsible for unusual designs, such as the Jahaz Mahal and Hindola Mahal at Mandu. The Kushk Mahal at Chanderi is a remarkable square building with intersecting long halls that divide the interior into four quarters, each with three storeys of apartments. Tilework provides colour at the tops of the walls and beneath the domes.

The first sultans of the Bahmani kingdom in the Deccan, whose palaces are seen in crumbling condition at Daulatabad and Firuzabad, built in a style similar to that of the Delhi and Mandu sultans. The mid-15th-century complex at Bidar demonstrates a revived interest in Persian and Central Asian models, with an emphasis on ceremonial arched gateways and portals, and a preference for coloured tilework. Persian influence is even more evident in the 16th century, when open pavilions have strictly symmetrical designs with monumental portals. The outstanding example of the Persianized Deccan style at this time is the Farah Bakhsh garden palace at Ahmadnagar. It is laid out on an irregular octagon with imposing portals in the middle of each side which lead to a two-storeyed domed chamber in the middle.

Palace architecture under India's early sultans reaches its climax at Bijapur and Golconda, the two most important Deccan capitals in the 17th century. Royal buildings continue to make use of Persian-style portals, as in the Gagan and Anand Mahals at Bijapur, and extensive vaulted halls become the principal feature of the Golconda palace. Decoration attains a new expression, with a profusion of curved brackets, *jalis* (stone screens), and ornamental parapets; cresting and miniature finials add lively interest to the upper parts of the royal buildings at Bijapur.

26

28,
31

32

34,
35

36–
40

Kotla Firuz Shah, Delhi's main citadel in the second half of the 14th century, was already decaying when sketched by Thomas and William Daniell at the end of the 18th century for their Oriental Scenery. *The circular watchtower and domed pavilion have since disappeared.*

Delhi

The Hindu citadel of Lal Kot, not far from the west bank of the Jumna River, was captured by Qutbuddin Aybak and, renamed Delhi, became the first capital of Muslim India. As it turned out, this was to be only the first of a series of royal cities established by successive sultans in the vicinity.

Nothing remains of royal buildings in the first two capitals. The third, however, **Tughluqabad**, preserves its massive perimeter walls of grey granite as well as the tomb of its founder, Ghiyathuddin (ruled 1320–25). Under the sultans of the Tughluq dynasty the Delhi kingdom reached its greatest extent, encompassing almost all of the subcontinent. The power of Ghiyathuddin, the first of the Tughluqs, may be judged from the impressive mausoleum that stands isolated in the middle of a vast reservoir (now dried up), joined to the city walls by a causeway. The royal stronghold, which is situated in the middle of the south side of the citadel, is enclosed by high walls with towers. The area

immediately to the west, similarly bounded by rubble fortifications, is set aside for Ghiyathuddin's own residence. A second causeway leads from the south-east corner of the citadel to **Adilabad**, a smaller fort added by his successor, Muhammad (ruled 1325–51).

While Tughluqabad continued to be the more important city, Muhammad concentrated most of his building activities at **Jahanpanah**, the fourth capital at Delhi. Several palace structures still stand there in a ruined condition. They are constructed of stone rubble and were once covered by fine plasterwork. The walls have characteristic sloping sides, broken only by unadorned arched openings; flattish domes and arched vaults are used throughout. The crumbling **Bijai Mandal**, or Wonderful Mansion, consists of a vaulted hall with a low octagonal pavilion on its western side, and a domed entrance chamber to the north. Excavations have uncovered the bases of wooden pillars of another structure on the south, possibly the remains of the audience hall described by Ibn Battuta (see pp. 32–33).

The palace complex in Delhi's fifth capital, **Firuzabad**, survives in a more complete form. The citadel is known as **Kotla Firuz Shah** after its royal founder, Firuz Shah (ruled 1351–88), one of Delhi's greatest builders and the first to establish his capital within sight of the Jumna. Firuzabad is divided into three rectangular walled areas. The northern and southern enclosures are now filled with modern buildings; the central enclosure contains the remains of an audience hall, a circular well, the Jami Masjid and a **ceremonial pyramid**. This last structure is a unique monument, with three diminishing tiers of vaulted chambers. On the top level stands an inscribed stone column dating from the period of Ashoka, the 3rd-century BC Maurya emperor, which was brought from Topra in Ambala District in 1357 at the express order of Firuz. The circular well, or *baoli*, nearby is surrounded by subterranean vaulted chambers.

Firuz Shah was also responsible for constructing another royal complex which occupies a large area on a forested ridge a short distance west of Firuzabad, where he erected a second pillar of Ashoka. The **Pir Ghaib** is a two-storeyed rubble building which functioned partly as a mosque. The floor and roof of the southern apartment are pierced by a hollow masonry cylinder, perhaps for making astronomical observations – a function suggested by its mention in contemporary accounts as Kishk-i Jahan Numa, or World-Showing Palace. Firuz also erected several hunting lodges outside Delhi, the most elaborate of which is the **Malcha Mahal**, with nine symmetrically arranged vaulted chambers.

After the death of Firuz Shah the Delhi kingdom became unstable and the Tughluq empire speedily disintegrated. Timur, ruler of Samarqand, dealt a final blow by savagely raiding the capital in 1398. An indication of Delhi's loss of power and prestige is the absence of any surviving royal buildings dating from the 15th century, the period when the city was ruled by the sultans of the Sayyid and Lodi dynasties. Not until the middle of the 16th century, under Sher Shah Suri and the newly arrived Mughals, was Delhi once again able to assert its power. (The later citadels at Purana Qila and Shahjahanabad are discussed on pp. 118–19.)

Mandu

Originally a hill post of the Hindu Paramara rulers, this fort was taken by the Delhi sultans in 1305, after which it became the headquarters of the Central Indian province of Malwa. In 1401 Dilavar Khan broke away from the Delhi régime, and the fort became the capital of an autonomous line of sultans under the name of Mandu, also known as Shadiabad, the City of Joy. The Malwa sultans waged war against the neighbouring kingdoms of Gujarat and the Deccan, sometimes allying themselves with local Rajputs. Hoshang Shah (ruled 1405–35) and Mahmud Khalji (ruled 1436–69) were the most powerful of Mandu's rulers. Despite several setbacks in their campaigns against the Rajputs of Chittor and the Bahmanis, these sultans steadily increased the territories of the Malwa kingdom. Mandu remained the capital

until 1531 when it was captured by the Gujarat sultan, falling to the Mughal forces soon after.

Mandu occupies an irregularly shaped plateau of incomparable beauty, its steeply wooded sides being strongly fortified with walls extending no less than 60 kilometres (37 miles) all around. The principal entrance, the **Delhi Darwaza**, is at the north end of the plateau, where many of the royal monuments are grouped together inside a separate walled enclosure. Other palace buildings are dotted all over the plateau, some perched on the southernmost edge to overlook the plain of the Narmada River, more than 350 metres (1,150 feet) below. Many buildings are associated with reservoirs, the names of which hark back to Paramara times.

The ceremonial approach to the main palace area is through the **Hathi Pol**, or Elephant Gate, with animals (now damaged) carved on the sides. Guard rooms flank the central arched entrance and there are bastions for mounting guns, a feature dating from the Mughal occupation. Inside is the **Palace of Gada Shah**, named after a local chief who flourished during the reign of Mahmud (ruled 1510–26). One building in this complex, now much ruined, has a large central chamber covered with transverse arches which

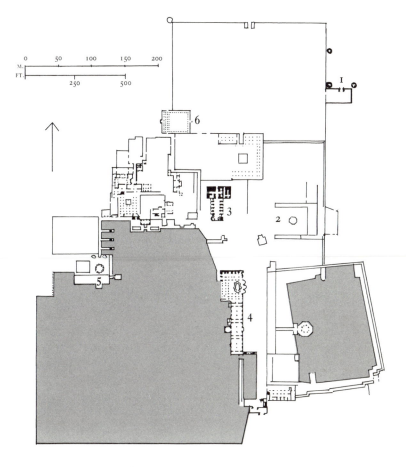

The main palace at Mandu. (1) Hathi Pol, (2) Palace of Gada Shah, (3) Hindola Mahal, (4) Jahaz Mahal, (5) Lal Mahal, (6) Dilwar Khan's Mosque.

may have served as a hall of public audience. Another building is two-storeyed: the lower level has arched openings and side apartments, while the upper level has a large chamber with a fountain from which water flowed through spouts carved with animal heads. The nearby **Hindola Mahal**, or Swing Palace, a name which refers to the shape formed by its sloping buttresses, consists of a main hall with a projecting entrance added later; the vaulted roof supported on transverse arches collapsed long ago. In front is a deep well with a labyrinth of underground rooms, serviced by an ingenious ventilation system, as well as a hammam and a small mosque. A complex of other courtly structures is situated behind the Hindola Mahal.

South of the Hindola Mahal is the **Jahaz Mahal**, or Ship Palace, built on a narrow strip of land between two reservoirs. The palace has three large halls arranged in a line, each with six domes. An extension to the north contains a bath with multi-curved sides. A long flight of steps at the south-east corner ascends to the spacious roof-top terrace where there are several viewing pavilions: that in the middle has a dome adorned with blue and yellow tiles; those at the end are roofed with combinations of pyramidal vaults and smaller domes. Here, too, is another bath; its water, originally raised by a mechanical pulley, flows through spiral channels set into the floor.

Among the other buildings distributed around the plateau is the **Hathi Mahal**, or Elephant Palace, with three arched openings on each side and a dome rising above the central bay. Though now serving as a tomb, it was originally intended as a pleasure pavilion. The **Lal Mahal**, or Ruby Palace, has a central chamber for reception and side rooms for dwellings; a ruined platform with a pavilion is situated in the middle of a spacious court in front.

The remaining courtly monuments are located at the southern edge of the plateau. The **Palace of Baz Bahadur** (ruled 1555–62) is approached by an impressive flight of steps bounded by a lofty arcade. Steps lead through an arched gateway into the outer court. The inscription over the main entrance assigns the construction of the complex to Nasiruddin (ruled 1500–1511), despite the fact that it is named after a later sultan. The main portion of the palace has an open court with a square pool surrounded by vaulted halls and rooms. An arcaded, part-octagonal pavilion projects outwards from the northern wing to give fine views of the garden. A smaller court to the south, surrounded by rooms and halls, was probably for attendants. The **Palace of Rupmati**, on the final crest of the hill beyond, is named after the consort of Baz Bahadur, but it is probably no later than the 15th century. The complex has two wings, one of which consists of a double-height chamber with two rooms at each end.

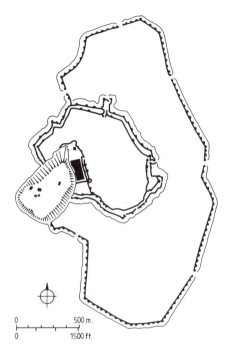

The citadel at Daulatabad.

Daulatabad

After the Tughluq conquest of the Deccan at the end of the 13th century, the Hindu citadel of Devagiri was occupied and renamed Daulatabad. It was to this fortified headquarters that Muhammad attempted to move the Delhi court from Jahanpanah in 1327, in a scheme to disperse Tughluq power. Although his enterprise failed, Daulatabad continued as the headquarters of Muslim power in the Deccan. In 1347 the local governor, Alauddin Hasan Bahman, proclaimed himself sultan, thereby initiating the Bahmani dynasty. Daulatabad was soon abandoned as a capital when the sultans moved their headquarters to Gulbarga, but the fort remained an important centre of military power throughout the 14th and 15th centuries. In 1500 it passed into the hands of the Nizam Shahi rulers of Ahmadnagar. The Emperor Shah Jahan saw Daulatabad as the key to his control over the Deccan, and it was taken by the Mughals in 1633.

The site is overshadowed by a hill some 200 metres (650 feet) high, with sheer, artificially excavated sides commanding a natural pass. The citadel at its summit is reached by steep flights of steps, some of which pass through rock-cut passages that re-use ancient Buddhist caves. Just beneath the summit is a pavilion in Mughal style with a projecting part-octagonal bay.

The base of Daulatabad's rock is surrounded by walls and a deep, rock-cut moat about 15 metres (50 feet) wide, crossed at only one point by a drawbridge. The innermost enclosure of the city, the **Kalakot**, is built up against the hill on its north-eastern flank. Several dilapidated royal buildings stand here. They include the **Chini Mahal**, probably a reception pavilion, which is named after the blue and white tiles that decorate its façade, now mostly fallen. An arched entrance leads to a long, double-height hall roofed with transverse arches; steps to the right ascend to two long chambers at the upper level. The residences opposite include suites of apartments symmetrically disposed around an inner court. The angled arches, plaster roundels, and wooden columns and brackets embedded in the walls are typical features of the Bahmani style.

A path descends from Kalakot to the outer enclosure, the **Mahakot**, once the residence of the court and of the military elite. This zone is protected by a double set of walls that enclose an approximately circular area fanning out from the rock on the north and east; elaborately defended gateways are positioned on three sides. The enclosure is traversed by an east-west road overlooked by the lofty **Chand Minar**, or Moon Tower, which dominates the lower town; a large tank and the spacious **Jami Masjid** are situated nearby. A further circuit of walls, extending to the north, east and south, defines the outer town, or **Ambarkot**.

Bidar

In 1424 this city became the capital of the Bahmani sultans when the capital was transferred here from Gulbarga by Shihabuddin Ahmad (ruled 1422–36). As the 15th century progressed, however, the Bahmani kingdom fragmented into a number of smaller states; in the 16th century, Bidar was the seat of a later line of sultans, the Baridis, the greatest ruler of which was Amir (ruled 1504–43). The Baridi dynasty lasted barely a hundred years, and by the beginning of the 17th century Bidar was absorbed into the Bijapur kingdom. The city was occupied by the Mughal army in 1656.

Bidar's fort and town are both approximately circular and of almost equal area. Each is surrounded by a ring of fortifications with numerous towers, mostly polygonal and massive, many with gun emplacements; above is a battlemented parapet. On the southeast side of the fort, the walls coincide with those of the town, rising above a triple moat hewn out of laterite. A sequence of gates here links the fort with the town. The first is the **Sharza Darwaza**, or Lion Gate, with two sculptured stone animals inserted into its façade; the second, the **Gumbad Darwaza**, or Domed Gate, has sloping walls, pointed arches, corner finials and a dome.

The palace begun by the Bahmanis and renovated by the Baridis provides the most complete picture of Deccan royal architecture in the 15th and 16th centuries. The first residential building inside the complex is the **Rangin Mahal**, or Coloured Palace. It is a multi-chambered pavilion with a six-bay hall facing northwards onto a small court. The wooden construction of the hall is intact in all of its carved detail, including intricately worked lotus capitals and brackets; the doorways are embellished with delicate inlays of mother-of-pearl, as well as with painted designs and poetic inscriptions in Persian. The royal **kitchen** adjoins the pavilion on the west.

The next court provides a setting for the **Solah Khamba Masjid**, or Sixteen-Columned Mosque, the principal place of worship within the palace. The court is known as the **Lal Bagh**, or Ruby Garden. Only the central cistern and axial channel survive; the latter once conducted water from the Tarkash Mahal, on the south side of the court, to a **hammam** with small domed chambers on the north. The **Tarkash Mahal**, or Turkish

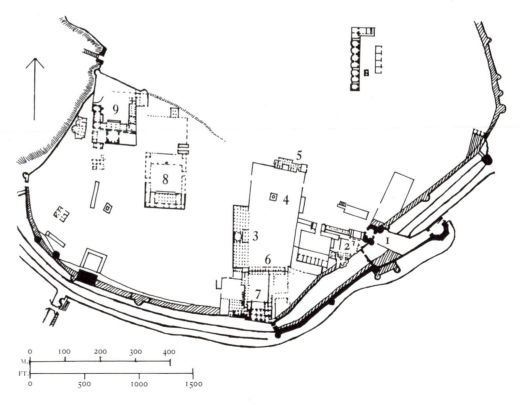

Palace area at Bidar. (1) Gumbad Darwaza, (2) Rangin Mahal, (3) Solah Khamba Masjid, (4) Lal Bagh, (5) hammam, (6) Tarkash Mahal (7) Gagan Mahal, (8) Diwan-i Amm, (9) Takht Mahal.

Pavilion, was a residence, possibly for a foreign queen as the name suggests. Though the building is dilapidated, the delicacy of the plaster decoration is still evident. To the rear is another residential complex known as the **Gagan Mahal**, or Sky Palace, with two series of north-facing chambers and a vaulted gateway.

A spacious terrace extends westwards from the Lal Bagh, commanding views over the surrounding landscape. Numerous cisterns, wells and guard rooms are situated here, as well as two large royal complexes, now decayed. The **Diwan-i Amm**, or Hall of Public Audience, has a raised colonnade of which only the finely carved footing blocks survive. The walls of the surrounding chambers are adorned with coloured tilework in an array of abstract foliate and geometric patterns; the floors have designs in inlaid stonework. The hall faces northwards onto a large square court surrounded by high walls.

A short distance to the north-west is another large complex, also surrounded by high walls, the **Takht Mahal**, or Throne Pavilion. The focus here is the tall portal in the middle of the west side of the court; finely worked stone bands define the pointed-arched recesses, while a hint of coloured tilework still remains in the spandrels. The imposing throne room is situated on the south side of the court, connected to a columned hall; suites of smaller chambers open off to the sides. An oval pool is the principal feature of a smaller court in the south-west corner of the complex. A short distance to the west is a pavilion with a part-octagonal bay looking down on the reservoir in the lower part of the fort.

Bijapur

This Bahmani period city became the headquarters of a new line of rulers founded by Yusuf Adil Khan in 1490. The fortunes of the Adil Shahis, as these rulers styled themselves, were greatly boosted after the defeat of Vijayanagara in 1565 (see p. 185). Ali Adil Shah and his successor, Ibrahim Adil Shah, were the greatest of the Bijapur sultans. During their reigns (1558–1627) the capital was strongly fortified and many imposing monuments were added, including the Jami Masjid and a variety of tombs, of which the Gol Gumbad, with its immense dome, is the largest. In 1599 Ibrahim ordered the construction of Nauraspur, intended as a twin city immediately east of Bijapur, which was never completed. In 1686 the Adil Shahi kingdom was incorporated into the Mughal empire.

Bijapur has two concentric circuits of fortifications, the royal citadel occupying the inner zone. The walls are of massive stonework with cylindrical towers protected by a moat; hooded slits and battlements are positioned high up. Of the broadly arched bridges that crossed the moat leading to the gateways, only those on the south and east have been spared. There are several small mosques inside the citadel, the finest being the **Mecca Masjid**, entirely surrounded by high walls. Palace structures here once benefited from a regular supply of water conducted through a network of aqueducts and subterranean water channels, the remains of which are still evident.

The **Gagan Mahal** or Sky Palace, which was erected in 1561 by Ali Adil Shah, faces northwards onto a large open space used for military displays. Its façade is dominated by a large central arch, with narrower arches on either side; plasterwork in the spandrels displays medallion-and-bracket motifs, the latter being fish-shaped (the fish was an emblem of the Adil Shahis). The wooden structure connecting the arches to the rear apartments has collapsed. The nearby **Anand Mahal**, or Palace of Delight, dates from 1589. It, too, has a triple-arched façade leading to a great hall, with smaller rooms opening off at the rear on two levels.

A large quadrangular court marks the core of Bijapur's citadel. Above the north-west corner, looking out over the moat, rises the **Sat Manzil**, or Seven[-Storeyed] Palace, dating from 1583, of which only five levels are intact. The façade presents unadorned arched openings, but the interior was once richly ornamented with murals. Immediately to the north is a small pavilion known as the **Jala Mandir**, ornately decorated with projecting brackets and eaves, and crowned with a petalled dome; it stands in the middle of a pool. To the east is a block of residential apartments, the interiors of which retain the remains of ornate relief plasterwork. On the south side of the Sat Manzil court is the **Chini Mahal**, so called because of the Chinese ceramics that were discovered nearby. The building extends across the whole width of the court, its central vaulted hall being almost 40 metres (130 feet) long.

Beyond the eastern moat, but connected with the citadel by a bridge, is the **Dad Mahal**, or Hall of Justice, erected in 1646; it was later converted into a shrine for a relic of the Prophet, and renamed the Athar Mahal. This gives the most complete idea of a typical Bijapur palace. It has a portico consisting of four double-height teak columns with elaborately carved brackets carrying a painted panelled ceiling. The portico faces eastwards onto a garden with a central square pool. Double suites of vaulted rooms on two levels inside include a large hall that opens onto the verandah. Small chambers at either end have murals depicting blue-flowering creepers and ornamental vases; scenes of courtiers, now mostly lost, date from the 18th century.

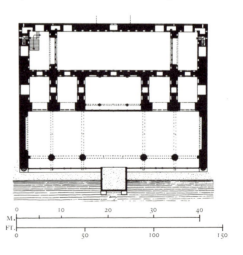

The Gagan Mahal at Bijapur.

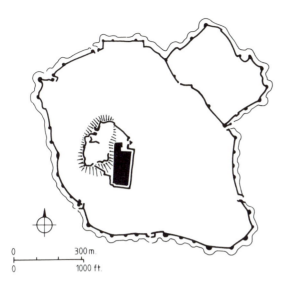

The citadel at Golconda.

Golconda

Another Bahmani fortress to become the capital of an independent line of rulers was Golconda, in the eastern part of the Deccan. At the beginning of the 16th century Quli Qutb al-Mulk (ruled to 1543) was responsible for transforming Golconda into the capital of the newly founded Qutb Shahi dynasty. The palace inside the fort was greatly expanded during the period of Ibrahim (ruled 1550–80), and many structures were added by later rulers. By the time Golconda was overrun by the Mughal army in 1687, it had become superseded by nearby Hyderabad as the Qutb Shahi capital.

The palace is dominated by a rugged hill overlooking a vast plain. The **Bala Hisar**, or Upper Fort, rising about 130 metres (425 feet) above ground level, is guarded by walls built of massive granite blocks that climb up and over the boulders. The ruined palace complex is laid out below the eastern slope of the hill, and is itself protected by a circuit of fortifications. These outer walls are strongly built, with sloping-sided cylindrical towers. Of the many gateways, the most imposing is the **Bala Hisar Darwaza** at the north-east corner. Its arched entrance has mythical beasts and lions worked in the stucco panels of the spandrels. Two free-standing portals, with vaults carried on quadruple arches, face the gateway from outside the walls. These ceremonial structures provide a focus for the main street of the town, which is lined with mansions, bazaars and barracks, many now in a neglected condition.

A monumental domed portico inside the Bala Hisar Darwaza signals the beginning of the fort. Immediately to the north is the royal **hammam**. The road proceeding west towards the citadel is flanked by **barracks**. Golconda's main palace structures, which extend southwards from this road, are laid out in a sequence of enclosures that provide a transition from public to private zones.

The buildings are now ruinous, with collapsing walls and vaults and decaying plasterwork.

The **Shila Khana**, or Armoury, dominates the outermost enclosure. The second enclosure is overlooked from the west by the **Taramati Masjid**, a royal mosque with fine plaster decoration. On the south side is the **Dad Mahal**, with a central vaulted chamber. An arcade leads by way of a lofty audience hall, with transverse arches supporting heavy vaults and domes, to the third enclosure, which belongs to the private zone of the palace. In the middle is a paved court with a twelve-sided pool set into the plaster floor; a part-octagonal chamber with arched openings surveys the court from the north-west corner. Residential apartments open off to the east and west. On the south side is the **Rani Mahal**, or Queen's Pavilion. Its raised terrace, probably once a colonnaded verandah with high wooden columns, now lost, opens onto a triple-vaulted hall. Delicate arabesques in the roundels above the side arches constitute the finest plaster decoration in the complex.

Continuing southwards, steps descend to a large hall, possibly for courtly assemblies, now ruined except for supporting piers that carried masonry vaults. Beyond, at the lowest level, is the **Shahi Mahal**, the fourth and final enclosure of the sequence, with a pavilion in the middle of a private garden. Now partly fallen, it has portals on four sides raised up on vaults. Additional enclosures, possibly for residential apartments, are situated to the east. A short distance to the west is a small mosque with its own arcaded court, completely concealed from view by high walls.

Steps climb to the summit of the Bala Hisar. The ascent is lined by stores and granaries and a **treasury** with six flattish vaults, dated by an inscription to 1624. Tanks and water channels all the way up are part of an elaborate system that raised water to the uppermost level. Immediately below the summit is **Ibrahim's Mosque**, distinguished by its prominent corner minarets; the courtyard in front extends onto the ramparts. The **Mahakali Temple** nearby is built into a large boulder, the sanctuary being actually cut into the granite.

The **darbar hall** of the Qutb Shahis occupies the highest point of the citadel. It is divided by substantial piers into vaulted bays; a raised chamber with triple arches opens off the rear wall. Its roof-top terrace has a pavilion with a stone seat for the Golconda sultans to enjoy uninterrupted views of the fort and surrounding landscape.

Imperial Mughal capitals

Fatehpur Sikri ❧ Agra ❧ Delhi

Fatehpur Sikri   The residences of the Mughal emperors are among the greatest masterpieces of Indian palace design. Akbar began the construction of his new capital at Fatehpur Sikri in 1571, only to abandon it fifteen years later. The inventive forms of many of its courtly buildings are remarkable for their synthesis of Persian-derived elements with indigenous features.

Despite its name, the Diwan-i Khass [41], or Hall of Private Audience, may actually have served as a ceremonial meditation chamber for the emperor. Its two-storeyed red sandstone façade, with angled eaves or chajjas and rooftop chhatris, conceals a double-height interior [45].

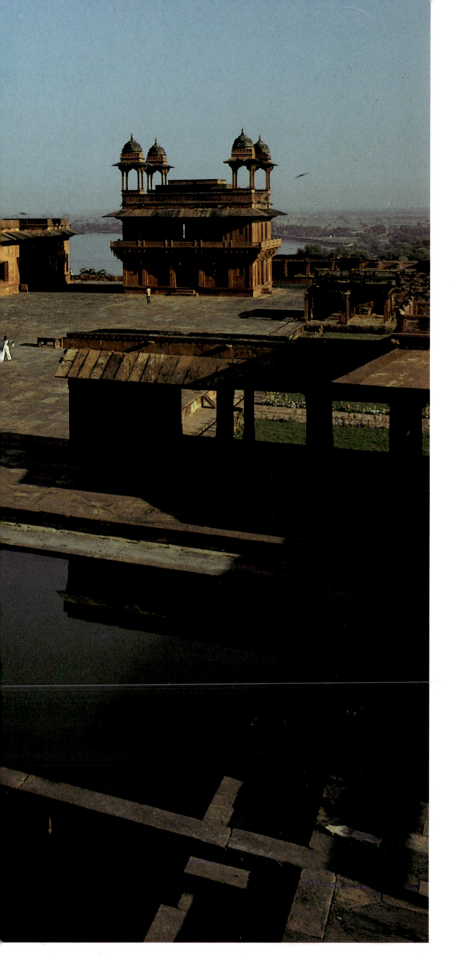

At Fatehpur the broad terrace of the Mardana [*42*] provides the setting for an ensemble of structures associated with Akbar's private administrative and personal business. The pavement has geometric motifs in different coloured stones, including a *pachisi* board where human beings served as pieces. In front is the Anup Talao, a square pool with bridges leading to a central platform, used as a seat. Beyond are the Panch Mahal, a whimsical five-storeyed pyramid of open terraces, and at the northern end the Diwan-i Khass.

At the southern end of the Mardana is the Khwabgah [*43, 44*], believed to have been Akbar's own sleeping chamber. The small pavilion, which is raised high on a colonnaded terrace, is surrounded by a verandah on four sides roofed with sloping slabs.

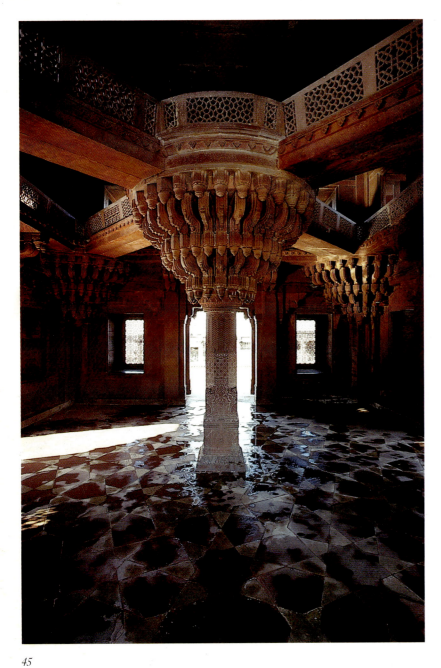

45

The interior of the Diwan-i Khass at Fatehpur [45; see also 41] is
remarkable for the pillar that stands freely in the middle. Clusters of
outward-springing brackets support a circular dais, reached by
diagonal walkways. While Akbar is sometimes supposed to have sat
here enjoying religious discourses, it is more likely that he used the
seat for ceremonial meditation.

The Turkish Sultana's House [46] is a small structure at one corner
of the Anup Talao. It is notable for its exquisitely carved surfaces,
from imitation tiles on the sloping roof to geometric patterns on
the walls.

46

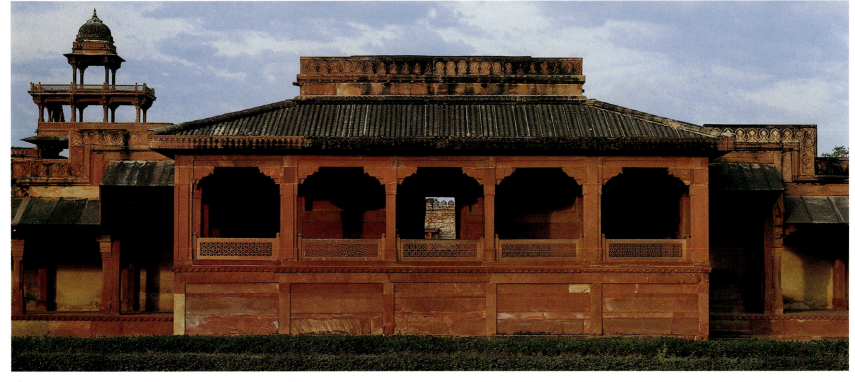

47

The strong, prismatic character of the red sandstone architecture of Akbar's period is perfectly displayed in the ghost city of Fatehpur. A pavilion in the Diwan-i Amm court [48] stands at the boundary between the public sphere and the more private Mardana, beyond which rises the Panch Mahal. More private still is Jodh Bai's Palace [47], a zenana (abode of women) in Rajput style with apartments paired across a square inner courtyard. Also residential was Birbal's House [49]; all of its surfaces, inside and out, have delicately carved decoration.

49

Agra

This city was the preferred capital of Akbar for much of his reign. The royal residence is known as the Lal Qila, or Red Fort, because of the colour of its sandstone walls. The main entrance is from the south through the Amar Singh Darwaza [see 6], which leads into a protective barbican. Here there is a further gate in the main ramparts, the Akbari Darwaza [50]. Its polygonal towers are capped with small domes and enlivened with brilliant tilework on the wall panels.

An inclined ramp ascends from the gateway to an extensive open area where stands the Jahangiri Mahal [51–53] – despite its name built in the 1560s–70s, and the only palace structure at Agra to survive from Akbar's era. With its windowless ground storey, it seems to have been a zenana. The arched entrance in the middle of the principal façade is boldly emphasized; octagonal towers with domed chhatris accentuate the corners. The interior has a square court, off which open a number of reception halls and residential suites. The long chhajja carried on brackets carved with pendant buds [53] is typical of the early Mughal style.

51

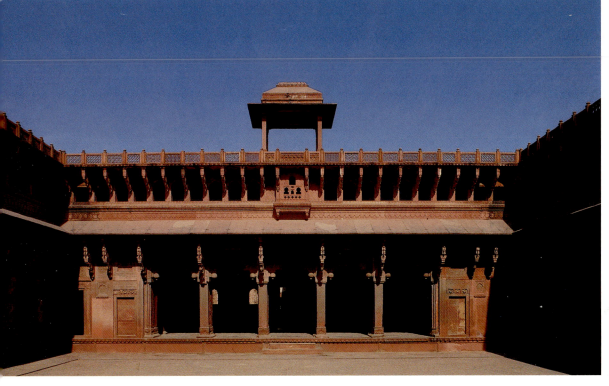

52

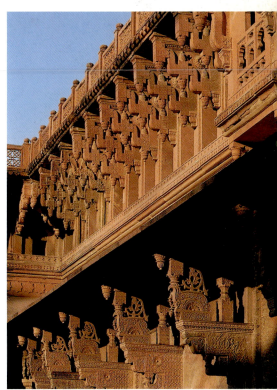

53

54

Substantial additions were made to the Agra palace by Jahangir and Shah Jahan in the first half of the 17th century. Shah Jahan's Diwan-i Amm [55] served as the main setting for formal receptions, known as darbars. Rows of faceted columns, doubled on the periphery, support broad arches with cusped profiles, a characteristic of mature Mughal architecture. Equally characteristic is the use of white marble, which also distinguishes the Moti Masjid or Pearl Mosque, built in 1655, that rises above the red sandstone walls beyond. A third hallmark of the period is the sumptuous inlaid decoration in semi-precious stones, usually referred to by the Italian term *pietra dura*. Particularly intricate decoration in this technique adorns a panel in the Musamman Burj, a pavilion in the private zone of the palace [54; see also 57].

55

56

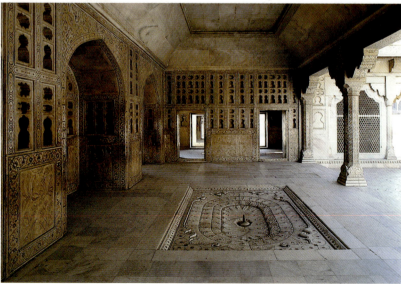

58

57

The Musamman Burj at Agra [56, 57; see also 54] is an octagonal tower looking out from a great height over the Jumna River that flows past the fort. It is surrounded by a verandah and capped with a dome sheathed in gilded copper. The landward inner chamber is an exquisite exercise in white marble and pietra dura inlay, even in the fountain set into the floor, which has layers of petal-like motifs.

The Khass Mahal [58] built in 1636, stands on a terrace between a formal garden and the river; arcaded openings on three sides are sheltered by an angled chhajja, and diminutive chhatris mark the corners of the roof. Flanking it are two pavilions with curved *bangla* roofs imitating the form of thatched huts in Bengal. The dome of the Musamman Burj rises at the far left.

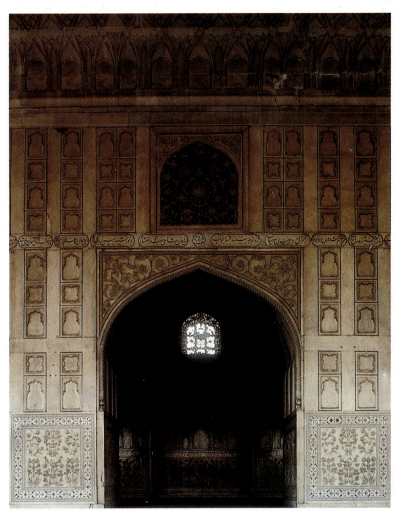

59

60

A distant view of the celebrated Taj Mahal is visible across a bend in
the Jumna from the Diwan-i Khass in the Agra fort [59], erected in
1637. The walls of this private audience hall [60] are cloaked with
relief carving and pietra dura inlay of consummate workmanship.
Though many designs are Persian in inspiration, the flowering plants
are purely Indian. On the broad terrace in front of the hall are seats of
white and black marble. The latter has a Persian inscription from the
reign of Jahangir carved on its rim [61].

61

Delhi

Built for Shah Jahan in the 1640s, the Lal Qila or Red Fort contains a formally planned palatial complex stretched out along the Jumna. The private apartments overlook the river; most visitors proceeded no further than the Hall of Public Audience [65]. As at Agra [see 55], the colonnaded Diwan-i Amm has a long façade with cusped arches. Inside is a free-standing marble throne in the form of an elevated seat under a curving canopy of bangla form [64, 65]. Panels set into the wall behind include some of Italian workmanship: one depicts Orpheus charming the beasts with his music [63], a symbolic illustration of the Indian concept of the ruler as world-master.

Equally expressive of the ruler's universality are the scales of justice, surrounded by the moon and planets, on a panel in the Khass Mahal [62]. The intricately worked marble screen is suspended over the central water channel [see 66].

64

65

66

67

68

In the Delhi fort, royal pavilions are aligned along a riverside terrace and linked by an axial water channel, the Nahr-i Bihisht or Stream of Paradise. It flows through the Khass Mahal [66] and Rang Mahal [69], where a lotus-shaped fountain pool has deeply cut undulating petals and leafy fronds, once inlaid with gold and silver.

The pavilions are approached through a sequence of courts guarded by the Naqqar Khana [67], where drums were sounded. It is the only building at Delhi with a red sandstone façade. Interior panels [68] have sculptured arabesques and inscriptions.

70

The finest of the royal pavilions erected by Shah Jahan at Delhi, the Diwan-i Khass, has a suite of apartments surrounded by an arcaded verandah. The exterior [71] is relatively simple, with an angled chhajja and small rooftop chhatris. The central chamber [72], however, is splendidly appointed. Painted and inlaid flowers and arabesques embellish the walls and piers, and the wooden ceiling was once entirely gilded, forming a worthy setting for the famous jewelled Peacock Throne until its removal in 1739.

Domed forms are restricted to non-residential structures, such as the Musamman Burj [70]. Like the example of Agra [see 56], it looks out over the river.

71

72

The principal place of
worship inside the Delhi
fort is the Moti Masjid or
Pearl Mosque, so called
after the white marble that
covers all of its surfaces.
The building was erected in
1659 by Aurangzeb, last of
the great Mughal emperors.
The triple-arched screen
between the courtyard and
the prayer chamber [74] is
overhung by a chhajja with
a central bangla curve; three
bulbous domes rise above.
The interior [73] has its
floor divided into individual
prayer zones by inlaid black
marble strips. Steps are for
the mimbar, or pulpit. The
domes above are treated as
fully opened lotuses.

73   74

THE MUGHAL era was initiated in 1526 at the battle of Panipat when Babur, warrior prince of a small Central Asian kingdom, defeated the Lodi ruler of Delhi. Babur's successful military exploits in India, as well as those of his son and grandson, Humayun (ruled 1530–43, 1555–56) and Akbar (ruled 1556–1605), led to the formation of an empire that encompassed almost all of the subcontinent, except for its most southerly part. Mughal preeminence was paramount until the end of the 17th century, when it was challenged by the rise of the Marathas in the Deccan; the British systematically annexed the Mughal territories during the course of the 18th century.

The unprecedented resources and wealth of the Mughals partly explain the magnificent architectural achievements of Akbar, Jahangir (ruled 1605–27), Shah Jahan (ruled 1628–57) and Aurangzeb (ruled 1658–1707). Like their predecessors, these four emperors took a personal interest in the arts, exhibiting considerable refinement in their culture and taste. The citadels at Fatehpur Sikri, Agra, Delhi and Lahore were universally admired not only for the formalities of the imperial court and the sumptuously appointed architecture of the palaces, but also for the consummate workmanship of the carpets, silk cloths, velvets, silver dishes, crystal goblets, miniature paintings and other luxury objects that were produced in the royal workshops.

Stylistic development

By the time the Mughals arrived in India, Persian features such as arches, vaults and domes had, as we have seen, already become part of Indian royal architecture. Akbar was particularly fascinated by the indigenous traditions of Central and Western India, with the result that *chhatris*, or domed pavilions, and *jalis*, or pierced stone screens, derived from Rajput palaces become an intrinsic part of Mughal architecture; yet another Rajput device is the *jharoka*, or projecting balcony with a small vaulted roof. The building types preferred by Akbar for his imperial residences at Fatehpur Sikri and Agra often have multi-storeyed apartments and terraces looking inwards to an enclosed court, in imitation of Rajput *mardana* palaces (see p. 153). Domed and vaulted pavilions rise upon the flat roofs, the corners of which are marked by freestanding chhatris; jharokas extend outwards from the walls, marking the location of the most important chambers within.

47, pp. 55 154

The Lahore Darwaza [75] connects the Lal Qila on the west with the Chandni Chowk, principal market street of Shah Jahan's capital, Shahjahanabad, known today as Old Delhi. The gateway is flanked by part-octagonal towers built in the same red sandstone as the walls. Accents of white marble are provided by diminutive chhatris and slender minaret-like finials over the entrance.

There is also a connection with Gujarat, from where many artisans were brought to work on imperial projects, especially after 1573 when the region was incorporated into the Mughal empire. Gujarati craftsmen are responsible for the exuberant carving of sandstone panels, brackets and jalis. This combination of Persian, Rajput and Gujarati traditions resulted in a highly original style that was cultivated by Akbar as an expression of his syncretistic outlook and delight in invention. It culminated in his masterpiece, the palace at Fatehpur Sikri.

Royal buildings erected by Jahangir, Shah Jahan and Aurangzeb are increasingly standardized. Imperial residences are conceived as symmetrically organized ceremonial complexes, with rigid alignments of monumental gateways, reception halls and royal apartments. The arrangements at Delhi and Lahore (not considered here, since it is now in Pakistan) are dictated by an overriding geometry that regulates the layouts of all buildings, together with their interconnecting courts and gardens. Halls of public and private audience, known respectively as Diwan-i Amm and Diwan-i Khass, are the principal focus of these complexes; they have lofty columns with broad cusped arches supporting flat ceilings. From the time of Shah Jahan onwards there is also a preference for Persian-style pavilions with vaulted halls in the middle and triple entrances on all four sides – hence the name, *baradari*, or twelve-doored. Arcaded verandahs are overhung by *chhajjas*, or angled eaves; small domed chhatris rise upon the corners of the roof. A characteristic feature of this period, thereafter a hallmark of the Mughal style, is the multi-cusped arch. It is used both structurally, to support broad spans, and also as a decorative motif to frame niches and panels.

Red sandstone and white marble are everywhere present in Mughal royal architecture (with a growing preference for the latter), and there was even an imperial monopoly on their use. Stone slabs set horizontally and vertically are manipulated with considerable skill to create vaults with pyramidal or tent-like shapes and even suspended flat ceilings. Domes have fluted and petalled profiles, and there is a fondness for a particular type of curved roof with a downward-sloping cornice imitating the thatched roofs of huts in Bengal, known accordingly as *bangla*. Jharokas with curved, bangla-like vaults assume a particular significance since they are used by the emperor to show himself before the public, and as emblems of the imperial presence, they are applied above royal thrones, as in the Diwan-i Amm at Delhi. Ribbed-fruit and pot-like finials, traditional Indian motifs, crown the apexes of vaults and domes, exactly as in tombs and temples. Columns are multi-faceted or have fluted sides with swelling, vase-like bases. Brackets are sometimes fashioned as animals and birds in full relief. Light is filtered to the interior through stone jalis carved with considerable skill to create bold geometric and floral designs.

p. 119

55
71

58

65

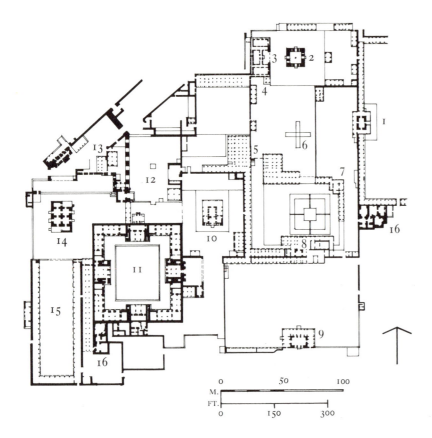

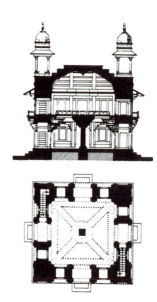

Fatehpur Sikri, the main palace area. (1) Diwan-i Amm, (2) Diwani-i Khass (section and plan above), (3) Daulat Khana, (4) Astrologer's seat, (5) Panch Mahal, (6) Anup Talao, (7) Turkish Sultana's House, (8) Khwabgah, (9) Daftar Khana, (10) House of Miriam, (11) Palace of Jodh Bai, (12) garden, (13) Nagina Masjid, (14) Birbal's house, (15) stables, (16) baths.

Mughal architecture is embellished throughout with stone carving and inlay as well as with painting and gilding. Akbar's red sandstone pavilions at Fatehpur Sikri and Agra have exquisitely detailed foliage patterns cloaking both inner and outer surfaces. Colouristic effects are achieved through different sandstones in combination with marble; there is even a limited use of coloured glazed tiles. Under Jahangir and Shah Jahan, semi-precious stones, such as jade, lapis lazuli, carnelian and jasper are set into white marble panels to create delicately tinted flowers and leafy arabesques. This inlay technique was imported, perhaps together with some craftsmen, from Italy (where it was known as *pietra dura*), to become a distinctive attribute of the mature Mughal style.

46–49

51–53

54

Fatehpur Sikri

The foundation of the palace city of Fatehpur Sikri was the direct result of Akbar's pilgrimage to Shaykh Salim Chishti, a Muslim saint who lived on Sikri hill, 37 kilometres (23 miles) south-west of Agra. Akbar had been concerned about his lack of an heir, and the saint assured him of three sons. After three of Akbar's wives had given birth to sons as predicted, the emperor honoured the shaykh by building a Jami Masjid and an imperial palace in the vicinity of the shaykh's residence. Akbar began the construction of his new royal city in 1571, making it the capital of his empire until about 1585. But the campaigns of his later years detained him in other

parts of the empire, and by 1600 the palace was already in disuse, never again to be occupied by Akbar or his successors.

Akbar's City of Victory – Fatehpur – is laid out as a vast fortified rectangle, more than 2 kilometres (1⅕ miles) long, enclosing the sandstone ridge of a hill running from south-west to north-east. The royal complex and Jami Masjid are built at the top of the ridge, while associated utilitarian structures, including stables, workshops and baths, are clustered against the lower slopes. Below the ridge to the south are the crowded streets of the modern town, inside which there are vestiges of Akbar's period, including a market. Fortifications with regularly spaced gateways surround the site on three sides. Gardens, orchards and a caravanserai once overlooked the bank of a great reservoir to the north.

The principal entrance to the city is from the **Agra Darwaza** at the north-eastern end of the ridge. Numerous structures line the approach to the palace complex, including caravanserais and the residences of nobles, some only recently exposed by archaeologists. Beyond the triple arches of the **tripolia** gateway are the remains of the **Chahar Suq**, or Four Markets, square. The bazaar that proceeds from here passes by the arcades of the quadrangular **karkhana**, where the royal workshops were accommodated. Kitchens, baths and other service structures, as well as a deep tank, are situated close by. (For these markets and utilitarian buildings see above, pp. 61–65.)

5

The commercial street leads directly to the **palace core** of the city. This consists of a sequence of interconnecting courts surrounded by colonnades and overlooked by pavilions. The courts are occupied by free-standing structures, pools and gardens, all strictly oriented to the cardinal directions; their distribution along the angled ridge produces an asymmetrical plan of considerable complexity. The royal buildings are of startling originality, unsurpassed in the history of Indian palace design. A consistency of technique and decorative detail is achieved through the use of local red sandstone. The first court is that of the **Diwan-i Amm**, the entrance to the emperor's own residence. A raised pavilion in the middle of the west side of the court, distinguished by the tile-like patterns incised onto the sloping stone slabs of the roof, was reserved for Akbar himself. The central bay, which is enclosed by jalis, connects with a vaulted chamber and a small doorway that provides direct access to the Mardana, which was probably dedicated to the emperor's private administrative and personal business.

The spacious terrace of the **Mardana** is partly paved in geometric designs of different coloured sandstones. At its northern end stands a structure usually called the **Diwan-i Khass**, despite the fact that it could never have functioned as an audience hall. (Many of the labels attached to individual buildings have no historical basis.) On the outside, the building has a surrounding balcony defined by low jalis and angled eaves above; both balcony and eaves are carried on rows of elaborately carved brackets. Domed chhatris rise from the four corners of the roof. The room inside rises the full height and is crowned by a lofty curved vault. In the middle is a solitary free-standing pillar, with petals at the base and delicately carved relief patterns on the faceted shaft. A cluster of carved brackets opens outwards in two tiers to support a circular dais. Diagonal walkways connect the dais to the surrounding walls, within which are narrow flights of steps. This unique structure is sometimes supposed to have been the place where Akbar listened to religious discourses; more likely, the pillar was intended as a ceremonial seat for the emperor to meditate and show himself symbolically as the pillar of the Mughal empire.

Immediately to the west of the Diwan-i Khass is the **Daulat Khana**, or Treasury, which probably accommodated offices, such as the accounts for the imperial household. The building has three rectangular chambers surrounded by narrow communicating passageways. The flat ceiling of the central chamber is supported by angled struts, with curved brackets emerging from monster heads. At its south-east corner is the **Astrologer's Seat**, which is a detached domed pavilion with four columns. Diagonal struts suspended between the columns take the form of traditional temple portals, imitating earlier traditions in Gujarat.

In the middle of the Mardana, south of the Diwan-i Khass, is a small stone seat positioned at the intersection of two lines of squares marked out on the surrounding pavement; these squares are for *pachisi*, a game resembling ludo, which was played here with people as pieces. On the west, the terrace is overlooked by the **Panch Mahal**, or Five[-Storeyed] Pavilion, perhaps intended for the ladies of the court. It is a whimsical structure with diminishing colonnaded storeys crowned by a single domed chhatri in pyramidal formation. The shafts and brackets of the columns are covered with geometric and foliage patterns. Jalis placed between the columns (now mostly removed) screened off the different levels.

The southern half of the Mardana is occupied by the **Anup Talao**, or Matchless Pool, a square pool with bridges leading from the middle of each side to a central platform, probably used by Akbar himself. The platform is bounded by low jalis, and has a raised seat in the centre. Dilapidated colonnades and apartments surround the water on two sides. Near to one corner is the **Turkish Sultana's House**, no more than a modest chamber opening off a verandah roofed with sloping slabs. The decoration is exquisite and pervasive: columns, brackets, beams and eaves are covered with fragile arabesques; walls and ceilings have chevron motifs imitating thatch construction as well as bold geometric patterns framing deep recesses; sensitive reliefs of flowering trees with animals and birds adorn the wall panels inside.

Elevated above the apartments and colonnades on the south side is a pavilion with sloping roof slabs on four sides; it is identified as the **Khwabgah**, or House of Dreams, Akbar's own sleeping chamber. To the south is the **Daftar Khana**, or Records Office, which opens off a spacious court intended for large assemblies. The central apartment is surrounded on three sides by a lofty verandah; the jharoka projecting outwards from the rear wall of the central apartment was probably used by Akbar for public appearances.

Small doorways connect the Mardana with the more private and residential courts to the west that constitute the **harem**, possibly the residence of the princes and women of the imperial household. The first court is occupied by the **House of Miriam**, a four-chambered apartment surrounded by a colonnaded verandah on three sides; a vaulted chhatri rises upon the roof. Murals once adorned the walls and ceilings, but only the barest traces of figures, animals and calligraphic panels survive. Immediately to the south-west is the **Palace of Jodh Bai**, actually a zenana in the Rajput style (see above, p. 55). It is entered on the east side through an impressive gateway with fringes of lotus buds and six-pointed stars decorating the principal arch; projecting balconies with roof-top chhatris are positioned at either side; the interior passageway, with two turns, is flanked by guard rooms and sculpture niches. The almost square court has apartments in the middle of each of three sides; those on the north and south have double-height chambers overlooked by internal balconies. The western apartment is distinguished by its temple-like columns and raised balcony seating; niches in the walls may have housed Hindu devotional sculptures. Pavilions elevated above the apartments have gabled roofs covered with blue ceramic tiles; vaulted chhatris stand in front. The corners of the roof are marked by freestanding domed pavilions.

The **Hawa Mahal**, or Palace of Breezes, which extends out from the northern apartment of Jodh Bai's Palace, has intricately worked jalis in the vaulted chamber of its upper floor; from here a small private garden could have been viewed. Next to the Hawa Mahal is an elevated walkway that leads to the outer walls of the complex, passing above the garden and subsidiary buildings. Domed chhatris and jalis at the end mark the favourite lookout spots. Beneath the pylons that support the walkway is the small **Nagina Masjid**, or Bird Mosque, the private place of worship for royal women.

49   **Birbal's House**, dated by an inscription to 1572, stands beyond the private garden. It comprises a quartet of apartments entered at either end through pyramidal vaulted chambers; domed chambers at the upper level are disposed in diagonal fashion. Walls and brackets, both outside and inside, are entirely covered with delicately carved decoration. Arched recesses and niches are edged with fringes of lotus buds; the ceilings display intricate lotus panels. The colonnaded **stables**, which are located directly to the

9 south, occupy three sides of a court more than 90 metres (some 300 feet) long. Stone rings and rope holes at ground level were used for tethering animals.

Near to the corner of the stables, outside the walls of the harem, are the remains of the **Ibadat Khana**, or House of Worship. This structure consisted of a sequence of square terraces with a seat on top where Akbar listened to the learned discourses of theologians and religious leaders. Another unusual building on the edge of the royal complex is the **Jesuit church** situated beyond the Mardana walls. The excavated remains indicate a small chapel with an altar.

Other features associated with the palace are located beneath the ridge to the north of the main complex, near to the bank of the great reservoir. In the vicinity of gardens and orchards stands the **Haram Sarai**, which is a caravanserai for visitors. It is surveyed

7 by the nearby **Hiran Minar**, or Golden Tower, an impressive 21-metre (70-foot)-high cylinder covered with polychrome stars and octagons; hunting trophies may have been displayed on its tusk-like, projecting spikes. The octagonal domed chhatri at the top is surrounded by a circular balcony of pierced stone.

Several **hammams** with small domed chambers are scattered along the bank of the great tank. Here too is a well contained in a large square structure with a deep octagonal shaft. The nearby **Hathi Pol**, or Elephant Gate – probably the imperial entrance to the palace – takes its name from the sculptured stone animals (now damaged) that flank its lofty arched entrance. The paved road passing through the gateway is the principal route of access to the royal complex from the north.

Agra

This city was the first major capital of the Mughals and, together with Fatehpur Sikri, the preferred residence of Akbar in his early years as emperor. It is laid out on the west bank of the Jumna at a point where the river turns eastwards. Though the citadel which dominates the town was strengthened and extended by Akbar between 1565 and 1573, most of the structures that stand within its walls belong to the reigns of his successors, Jahangir and Shah

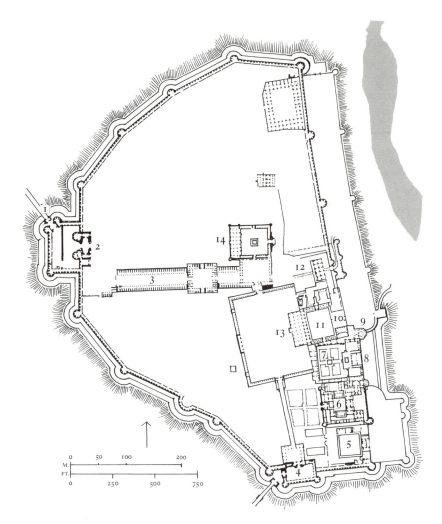

Agra, Lal Qila. (1) Delhi Darwaza, (2) Hathi Pol, (3) Minar Bazaar, (4) Amar Singh Darwaza and Akbari Darwaza, (5) Akbari Mahal, (6) Jahangiri Mahal, (7) Anguri Bagh, (8) Khass Mahal, (9) Musamman Burj, (10) Diwan-i Khass, (11) Macchi Bhavan, (12) Nagina Masjid, (13) Diwan-i Amm, (14) Moti Masjid.

Jahan. The fort is a massive construction with walls enclosing a semi-circle facing the river. The narrow streets of the town which surrounds it on three sides contain numerous monuments of the Mughal period, including the Jami Masjid. Pleasure gardens once lined the river on both banks, but these have largely been obliterated by recent urban expansion. Two Mughal emperors are buried at Agra in impressive garden mausoleums: Akbar in his tomb at Sikandra, 6 kilometres (3¾ miles) north-west of the city, and Shah Jahan, together with his favourite wife, Mumtaz Mahal, in the Taj Mahal a short distance east of the fort.

59   The **Lal Qila**, or Red Fort, is protected by massive double ramparts of red sandstone separated by a deep ditch. They form a continuous circuit of more than 2 kilometres (over 1 mile), and are protected by a deep moat on all sides, except that of the river,

which originally came up to the walls on the east. The **Delhi Darwaza**, the principal entrance on the west, has a rectangular barbican entered through a side gateway. A further walled enclosure in front was removed in 1875; the inner archway carries the date 1600. Inside, a paved ramp climbs gradually to the **Hathi Pol**, a gateway flanked by part-octagonal towers ornamented with white carved animals and birds; domed chhatris rise above. The two stone elephants with riders that once stood guard have been removed. The **Minar Bazaar**, or Lamp Market, inside is lined with small shops along its entire length (see above, p. 62). The **Akbari Darwaza**, the principal entrance to the fort from the south, is enlivened with brilliantly coloured geometric tiles on its polygonal towers. An inclined ramp for animals and wheeled vehicles inside ascends to the elevated ground within the fort.

Various royal pavilions stand here, formally arranged in a line, each benefiting from a splendid view of the river to the east. The earliest and most southerly, the **Akbari Mahal**, has now collapsed; the only remaining evidence is the plan, with apartments arranged symmetrically around a square inner court. Immediately to the north is the **Jahangiri Mahal** which, despite its name, was erected by Akbar; it is, in fact, the only complete building at Agra that belongs to his reign. The lack of exterior openings at the lower level suggests that it may have served as a zenana. It faces west onto an open area where there is a stone cistern hewn from a single block of marble; a Persian inscription incised on the rim is dated to 1611. The robust red sandstone façade of the Jahangiri Mahal has a prominent arched gateway in the middle decorated with six-pointed stars and other geometric patterns in white marble inlays; jharokas project on either side. Rows of niches on the outer walls are outlined in white marble, with fringes of lotus buds and panels of relief geometric designs below. The corners have projecting octagonal towers crowned with domed chhatris.

The entrance chamber of the Jahangiri Mahal is roofed with a petalled dome. The court beyond is surrounded on four sides by apartments with upper colonnades concealed by jalis; angled chhajjas are supported on elaborate brackets with pendant buds and arabesque ornament, while vaulted chhatris protrude above the roof. On the north side of the court is a double-height columned hall; its flat ceiling is supported on diagonal struts carved with serpentine brackets emerging from monster mouths. Relief geometric ornament entirely cloaks the columns, brackets, beams and ceiling, the last with a central lotus medallion. The lofty vaulted hall on the south side has pierced wall panels permitting communication with the surrounding narrow passageway. The chamber on the east leads to a portico which faces onto a court with an ornamental pool. Screened balconies beyond frame views of the river.

An inconspicuous gateway at the north-east corner of the Jahangiri Mahal leads to the **Anguri Bagh**, or Grape Garden – a formal composition, with geometric flower beds outlined in marble and a square pool reached by raised walkways. The labyrinth of underground chambers beneath is a **taikhana**, or hot-weather retreat; perhaps also a dungeon. The garden is surrounded on three sides by two-storey apartments; on the east is a raised terrace with a square pool. A symmetrical arrangement of white marble buildings opens onto the terrace. The **Khass Mahal**, or Private Pavilion, in the middle dates from 1636. A verandah with cusped arches leads to the inner chamber; its walls are pierced with ornamental niches, while stalactite patterns enrich the arches and half-vaults; jalis look out over the river. Smaller pavilions at either side each have three vaulted chambers, the central ones fronted by open arcades with bangla roofs covered with gilded copper sheets.

Steps at the north-east corner of the Anguri Bagh ascend to the **Musamman Burj**, or Octagonal Tower, distinguished by its copper-sheeted dome. An octagonal room with a verandah projecting outwards and its adjoining rectangular chamber, both in white marble, are exquisitely ornamented with carved panels and multi-coloured stone inlays; the geometric designs of the jalis are particularly delicate, as is the treatment of the fountain set into the floor. It is in this tower, which dates from the period of Jahangir, that Aurangzeb confined Shah Jahan, who is supposed to have spent his last years gazing out across a bend in the river towards the Taj Mahal.

The **Diwan-i Khass**, erected in 1637 to the west of the tower, has its walls, columns, brackets and cusped arches entirely covered with low relief carving and inlay stonework. The hall stands at the south end of a broad terrace on which there are two thrones, one of white and one of black marble; the latter has an elegant Persian inscription of Jahangir, dated to 1603. To the east is an uninterrupted view of the river, while to the north is the royal **hammam** for which water was brought up from a well more than 20 metres (some 65 feet) below. Beneath the west side of the terrace is the large rectangular court known as the **Macchi Bhavan**, or Fish Pavilion, suggesting that a fish tank was once located here. Colonnades on two levels are interrupted on the north by an arched gateway. Opposite, on the south side, is a domed marble pavilion projecting outwards from the upper level. The **Nagina Masjid**, or Bird Mosque, which opens off the north-west corner of the court, was erected by Shah Jahan for the ladies of the zenana; it is a small white marble structure capped by triple domes.

A passageway on the upper west side of the Macchi Bhavan descends to the **Diwan-i Amm**, also dating from Shah Jahan's reign. This is an impressive structure, open on three sides, with tall, multi-faceted marble columns, paired on the periphery and quadrupled at the corners, supporting broad arches, each with nine cusps. The triple-arcaded alcove set into the east wall, which served as the imperial throne, is richly ornamented with pietra dura inlay. The hall faces westwards onto a large rectangular court, in the middle of which is a circular well lined with sandstone. The court is entered on the north and south sides through monumental red sandstone portals, that on the south being linked to the Akbari Darwaza.

The surviving portions of the market street are reached beyond the northern gate; further north is the **Moti Masjid**, or Pearl

Mosque, dating from 1655. The projecting entrance gateway on the east side of this mosque is approached by a double staircase. Its white marble court is surrounded by a colonnade on three sides; in the middle is a square ablutions pool with a central octagonal pillar that functioned as a sundial. The prayer chamber has three aisles, each with seven bays; three domes with petalled ornament rise above, while octagonal towers crowned with small chhatris are positioned at the four corners. Coloured marble strips set into the floor define individual spaces for prayer.

Delhi

The **Purana Qila**, or Old Fort, on a site overlooking the Jumna with no less than two thousand years of recorded occupation, represents the earliest efforts by the Mughals to provide Delhi with a palace citadel. The fortifications were begun by Humayun, but completed by Sher Shah, the ruler who temporarily banished the Mughals from India between 1543 and 1555. They enclose a vast rectangle with impressive gateways on three sides, each flanked by cylindrical towers with chhatris on top. The arches over the gateways are built in finely dressed sandstone, of contrasting buff and red colour. The west gateway has six-pointed stars in black and white marble in the spandrels; traces of coloured tilework survive on the projecting balconies above.

The only buildings that stand within the Purana Qila are the **Qala-i-Kuhna Masjid**, erected by Sher Shah, and the **Sher Mandal**. The latter is an octagonal two-storeyed royal building entirely built in red sandstone, with arched porticoes on each level and an octagonal domed chhatri on top. It was almost certainly built by Humayun, and it is traditionally associated with the library down whose steep steps he fell to his death.

p. 6 The **Lal Qila**, or Red Fort, overlooking the Jumna at a site further north, was the imperial headquarters of Shah Jahan's new capital, named after him as **Shahjahanabad**, begun in 1639. The palace inside the fort, mostly completed by 1648, became the principal residence of Shah Jahan and, with the exception of Aurangzeb, all of the later Mughal emperors. It was raided twice in the 18th century by Persian and Afghan sultans and eventually captured by the British, who, after 1857, demolished many of the buildings.

The fort is conceived as a rectangle with chamfered corners, the east side of which runs parallel to the river bank; an extension to the north-east originally contained a tributary of the river. The principal entrance on the west is the **Lahore Darwaza**. Extending outward from it is the **Chandni Chowk**, or Moonlight Market, the principal commercial street of Shahjahanabad, and the central east-west axis of the great arc of walls which contains the city. The **Delhi Darwaza** on the south leads directly to the Jami Masjid, the largest in India, which is located on a small rise; it was completed by Shah Jahan in 1658.

75 The **Lahore Darwaza** is flanked by impressive part-octagonal towers ornamented with plain blind arches, as well as by slender ornamental minarets; a string of chhatris above lends delicacy to the façade. The barbican in front was added by Aurangzeb. The gate leads directly to the **Chhatta Chowk**, a vaulted street some 70 metres (230 feet) long flanked by arcaded chambers, interrupted only by an open octagonal court, now serving as a market for antiques and souvenirs but originally a market for the palace (see above, p. 62). The bazaar terminates in an open square, of which the side arcades and central tank have been removed. In the middle of the east side is the **Naqqar Khana**, or Drum House, where kettle-drums were beaten at different times of the day. The building is of red sandstone, with delicate carved ornament in shallow cusped niches; small chhatris rise above the corners of the roof. All visitors, except royal princes, had to dismount from their horses at this point.

67, 68

Beyond the Naqqar Khana lies an inner court, once surrounded by arcades but now an open lawn overlooked from the east by the impressive red sandstone **Diwan-i Amm**. Nine bays wide and three deep, the hall is severely plain on the outside, the only interest being the angled chhajja and diminutive corner chhatris. Twelve-sided columns, paired on the outside and quadrupled at the corners as at Agra, support broad cusped arches. The throne of the emperor, which stands in the middle of the east wall, takes the form of an elevated seat sheltered by a canopy with a bangla roof. Both base and canopy are of white marble, ornamented with carving and inlays of semi-precious stones. Several of the pietra dura panels set into the rear wall are of Italian workmanship; one depicts Orpheus charming the beasts – a scene of symbolic significance for Shah Jahan (see above, p. 16).

65

64

63

The private portion of the palace, the harem, which extends to the east between the Diwan-i Amm and the river, consists of a continuous sequence of garden courts and white marble pavilions. The royal buildings, raised on a terrace that overlooks the river, are mostly of the baradari type, with triple arches on all four sides sheltered by overhanging chhajjas; small chhatris rise above the corners of the flat roofs. The pavilions are linked by a water channel, the **Nahr-i Bihisht**, or Stream of Paradise, which runs the whole length of the terrace, passing beneath the floor slabs where necessary. Only five pavilions are still intact. The **Mumtaz Mahal**, the southernmost, is now a museum. To the north, on axis with the Diwan-i Amm, is the larger and finer **Rang Mahal**, or Coloured Pavilion, which faces a private garden with a central pool. Its main hall has fifteen arcaded bays with apartments at the ends; a lotus-shaped marble fountain is set into the floor.

69

The channel passes through the innermost suite of the **Khass Mahal**, or Private Pavilion, to flow beneath a perforated marble screen of remarkable delicacy which is surmounted by a semicircular panel that shows scales of justice surrounded by planets, with the crescent moon below. The **Musamman Burj**, or Octagonal Tower, protrudes outwards from the Khass Mahal onto the ramparts; its roof is a domed chhatri. From here the emperor looked down on the open area between the fort walls and the river where animal fights took place. On the northern side of the pavilion is another suite of three rooms used by the emperor as a retreat for prayer. Throughout, the ceilings are exquisitely painted

66

62

70

Delhi, Lal Qila. (1) Lahore Darwaza, (2) Delhi Darwaza, (3) Chhatta Chowk, (4) Naqqar Khana, (5) Diwan-i Amm, (6) Rang Mahal, (7) Khass Mahal, (8) Musamman Burj, (9) Diwan-i Khass, (10) baths, (11) Moti Masjid, (12) Hayat Bakhsh Bagh, (13) Hira Mahal, (14) Shah Burj.

with stylized arabesques; flowers in vases, both painted and inlaid, adorn the walls.

The northernmost pavilion, the **Diwan-i Khass**, is the most splendid of all. Here stood the famous gem-encrusted Peacock Throne (see above, p. 35) before its seizure by Nadir Shah of Persia in 1739. Cusped arches define the central chamber, which has a decorated wooden ceiling; painted and carved flowers and arabesques embellish the wall spandrels, while inlaid floral panels adorn the piers. Immediately to the north is the **hammam**.

The **Moti Masjid** immediately west of the hammam was added in 1659 by the austere and devout Emperor Aurangzeb as a place of private prayer. Its unadorned exterior contrasts with the carved marble panels of its interior court. The triple-arched entrance to the prayer chamber is overhung by eaves with a central bangla curve; three bulbous domes rise above. The **Hayat Bakhsh Bagh**, or Life-bestowing Garden, lies immediately to the north of the mosque; only some of its plots are intact. White marble pavilions stand at either end of the main north–south channel, in contrast to the red sandstone pavilion in the middle of the pool, which was added in 1842 by Bahadur Shah Zafar, the last of the Mughal emperors. The same ruler was also responsible for the **Hira Mahal**, or Golden Pavilion, on the east side of the garden, overlooking the river. The **Shah Burj**, or King's Tower, at the north-east corner of the fort has a domed octagonal chamber ornamented with inlaid mirrorwork; the adjoining vaulted portico shelters an inclined chute of white marble over which water once ran.

Rajput forts

Gwalior ❧ Orchha ❧ Datia ❧ Chittor ❧ Udaipur

Bundi ❧ Kota ❧ Amber ❧ Jaipur

Dig ❧ Jodhpur

Gwalior The magnificent fortified residences erected by the Rajput rulers of Western and Central India are unsurpassed for their dramatic locations [see *136*]. None presents a more glorious exterior than the Man Mandir at Gwalior [*76*], headquarters of Man Singh at the end of the 15th century. Cylindrical towers act as reinforcing buttresses, while providing vertical divisions for the long and highly decorated east façade. Walls are patterned with ornamental merlons and friezes of birds and beasts, all in brightly coloured tilework. Relief carving, delicate cresting, and pierced screens incorporating animal shapes add to the overall richness of effect.

The Hathi Pol [77], or Elephant Gate, serves as the principal entrance to the Man Mandir at Gwalior. Though the sculptured animals once positioned here are now missing, interest is achieved through boldly carved brackets supporting the arch and overhanging chamber.

The palace interior focuses on two courts. In the first, the hall on the north side [80] has piers with swelling capitals; above them are stone screens with geometric designs derived from dancing figures. Brackets on the south side are conceived as fully modelled rearing beasts [79]. From the second court, an ornately vaulted hall opens off to the east [78]: here the walls are carved with semicircles of lotus petals and ornamental merlons.

78

79

80

83

Orchha

The capital of the Rajput state of Bundelkhand in Central India preserves a trio of fine palaces, built in the century following its foundation in 1531. They stand on an island in the Betwa River, in line with the pinnacles of the Chaturbhuja Mandir, the main temple in the town on the other side [81]: nearest to the temple is the Raja Mahal; beyond rises the Jahangiri Mahal, whose towering bulk conceals the Ramji Mandir farther away. To the north of the palaces is the Praveen Raja Mahal [82], a small garden pavilion facing on to a formal arrangement of flower-beds.

The Jahangiri Mahal [81, 83, 84] was erected by Bir Singh Deo at the beginning of the 17th century. The emphasis on groups of domed chhatris and vaulted chambers rising above the skyline and surrounding a courtyard is typical of the Rajput style; so too is the use of flattish domes and angled chajjas.

84

85

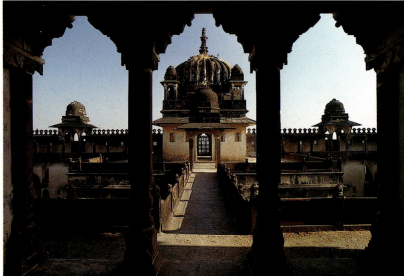

86

88

87

Datia

The climax of Bundelkhand architecture is the Govind Mandir, another residence of Bir Singh Deo of Orchha, built in about 1620. Its exterior [89] presents a symmetrical mass relieved by domes on projecting corner towers. The interior is of unusual interest for the massive multi-storeyed tower [88] that stands in the middle of an open court. Its dome rises higher than those at the corners.

Colonnaded walkways and bridges connect the apartments of the tower with those on the periphery of the court. In the view of the covered passage [87] we are looking in towards the centre; on the next level up [86], we are looking out from one of the triple-arched openings. The topmost level, which contains the king's own sleeping chamber [85], is distinguished by a shallow petalled dome.

90

Chittor

The rulers of the Mewar state of Western India occupied the fort here until the middle of the 16th century. The long plateau strengthened by continuous ramparts is dotted with numerous courtly buildings and other structures, including the Palaces of Rana Kumbha and of Patta [90, left distance and right foreground]. The Jaya Stambha [91], or Tower of Victory, erected by Rana Kumbha to celebrate his defeat of the Malwa forces in 1440, is conceived as a vertical temple, with balconied chambers at the summit.

Elevated domed chambers and rooftop chhatris are typical of the early Rajput style. Decoration is restricted to coloured tilework and lines of merlons. Multi-storeyed arrangements served as self-contained apartments, with towers at either side of a small interior court, as in the quarters of the Kanwar Pade, or Heir Apparent, in the Palace of Rana Kumbha [92]. Elsewhere, as in the early 16th-century Palace of Ratan Singh [93], chhatris look down on a central open space.

The Palace of Padmini, with its small pavilion [94] standing in the middle of an artificial lake, was built in the late 19th century, still in the same traditional style.

91

94

92

93

Udaipur

95

Capital of the Sisodia Rajputs after their move from Chittor, Udaipur occupies an incomparable site on the edge of Lake Pichola. The City Palace [*96*] is a maze of reception halls, residential suites and internal courts built on a ridge above the water. Work was begun by Udai Singh towards the end of the 16th century, and has continued ever since. The latest addition is the Shiv Nivas, a semicircular wing for royal guests. It projects beyond the domed corner turrets of the Shambhu Nivas, residence of the princely family today. Pleasure pavilions on various islands seem to float on the lake. The best preserved is the complex on Jag Mandir [*95*].

96

The entrance to the main block of the City Palace at Udaipur is a modest door off the Ganesha Deodhi terrace [97; see also 13]. Whitewashed walls on either side are brightly painted with martial animals in the traditional Rajput manner. The uppermost court inside the complex is a raised garden, the Amar Vilas, on to which faces the Badi Mahal [98; see also 14]. This pleasure pavilion has cusped arcades in the Mughal manner framing a square marble tub.

The most elaborate of the inner courts is the Mor Chowk or Peacock Court [99, 100]. On its walls are peacocks modelled in high relief and faced with coloured glass mosaic. A projecting balcony, or jharoka, at the upper level is flanked by inserts of coloured glass. The Badi Chatur Chowk is a smaller court for private use. Its screen wall [101] has painted and inlaid compositions depicting European men and Indian women.

97

98

99

100

101

102

103

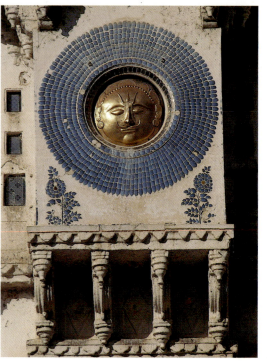

104

The Manek Mahal is a formal audience chamber for the Udaipur rulers, with a raised alcove entirely cloaked in mirror glass [102]. Gleaming brass sun-face emblems of the Sisodia family occur throughout the City Palace. The largest is on the wall of the Surya Chopar [103], a reception room at the lower level. Another is prominently displayed on the façade of the Manek Chowk [104], where it can be seen from the outermost court below.

105

Islands in the lake provide sites for refreshment like the Jag Mandir [105; see also 95] and the Jag Nivas or Lake Palace Hotel, which retains several original pavilions [106]. The use of chhatris in combination with curving bangla roofs is common in 18th-century Rajput architecture, as is the clustering of fluted domes and curved vaults. The Monsoon Palace on the summit of a hill overlooking the lake served as a weekend retreat.

106

107

Bundi

The small state of Bundi nestles in the hills east of Mewar. The main palace presents an imposing bulk rising in tiers above the houses of the town [*108*; see also *11*]. It is approached by a long paved ramp that ascends to the Hathi Pol [*107*]. Fully modelled elephants stand on brackets projecting outwards from octagonal towers on either side; the animals' trunks form an extra arch over the entrance. The doorway leads directly to a court overlooked by the Ratan Daulat [see *109*], audience hall of Ratan Singh, 17th-century ruler of Bundi.

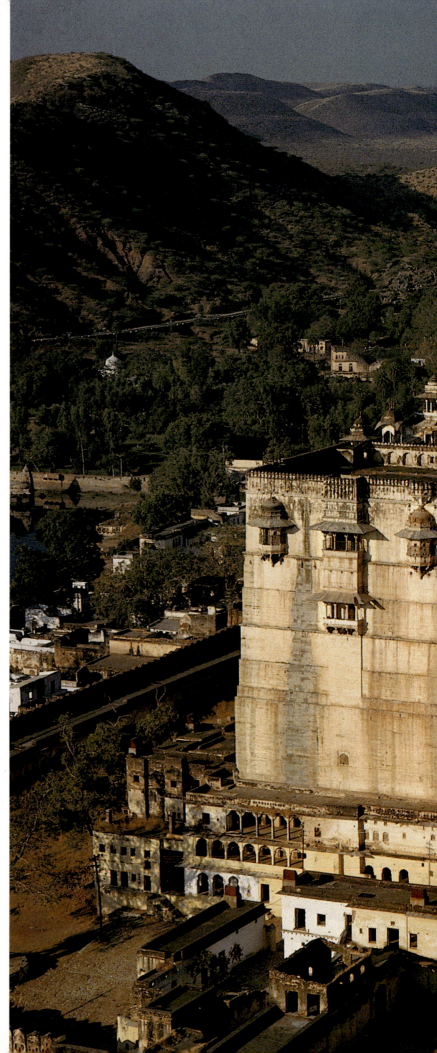

108

The marble seat of Ratan Singh of Bundi [109], surrounded by marble screens, is placed at the edge of the Ratan Daulat, the audience hall overlooking the entrance court [see 107]. The pillared Hathi Shala [110], with brackets in the shape of elephants, was also used for formal meetings. A mural panel elsewhere in the palace [111] portrays the Bundi king seated in this hall, recognizable by its elephant brackets.

109

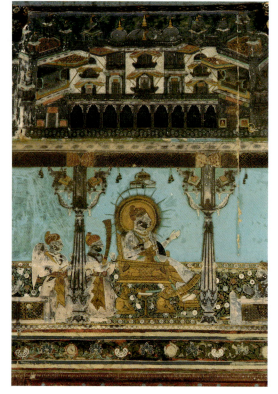

111

110

Paintings adorn the Chitra Shala [112], which is a veritable picture gallery, with legends and scenes of royal life covering the walls. Executed in the decades around 1800, they include depictions of the maharaja with his retinues, ladies and visitors in audiences, courtly entertainments, and temple ceremonies [114]. Ceilings too are treated decoratively. That in the Badal Mahal [113], the royal sleeping chamber, has a multi-faceted vault covered with tiny figures.

112

113

114

115

Kota

The palace of this independent Rajput dynasty
is entered through a Hathi Pol adorned with
brightly painted elephants; pavilions at multiple
levels add to its picturesque quality [*116*]. The
main reception hall is the Raj Mahal [*115*]: here
the columns are covered with glasswork, and the
walls with paintings of landscapes, royal
meetings and mythological episodes. The simple
throne covered with a canopy is that of Rao
Madhosinghji, ruler of Kota in the second
quarter of the 17th century.

   Paintings of a similar mix of subjects adorn
the walls of the Badah Mahal [*117*], a small
chamber in the private wing. Murals show
boating trips on the nearby Chambal River and
picnics in the palace gardens, while miniature
paintings on paper are encased in glass and set
into the walls below.

116

140 · *Rajput forts*

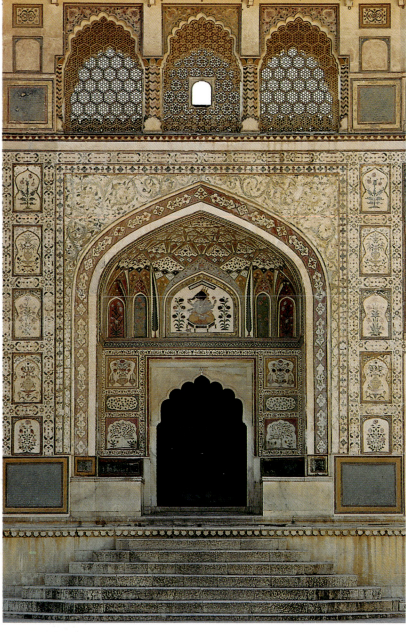

122

The Ganesh Pol at Amber [*122*] takes its name from a painted panel with the elephant-headed god Ganesha over the entrance. The Sohag Mandir, placed above, has jalis through which women observed the public activities in the second court of the palace.

The gateway gives access to the third court, which is conceived as a private garden with the residential apartments of the Jai Mandir on one side. The central chamber of that complex [*123*] is treated as a shish mahal, or mirror pavilion, the walls and ceilings being coated with mirrorwork laid in intricate multi-faceted patterns.

123

124

125

126

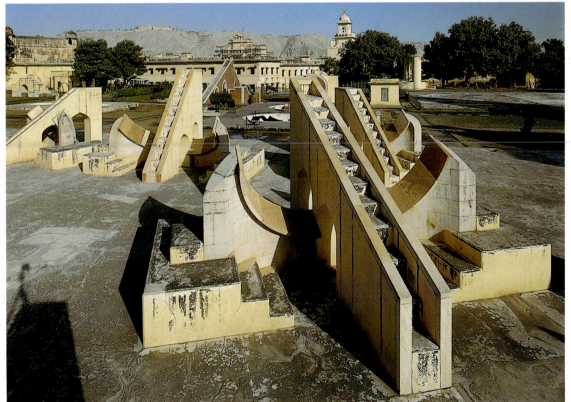

127

Jaipur

Sawai Jai Singh founded his new city on 18 November 1727, a date determined by the court astrologer. A believer in astronomy as a guide to wise rule, he included an observatory, the Jantar Mantar [*127*], in his palace complex. Near it the Hawa Mahal or Palace of the Breezes, of 1799, provided a screened vantage-point from which courtly women could observe life in the town street outside [*126*; see also *17*].

The first inner court of the palace contains the Mubarak Mahal [*125*], built in the late 19th century by the British architect Samuel Swinton Jacob. Its multi-storeyed exterior contains a double-height hall. Public and private zones meet in the second inner court [*124*]. Here stands the original Diwan-i Amm; giant silver vessels held Ganges water for royal rituals. To the left is the private zone, entered through the Ganesh Pol. Beyond rises the most important residential building, the Chandra Mahal.

Dig

The 18th-century residence of the Jats of Bharatpur is one of the finest Rajput pleasure palaces. It consists of a number of detached pavilions formally disposed in an elaborate garden, complete with axial water channels and fountains [*128*].

The flat-roofed Gopal Bhawan is flanked by the Sawan and Bhadon Bhawans [*130*], named after the monsoon months, each with a curved bangla roof in the Mughal style. This trio of pavilions projects over an artificial lake, the waters of which reflect their arcaded façades and screened balconies. One apartment inside the Gopal Bhawan [*129*] has cusped arches framing a secluded seating area used for private entertainments. The adjacent eating chamber [*131*] has a stone table around which the diners sat; attendants served from the middle. Secluded in a far corner of the garden is the white marble Suraj Bhawan [*132*], where the delights of water and gardens could be further enjoyed.

128

129

130

131

132

Jodhpur

Capital of the Marwar kingdom in the desert of Western India, this was the seat of a powerful dynasty of rulers from the 15th century onwards. The palace stands inside a great fort [see *136*], approached by a steep path that passes a whitewashed temple below the north promontory [*133*] and then traverses seven arched gateways. Beside the Loha Pol, or Iron Gate, is a slab carved with hand-prints [*134*] that commemorate the ritual suicide of fifteen royal wives.

The Moti Mahal [*135*] was added in the 18th century as a hall of public audience. Its cusped arcades and painted designs betray Mughal influence. Framed paintings on the polished plaster walls illustrate the dynastic succession of the Jodhpur maharajas.

134

133

135

As the sultans of Delhi extended their territories into Central and Western India they encountered resistance from a number of Hindu warrior clans, known collectively as Rajputs, with whom they struggled for supremacy. The final break in Rajput power came in 1567, with the siege and conquest of the fort at Chittor by the Mughals. Thereafter, peace reigned in the region, and the Rajputs were permitted to retain their territories as long as they did not engage in warfare. Marriages took place between Rajput princesses and Mughal emperors, and many Rajput princes were enlisted as commanders and governors in the imperial service. But as the Mughal empire disintegrated in the course of the 18th century, the Rajputs asserted their autonomy. They later secured treaties from the British, guaranteeing their survival into the modern era. Many Rajput states were unified by the British into Rajputana, 'Land of the Rajputs', now the modern Indian state of Rajasthan.

Stylistic development

p. 154

The oldest parts of the Rajput palaces at Chittor, Gwalior, Udaipur and Amber belong to the 15th and 16th centuries, contemporary with the royal buildings of the early sultans. There is, however, a basic difference. The typical residence of the Rajput maharaja, where his family, retinue and retainers are accommodated, is the *mardana*. This is a fortified square or rectangular palace, with suites of apartments on four sides of a central court, known as a *chowk*. Residential chambers and sub-courts are arranged on different levels, often stepped back to create upper terraces and walkways. Mardana exteriors present solid walls, many storeys in height, strengthened by buttresses, string-courses and corner towers. The surviving walls are generally undecorated, an exception being the brightly coloured tilework and sculptured designs at Gwalior. The severe effect is broken by tiers of *jharokas*, or projecting balconies, with *jalis*, or pierced stone screens. Roof-lines have rows of the domed chambers or open pavilions known as *chhatris*, creating picturesque silhouettes.

76

During the period of the Rajput alliances with the Mughals in the 16th and 17th centuries, new mardana complexes continued to be erected. Those at Orchha and Datia still preserve their original schemes, the Datia residence being the only one to have a tower rising upwards from the middle of the chowk. As older palaces were enlarged, the early blocks were converted into zenanas, used for courtly women only. The extensions to the Udaipur, Amber and Gwalior citadels, as well as the newer complexes at Jodhpur,

81–89

118

Bundi and Kota, are all assemblages of different mardana blocks, each focusing on an inner chowk, with connecting passageways and steps and intermediate courts. Chowks are overlooked on four sides by colonnades, arcades and centrally placed jharokas, the last with balcony seating carried on sculptured brackets and sheltered by small half-vaults; domed chhatris crowd the roof-top terraces. Apartments at different levels open off the chowks in symmetrical and axial arrangements, creating interiors with balanced designs that contrast markedly with the apparently haphazard effect of the exteriors.

108

90

An innovation dating from the 17th century is the introduction of the diwan-i amm, modelled on the Mughal hall of public audience, such as that erected in the second court of the Amber palace. Another sign of Mughal influence, especially in the 18th century, is the repeated use of cusped arches for interiors and openings, as at Jodhpur and Jaipur. Gateways become imposing structures, sometimes axially aligned in a sequence, with balconies on top for drummers and musicians. *Hathi pols*, or elephant gates, are provided with large animals carved in full relief in front of the entrance arches, as at Bundi and Kota. *Tripolias*, or triple-arched gateways, are erected as ceremonial entrances to the public parade grounds in front of the palaces, one of the finest being at Udaipur.

120

107,
116

A characteristic of 18th-century Rajput palaces is the dissolution of the solid exteriors. Walls become tiers of continuous arched openings filled with jalis and regularly punctuated by projecting jharokas, as at Jodhpur and Bikaner. Another feature is the increased use of curved *bangla* roofs with sloping cornices (following the usage of the Mughals, who introduced this Bengali roof form), for balconies and roof-top pavilions. As the need for security lessened, palaces became more open in plan, and the central chowk is expanded into a formal garden with a central pool and axial waterways, again in the Mughal manner. The core of the Jaipur city residence, the most ambitious royal project of this era, is a multi-storeyed wing facing a great formal garden. There is also a fascination with internal decorative effects. Apartments are treated as *shish mahals* (mirror pavilions), with walls, vaults and domes adorned with coloured glass and small pieces of mica or mirror to create dazzling effects. Murals adorning walls and ceilings often illustrate mythological subjects, as well as more contemporary scenes of battles and courtly receptions.

105

14,
123

Perhaps the most impressive of all Rajput strongholds is Meherangarh [*136*], the fort that has dominated the city of Jodhpur since the mid-15th century.

Gwalior

From the 8th century onwards the citadel at Gwalior in Central India was the headquarters of a succession of Rajput rulers whose shrines still stand on the level top of the hill. The fort was taken by the Delhi sultans in the early part of the 13th century, but then recaptured in 1398 by Bir Singh Deo, who made it the capital of the Tomar Rajputs. The most powerful of these rulers was Man Singh (ruled 1486–1516), whose palace is the most complete royal complex still standing at the site. Tomar control of the region did not survive Man Singh's death, and in 1518 Gwalior was occupied by the Mughals. The 18th century witnessed a period of confusion, with the fort finally being taken by the Scindia Rajputs.

Gwalior's citadel occupies a 3-kilometre (1¾-mile)-long sandstone hill with steep escarpments, rising 90 metres and more (up to 300 feet) above the town. The sides of the hill are strongly fortified with formidable ramparts that line the edge of the plateau, except on the south-west where the walls traverse a deep gorge. The main entrance to the fort is at the north-east, through a sequence of gateways that protect the road ascending the hill. The lowest is the **Hindola Pol**, or Swing Gate, with fringes of lotus buds on the arches. Its cylindrical towers are ornamented with friezes of geese, originally in coloured tilework; small pavilions are placed at the top.

Immediately inside the gateway is the **Gujari Mahal**, or Gujarati Pavilion, now an archaeological museum, erected in about 1510 by Man Singh for his Gujarati wife, Mriganayana. It follows the standard mardana pattern, being regularly laid out on a square plan with a large central chowk. Double-height chhatris and jharokas are positioned at the corners and in the middle of each side. One balcony has serpentine brackets supporting angled eaves; a sculptured elephant stands inside another. The interior apartments, which have now mostly collapsed, each consisted of a suite of chambers opening off a private sub-court.

The gateway at the top of the ascending road is the **Hathi Pol**, now missing its elephants, but with an arch fringed with lotus buds. It adjoins the south side of **Man Mandir**, the palace of Man Singh, with which it forms the impressive façade that dominates the east flank of the fort. The palace exterior is broken by regularly spaced cylindrical towers topped with domed pavilions. The walls, patterned with bright turquoise blue, yellow and green tilework, have ornamental merlons and friezes of geese and *makaras* (aquatic monsters) with entwined tails on the south side, and vivid green banana trees and solar emblems on the east. Relief is added by projecting cornices and a row of pilasters joined by angled lintels. The parapet wall between the towers and projecting balconies has jalis with animal designs.

Man Mandir's interior is intricately planned, with passageways leading from the entrance on the west to suites of apartments disposed symmetrically about two inner courts. Their façades are elaborate compositions, with jalis suspended between some of the columns, brackets carved with lotus petals or beasts, and struts fashioned as peacocks and *yalis*, or hybrid monsters. The eaves

The palaces at Gwalior include the Gujari Mahal (above) and the Man Mandir (below). (1) Hathi Pol, (2) first court, (3) second court, (4) servants' quarters, (5) Vikramaditya Mahal.

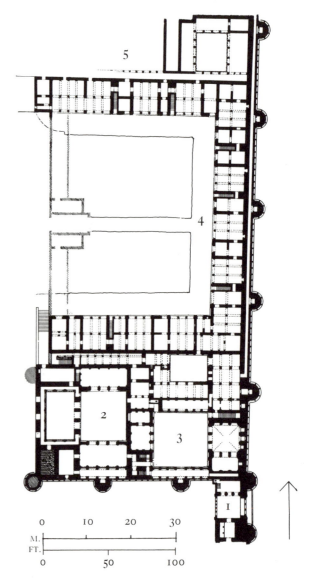

have angled or corrugated profiles; friezes on the walls above have blue and green or yellow tilework in parapet-like patterns. Upper balconies project from one or more sides of the courts. The interiors of the apartments are no less ornate. Around the **first** court, the north chamber is distinguished by a pyramidal vault carried on jalis that conceal the upper galleries. The screens are enlivened with abstract motifs derived from dancing women holding sticks. The west chamber has its walls covered with geometric relief patterns; small square holes communicate with surrounding passageways. From the **second court**, the east chamber looks out over the ramparts. It has large semi-circular designs of lotus petals and merlon motifs carved on the walls and cross-vault.

The **servants' quarters**, now partly ruined, extend from the north side of the Man Mandir. They are arranged in two colonnaded storeys around three sides of a large court, entered on the west through a deep gateway. Further north is **Vikramaditya Mandir**, named after Man Singh's son. The dilapidated structure has a pyramidal vault, with chhatris at the apex and at the four corners. A passageway concealed in the ramparts connects this palace with the Man Mandir. Opposite, on the other side of an overgrown court, is a large Mughal-style pavilion with a spacious interior roofed by a ribbed vault. Nearby is the **Karan Mahal**, a modest two-storeyed structure with roof-top apartments linked by a terrace; the façade is punctuated by three jharokas.

Towards the northernmost point of Gwalior's plateau is the **Jahangiri Mahal**, also known as **Kirtti Mandir**, after its founder Kirtti Singh (ruled 1454–79). The ruined complex consists of a large square chowk with a pool in the middle. The court is surrounded by rows of vaulted chambers, with domed chhatris in the middle of each side. At the furthest end is a collapsed set of apartments. Its central chamber has a double-height vault with arcades on two sides; projecting jharokas provide excellent views of the Gujari Mahal below.

Orchha

Laid out on an island in the Betwa River, Orchha was founded as the capital of the Rajput state of Bundelkhand in Central India by Rudra Pratap in 1531. Though his nephew, Madhukar, was defeated by the Mughals in 1577, the Orchha maharajas continued to control the region. Prominent among them is Bir Singh Deo (ruled 1605–27), a contemporary of the Mughal Emperor Jahangir with whom he enjoyed good relations. The 17th century is the period of greatest political power and artistic achievement for Orchha, followed by decline and invasion by the Marathas and Jats.

Orchha has three palaces in a line on the island; they succeed each other in date and in architectural complexity. The first to be built, the **Ramji Mandir**, belongs to the reign of Rudra Pratap and his son and successor Bharti Chand (ruled 1531–54). It is a square structure with apartments overlooking the square interior chowk. Only those on the north and west survive to their original

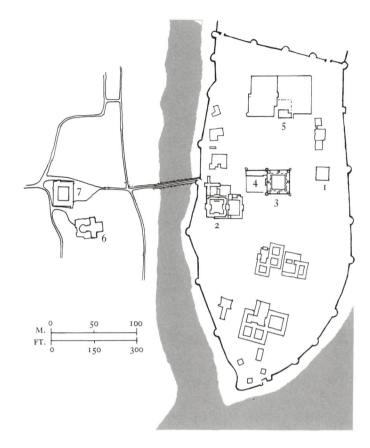

Orchha's citadel occupies an island in the Betwa. (1) Ramji Mandir, (2) Raja Mahal, (3) Jahangiri Mahal, (4) Shish Mahal, (5) Praveen Rai Mahal. In the town opposite: (6) Chaturbhuja Mandir, (7) Ram Mandir.

height of two storeys. Domed pavilions surrounded by chhatris are positioned at the uppermost level.

The second palace to be constructed, the **Raja Mahal**, built for Madhukhar (ruled 1554–91), overlooks the town, which is reached by a connecting bridge. It is laid out in the same way as its predecessor, but is three storeys high. The two upper storeys have vaulted apartments in the corners and in the middle of each side, connected to one another by terraces. Domed chhatris surmount the outer walls which contain corridors on each level. Paintings belonging to the 18th century cover the walls and ceilings of several apartments: on the ground floor, the coronation of Rama and the incarnations of Vishnu appear in the vaulted north-east chamber, and there are scenes from Krishna stories and depictions of courtly women in the central chamber on the south side.

The **Jahangiri Mahal**, immediately to the east, built by Bir Singh Deo at the beginning of his reign and named in honour of the Mughal emperor, is the largest and most evolved of the Orchha series. Its exterior presents tiers of galleries with stone screens; these run between cylindrical towers at the corners and projecting balconies in the middle of each side. The main gateway on the east combines curved lintels and arches with fringes of lotus buds.

Sculptured elephants in pavilions are placed at either side. Traces of painted geese and geometric designs, also some tile inlays, suggest the original turquoise blue and green colour scheme of the exterior. The square chowk, reached via an angled entrance, is surrounded on four sides by apartments that step back to create a series of roof terraces. The ground level has arched doorways framed by elephant brackets. The first upper level has rectangular vaulted chambers in the middle of each side, with square domed chambers at the corners; chhatris dot the connecting terraces. The second upper level has square domed chambers in the middle of each side and at the corners; small chhatris cluster against the domes, which are fluted on the corners. Connecting covered walkways are partly concealed by screens, while the parapets above are adorned with turquoise tiles.

Between the Jahangiri and Raja Mahals is the **Shish Mahal**, which is not a mirrored pavilion but a small columned hall with side chambers, now converted into a hotel. It opens directly off a parade ground situated between the two palaces. Immediately to the north of the Jahangiri Mahal is a small palace, the **Praveen Rai Mahal**, overlooking a formal garden with a systematic pattern of octagonal flower-beds. Water is supplied to each bed along conduits connected by channels to the river.

The town of Orchha is dominated by the **Chaturbhuja Mandir**, a temple higher and more imposing than any of the palaces. Erected by Bir Singh Deo to enshrine his guardian deity, Krishna, it flanks the side of an open plaza, onto which faces another palace, the **Ram Mandir**. Though this royal residence now serves as a temple itself, its arrangement of domed apartments, as preserved on the north and west sides of the central square chowk, resembles that of the other palaces. Slender towers rising high above the plaza trap wind to create a cooling effect in the chambers beneath, which were used as warm-weather retreats.

Datia

In 1626 Bir Singh Deo of Orchha granted a portion of his territories, including the town of Datia 25 kilometres (15 miles) north-west of Orchha, to his son Bhagawan Deo; thereafter, Orchha and Datia were separate states. The **Govind Mandir** erected by Bir Singh Deo in about 1620 is the last and most architecturally evolved palace of the Bundelkhand series. It stands on a hill west of the town, presenting a lofty though somewhat austere exterior, except for the east façade which has jharokas rising in tiers. The projecting arched entrance on this side has warriors on dragons painted in the spandrels. Ribbed domes surrounded by chhatris are set above chambers at the corners and in the middle of each side.

Steps ascend through three storeys of arcades and corridors to the **chowk**, which occupies the fourth level of the palace. The arrangements here repeat the basic scheme of the Jahangiri Mahal at Orchha, but with the innovation that the middle of the court is occupied by a square **tower**. It rises high above the peripheral apartments, providing the palace with a dramatic internal focus.

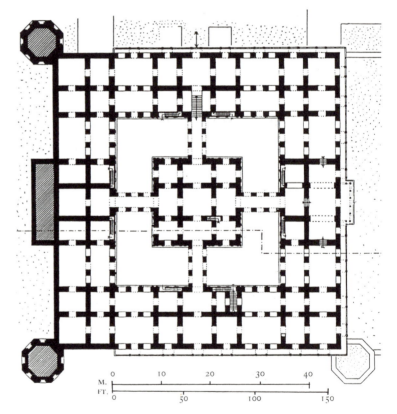

Section and upper floor plan of the Govind Mandir at Datia.

Palace of Rana Kumbha at Chittor. (1) Tripolia, (2) Sabha, (3) stables, (4) apartment of the Kanwar Pade, (5) other residential suites.

87, 86

At its first and second levels, the tower is connected to apartments on four sides by bridge-like arcades; the third and fourth levels have blind arcading and surrounding balconies supported on finely carved curved brackets; on the fifth level, a terrace surrounds a flat-vaulted darbar hall; and at the sixth – topmost – level is the royal sleeping chamber, distinguished by a shallow petalled dome. The silhouette is further enlivened by jharokas, chhattris, and merlons, the latter forming a crest around the fifth level and patterned in blue and green tiles on the uppermost parapet. Compared with the Orchha palaces, the Govind Mandir betrays considerable Mughal influence; this is best seen in the plasterwork of domes and vaults, and the painted petal designs, arabesques and geometric patterns.

85

Chittor

In Western India, the principal focus of the Rajputs was the fort of Chittor, which was the headquarters of the state of Mewar under the Guilhots and later the Sisodias. During the 16th century it was twice sacked, and then finally abandoned as the capital of Rajput power, never again to be occupied. The fort occupies a narrow ridge almost 5 kilometres (3 miles) long, rising abruptly some 150

90

metres (500 feet) above the plain. Impressive walls contain the plateau at the crown of the ridge. The main ascent is from the west by a winding road which passes through a sequence of gateways, mostly with arches. At the top is the **Ram Pol**, dating from 1459, flanked by polygonal buttresses adorned with relief carvings of elephants, horses, soldiers, courtiers and dancers. The entrance has sculptured jambs and lintels covered with animals, birds and scrollwork.

The largest and earliest royal residence at Chittor that still stands is the **Palace of Rana Kumbha** (ruled 1433–68). This monarch erected many of the temples in the fort as well as the **Jaya Stambha**, or Tower of Victory, to commemorate his triumph over the Malwa forces in 1440. The palace is entered on the east through the **Tripolia**, a gateway with part-octagonal towers crowned by domes. This leads into a large outer court overlooked on the north by a raised columned hall, the **Sabha**, which served as a formal assembly chamber. The Sabha conceals a flight of steps which ascend to the first inner court, provided with **stables**, including a ramp on the north for horses. The court is overlooked by small chambers at different levels, now much ruined. A long passageway connects the stable court with the private portions of the palace where separate buildings stand, each with suites of rooms arranged at different levels.

90

91

The best-preserved of the individual apartments in the Palace of Rana Kumbha is that of the **Kanwar Pade**, or Heir Apparent, in the south-west corner of the complex. Its asymmetrical, tripartite arrangement consists of a central court partly open to the sky, flanked on one side by a three-storeyed domed tower and on the other by a single-storeyed chamber with a roof-top terrace. The outer walls are enlivened by projecting jharokas carried on carved brackets, and jalis in rectangular openings; angled eaves and merlons crown the walls. Traces of turquoise tilework indicate that the palace was once decorated with brilliant colours.

The next important royal residence at Chittor is the **Palace of Ratan Singh** (ruled 1528–31), situated at the northern extremity of the fort next to a small lake. Polygonal towers crowned by domes are positioned at the corners and at intermediate points along the outer walls. The gateway at the south-east corner has an arched entrance crowned with merlons. The interior is partly occupied by a large court with buildings on the north. The principal apartments consist of two suites of domed and vaulted chambers opening off a broad terrace. Staircases concealed in the walls lead to roof-top chhatris. A domed chhatri on the north side of the terrace looks out over the edge of the fort.

South of Rana Kumbha's palace are the **Palaces of Patta and Jaimal**, two 16th-century noblemen. These small residences each have a large central chamber, now open to the sky since the roofs have collapsed, flanked by vaulted apartments on two or three levels. The standing portions have sharply delineated eaves mouldings, broken in the middle of each side by projecting balconies. Domes set between pyramidal vaults crown the upper chambers. Cornices and medallions with turquoise tilework add colour to the exteriors. Further south is a ruined complex known as **Chonda's Palace**, after the brother of an early 15th-century ruler of Chittor. Only its three-storeyed domed tower still stands.

Other palaces at Chittor, though traditionally Rajput in appearance, are actually late 19th-century constructions dating from the reign of Fateh Singh (ruled 1884–1930) of Udaipur. They include the **Palace of Padmini**, which surveys a reservoir with a small pavilion in the middle, and the **Fateh Prakash Palace**, now used to exhibit antiquities.

Udaipur

With the sack of Chittor by the Mughals in the 16th century it became apparent that the ancient citadel of the Sisodia Rajputs could no longer be successfully defended. A new capital of the Mewar kingdom was established, named Udaipur after its royal founder Udai Singh (ruled 1567–72), at a more easily defended hilly site some 100 kilometres (60 miles) to the west. Its focus is the picturesque Lake Pichola, artificially created by the building of a dam wall between two hills. The town on the east bank is dominated by a massive palace complex begun by Udai Singh during his short reign. Building work resumed only in 1614, during the reign of Amar Singh, and then continued without

interruption into the 18th century, with more recent extensions in the present century.

The **City Palace**, as it is commonly called today, overlooks Lake Pichola. The principal access to the complex is from the town bazaar through the **Badi Pol**, or Great Gate, which leads via a paved ramp to the triple-arched **Tripolia** situated at the north-east corner. Passing through the Tripolia, a large court is reached, the **Manek Chowk**, actually a terrace supported on vaulted structures, with service quarters on the eastern and southern sides; a formal garden in the middle replaces the original parade ground. The main block of the palace dominates the west side of the court. Despite its lack of symmetry, due to more than two hundred years of building additions, architectural unity is achieved through the repeated use of jharokas and domed chhatris that punctuate the upper parts of the walls, as well as by cornices and buttresses. A gilded sun-face, which served as the emblem of the Sisodias, is prominently displayed.

The arched entrance of the **Suraj Pol** at the south-eastern corner of the court faces towards the **Toran Pol**, which gives access to the **Zenana**, lying to the south – the oldest part of the palace and the original mardana block. The exterior walls are massive and unadorned, with part-octagonal buttresses crowned by octagonal domes. The interior court, the **Lakshmi Chowk**, is partly occupied by an open pavilion erected in the 18th century. It is surrounded by colonnaded apartments; those on the upper level, with pairs of domed chambers and intermediate lobbies, are set back to create a roof-top terrace. Later extensions on the south and east sides house the royal collection of paintings, armoury and costumes.

The **main block** of the palace to the north of the Zenana has been continuously expanded to present a complicated sequence of courts and apartments at different levels. The **principal entrance** from the Manek Chowk is through a small doorway approached by a flight of steps. The doorway has triple sets of cusped arches overhung by an angled chhajja; the British-style coat of arms of the Sisodia family, in embossed brass, which appears here is obviously a modern addition. Immediately to the south of the entrance chamber is the **Sabha**, the original formal audience hall of the palace; to the north are the vaulted chambers of the **Shila Khana**, or Armoury. Beyond lies the **Moti Chowk**, off which open the kitchen and other service structures.

The **Ganesha Deodhi** is a raised terrace that looks down on the Moti Chowk from the north side. It leads to a modest doorway that marks the beginning of the private zones of the palace. A wall niche facing this doorway is decorated in brilliantly coloured glass and mirrorwork; it houses a worn stone image of Ganesha. A steep flight of steps ascends to the **Rajya Angan Chowk** which is enclosed on four sides by apartments. On one side is the **Shrine of Dhuni Mata**, protective goddess of the Sisodias. The formal set of chambers opposite includes the **Daulat Khana**, or Treasury. Among the suites of private apartments that overlook the court from the uppermost level are the **Chandra Mahal** (Moon Pavilion) to the west, with a central water basin, and the **Dilkhush**

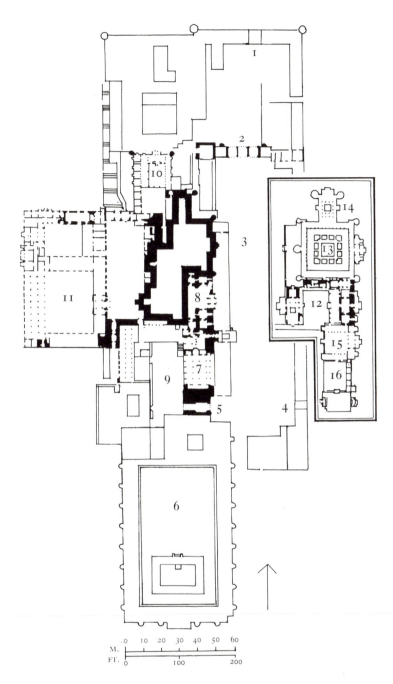

Udaipur's City Palace. (1) Badi Pol, (2) Tripolia, (3) Manek Chowk,
(4) Suraj Pol, (5) Toran Pol, (6) Lakshmi Chowk, (7) Sabha,
(8) Shila Khana, (9) Moti Chowk, (10) Mahendra Sabha,
(11) Karan Nivas. On the upper levels (inset, right): (12) Rajya
Angan Chowk, (13) Amar Vilas, (14) Badi Mahal, (15) Badi Chatur
Chowk, (16) Mor Chowk.

Mahal to the east, with paintings showing processions, festivals and courtly receptions. Centrally placed jharokas permit views of the activities in the court below.

Steps and corridors concealed in the walls ascend to the highest part of the palace, the garden court known as **Amar Vilas** after its builder, Amar Singh (ruled 1698–1710). It is raised on an artificial terrace supported by massive walls that conceal a natural hill. The **Badi Mahal**, or Great Pavilion, on the north side is a deep hall *98* with receding rows of cusped arches. A square marble bath with curved sides fills the centre. Jharokas with coloured glass panels *14* offer spectacular views of both the lake and the town.

Corridors lead from the Amar Vilas to the **Badi Chatur Chowk**, a small court for private use with pavilions on three sides capped with roof-top chhatris. The screen wall on the west, with windows and a door framing views of the lake, has painted and *101* mirror-inlay compositions depicting Indian ladies with European paramours holding flowers. On the east side is the **Badi Chatur Shala**, distinguished by the blue ceramic tiles that ornament the columns and ceilings; tiles also extend onto the outside of the jharoka that surveys the Manek Chowk below.

The last private zone is the **Mor Chowk**, or Peacock Court, *99,* named after the birds modelled in high relief and faced with *100* coloured glass that are set into the walls. Similarly brilliant glass mosaics adorn the upper level of the east side of the court, where male attendants are shown holding fly-whisks and flags. At the lower level on the south side is the **Surya Chopar**, a reception room dominated by the sun-face emblem in high relief on the *103* walls. On the north side is the **Manek Mahal**, with mirrored *102* interior apartments.

Below the walls on the lake side of the palace is the **Mahendra Sabha**, originally the law court linked with the palace. Nearby is the **Karan Nivas**, once the accounts office and now a museum housing antiquities and other exhibits. A ramp descends to the town from the court in front of the Karan Nivas.

Additions made to the palace in the 20th century extend to the south of the Zenana. Here stands the multi-storeyed **Darbar Hall** overlooking the lake, built in a revived Rajput style. The **Shambhu Nivas**, the current residence of the descendants of the *96* Udaipur monarchs, is recognized by its domed corner pavilions. It adjoins the **Shiv Nivas**, a remarkable semi-circular residential wing with an internal court, originally intended for royal guests and now a luxury hotel. Many of its apartments employ brightly coloured mirror mosaic, tile, glass and enamel to create opulent *24* and glittering interiors.

Lake Pichola provides a transcendental setting for several island pavilions. **Jag Nivas**, now the Lake Palace Hotel, dates *106* from the period of Jagat Singh (ruled 1734–51) but has been extensively renovated in recent years. Its picturesque balconies at different levels look out over the water, while the inner courts are treated as gardens with fountains and trees. The main palace on **Jag Mandir**, another island, is the **Gul Mahal**. This pavilion has *95,* three circular domed chambers, one above the other, each entered *105* through a small columned hall. White marble is used for the two

The Amar Vilas at Udaipur
served not only as a private
pleasure garden but also as a
place of formal reception. In
this large painting on cloth,
Rama Sangram Singh II
(ruled 1710–34) is shown in
darbar in the adjacent Badi
Mahal, attended by courtiers,
receiving the Dutch embassy.
The architecture is depicted
in detail, including the cusped
arcades, stained glass panels
to the rear (see plate 14),
and rooftop pavilions.

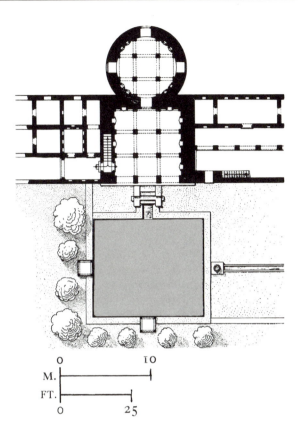

Plan of the Gul Mahal on Jag Mandir island in Lake Pichola at Udaipur.

chhatris with sloping cornices that rise above the main façade, as well as for the interior of the topmost chamber. Nearby, a trio of similar but smaller pavilions face each other across a pool with multi-curved sides in the middle of a walled garden. Arcades with cusped arches fringe the edges of the island where there are life-size elephants carved in the round, their trunks dipping into the water.

The hunting pavilions that dot the hills overlooking Lake Pichola include the **Khas Odi**, a lodge built in the 19th century. Among the pleasure gardens on the outskirts of the city is the **Saheliyon-ki Bari**. Its central pavilion has an inner court with a square pool in which stands a circular chhatri, its arcades and eaves almost completely obscured by sprays of water.

Bundi

This comparatively small state ringed by hills to the east of Mewar was controlled by the Hara Chauhan clan of Rajputs, who adopted the title of *rao*. Relations with Mewar were never peaceful, and in 1531 Suraj Mal of Bundi and Ratan Singh of Chittor killed each other on a hunting expedition! Bundi was among the first of the Rajput states to succumb to the Mughals, and in 1658 the rao of Bundi was killed in the Mughal civil war that broke out when Aurangzeb usurped the Delhi throne.

The 150-metre (500-foot)-high hill that dominates the north-ern edge of Bundi is crowned by **Taragarh**, a formidable citadel with prominent cylindrical towers. It dates back to the 14th century when the Bundi state was founded. The **main palace** is situated below, provided with its own high and thick walls. Paved ramps lead from the elephant stables and service courts up to the **Hathi Pol**, the main entrance to the palace on the east. It is flanked by part-octagonal towers with chhatris above. Brackets support two large sculptured stone elephants, once brightly painted, their tusks meeting in front of the entrance arch. The passageway is flanked by double colonnades, with a finely worked screen over the inner arch. The gate leads into the **Nauthana-ka Chowk**, or Court of Nine Horses, around which is an arcade once used as stables. A staircase ascends to the colonnaded **Ratan Daulat**, erected by Ratan Singh (ruled 1607–31) as an audience hall. A white marble seat sheltered by a vaulted chhatri overlooks the court below.

Extensive additions were made by Ratan Singh's successor, Chatar Sal (ruled 1631–58), whose major contribution was the high-level court to the south of the entrance. It has a small square marble pool in the middle, surrounded by apartments and open colonnades with viewing chhatris. The hall which opens to the west is known as the **Hathi Shala**, or Elephant Hall, after the animals carved on the column brackets. The hall to the east, the **Chhatar Mahal**, is of imposing proportions, with twelve-sided marble columns. Inlaid ivory doors in the rear wall give access to a rectangular apartment with walls of polished stone, where little sculptures of elephants serve as pegs for clothes. The small chamber that opens off to one side is adorned with paintings that illustrate views of the palace and of the courtly activities that took place within it, such as processions of the Dasara festival and assemblies of nobles; the ceiling and dado have floral designs in gold on a red background.

To the north of the palace entrance, and at a higher level, is the **Chitra Shala**, or Painted Hall. This opens off a garden with a central square pool and seating on four sides from where the palace's outer walls and entrance court can be viewed. The Chitra Shala consists of a small court surrounded on three sides by arcaded apartments. Paintings on the rear walls and ceilings of these apartments are among the finest examples of Rajput mural art. They mostly date from the period of Vishnu Singh (ruled 1773–1821), and depict mythological subjects, such as scenes of Krishna with Radha and the *gopis*, or herdswomen, love stories and court processions; the prevailing colours are blue, green and turquoise. A shish mahal, once cloaked entirely in mica, is recessed into the rear wall of the central apartment.

A separate staircase from the entrance court ascends to the **Zenana** which occupies the upper part of the palace on the west side. Among the columned halls in this zone is the **Badal Mahal**, or Cloud Hall, situated above the Hathi Shala.

Bundi is well endowed with pleasure palaces. Overlooking the waters of the **Phul Sagar** west of the town is a walled garden with a small house built in 1602 for a concubine of Bhoj Singh (ruled

11

108

107

109

110

112,
114

113

1585–1607). Its upper windows have louvres to trap the wind. To the north of the town are the **Shikar Burj**, or Hunting Tower, and the **Sukh Mahal**, the latter built on the dam wall of a large reservoir.

Kota

Some 38 kilometres (24 miles) south-east of Bundi and originally part of its territories is Kota, also founded in the middle of the 14th century. In 1625 it became the capital of a semi-independent state given to Madho Singh (ruled 1625–48) by his father Ratan Singh. Like Bundi, Kota also experienced difficulties with Mewar, but was eventually taken over by the Mughals, thereafter participating in the upheavals and struggles of the empire as an important province.

The **main palace** of the Kota Rajputs stands at the south-western corner of the fort overlooking the Chambal River. The residence is entered on the east through a parade ground contained within a broad sweep of fortifications. On the outside, the lower storeys of the palace present solid walls, with upper pavilions and jharokas, many with curved roofs arranged in an asymmetrical and picturesque manner. In the middle of the east front is the **Hathi Pol**, provided with the usual pair of brightly painted elephants with outstretched trunks and crowned with a domed pavilion. The gateway belongs to the era of the founder of the palace, Madho Singh, but the elephants are 18th-century additions. It leads into the first inner court, overlooked on the west by the **Akhada-ka Mahal**, a lofty hall originally intended for wrestling matches added by Durgan Sal (ruled 1723–56), now serving as a museum. On the north is the **Raj Mahal**, the darbar hall of Madho Singh. Its decoration dates from the 18th and 19th centuries, especially the glasswork covering the columns, and the paintings on the walls and ceilings depicting landscapes, royal receptions and mythological scenes.

Corridors and steps lead to the more private apartments located in the eastern wing of the palace. The **Arjun Mahal**, an 18th-century addition on top of the Hathi Pol, consists of a sequence of chambers covered by a large bangla roof. The projecting balcony on the east has peacock and elephant brackets. Immediately to the north is the **Lakshmi Bandar Tribari**, a small chamber with two adjoining shrine rooms. Its walls are decorated with murals of festivals such as Holi. Above is an open columned hall, the **Baroh Dari**, a formal reception room open on two sides erected by Madho Singh, beyond which are two private apartments, one above the other, contained within a Mughal-style pavilion. At the upper level is the **Badah Mahal**, notable for the delicate marble reliefs of hunting scenes and miniature paintings set into the walls. The chambers at the rear have murals illustrating the history and legends of Kota.

The original **Zenana** is detached from the main palace on the south. Its east front looking over the parade ground has regular projecting bays provided with tiers of arched openings with jalis; the west front is more open and varied since it gives access to a private garden. A new wing, added by Bhim Singh (ruled 1707–20), stands at the north end of the palace's main front, projecting eastwards. Another addition is the **Hawa Mahal**, or Palace of the Breezes, built next to the entrance to the fort; it is little more than an ornamental façade decorated with shallow pavilions defined by curved cornices and shallow domes. In the late 19th century Umed Singh (ruled 1888–1940) built two zenana buildings, one for each of his two wives. They are multi-storeyed structures in the traditional Rajput style, with tiers of screened openings separated by angled eaves and flat domes flanking a central pavilion.

Amber

One of the most important of all Rajput cities, Amber was the headquarters of the Kacchwaha Rajputs from the 12th century until the foundation of Jaipur in the early 18th century. Man Singh (ruled 1592–1615) is the outstanding personality here. He renovated **Jaigarh**, the fort that overlooks a strategic pass, and initiated construction on the new palace, the **Raj Mahal**, below. He was also responsible for erecting several Hindu temples in the nearby ravine. Memorial chhatris of the Amber rulers are situated about 600 metres (650 yards) north-east of the town.

A broad ramp ascends from the main road to the outermost court, the **Jaleb Chowk**, on the north side of the Raj Mahal, added to the original palace in the 18th century by Sawai Jai Singh II (ruled 1699–1743). The court, which is surrounded by guards' quarters and administrative offices, is entered on the east through the **Suraj Pol**, or Sun Gate, with a lofty arch flanked by jharokas. A flight of steps in the south-west corner leads to the **Singh Pol**, or Lion Gate, with painted designs in the spandrels above the opening and on the walls at either side. Concealed behind and beneath the steps leading up to this gate is the small **Shila Devi Temple**, which enshrines the protective goddess of the Kacchwahas. The image worshipped here was installed by Man Singh in 1604, having been brought from Bengal at the end of the 16th century. The shrine has a marble courtyard surrounded by delicately worked columns with cusped arches. Shila Devi is housed in a small recess, with banana trees carved in shallow relief on the marble panels flanking the doorway.

The Singh Pol gives access to the second court, which is situated at a higher level. The **Diwan-i Amm** stands at the north-east corner, surveying the lower chowk as well as the surrounding landscape. This hall belongs to the period of Mirza Jai Singh (ruled 1623–68). Double columns on the periphery and extended brackets carved as elephants carry the angled eaves; interior columns support a canopy-like vault of white marble. The **Ganesh Pol** gives access to the private apartments of the palace. It dates from 1639, but was ornately decorated in the 18th century with painted floral panels and a figure of the elephant-headed god Ganesha seated over the arch. The chamber above, the **Sohag Mandir**, has pierced marble screens through which ladies of the court could observe the activities below. It is roofed with a vault flanked by octagonal domes.

The third court, which is reached after passing through the Ganesh Pol, is another addition of Mirza Jai Singh. The chowk is partly occupied by a formal garden with pavilions on two sides. The **Sukh Nivas**, on the west, is little more than a deep verandah. The pavilion on the east is a two-storeyed building facing onto its own terrace with a shallow pool. The **Jai Mandir**, on the lower level of this pavilion, served as a hall of private audience. It has arcaded verandahs on three sides of a suite of vaulted chambers. The walls and ceilings have mirrorwork laid in intricate patterns to produce a glittering shish mahal; coloured glass is set into arched niches and window frames. The walls are panelled with carved marble slabs in the finest Mughal manner, with bunched flowers in vases the most frequently repeated motif. The **Jas Mandir**, on the upper level, functioned as the maharaja's private apartment. It is covered with two octagonal domes and a central curved vault; jalis at the rear offer spectacular views of the landscape. The interior is decorated with painted panels and ornate mirrorwork. A small

marble-lined **hammam** and a dining hall, the **Bhojana Shala**, are incorporated into the apartments that surround the sides of the court.

A labyrinth of steps, ramps and bent entries leads to the fourth and innermost court, the **Zenana Mahal**, the oldest part of the complex, originally erected by Man Singh as a mardana palace. The rectangular chowk was once occupied by a formal garden, and in the middle stands a small Mughal-style pavilion with cusped arcades. Separate apartments, now roofless, are disposed on two levels all around, separated from one another by high walls with concealed passageways. Domed chambers are raised up at the northern end; those at the southern end have angled masonry roofs with carved tile-like patterns. Additional small domed chhatris overlook the court from the higher levels.

The severely plain exterior of the Zenana Mahal is partly relieved by jharokas which, on the east side, look down on an artificial lake beside the road. A **formal garden** protrudes into the

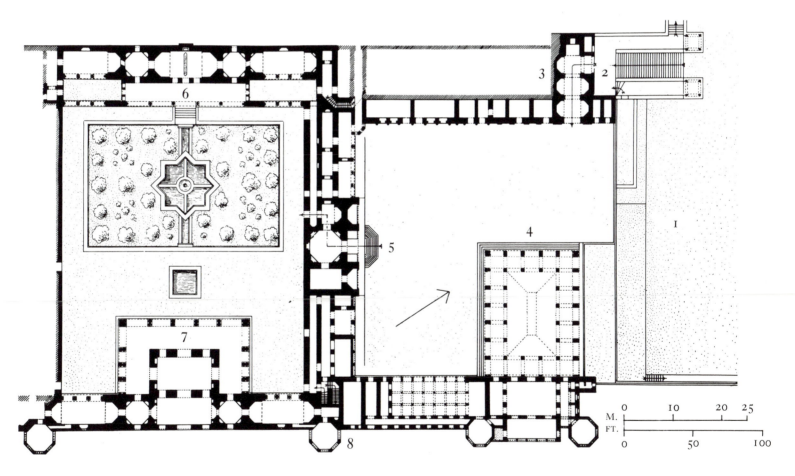

Second (right) and third courts of the Raj Mahal at Amber. (1) Jaleb Chowk, (2) Singh Pol, (3) Shila Devi shrine (below), (4) Diwan-i Amm, (5) Ganesh Pol (below) and Sohag Mandir (above), (6) Sukh Nivas, (7) Jai Mandir (below) and Jas Mandir (above).

lake, originally surrounded by water on three sides. Its descending terraces have geometrically patterned flower beds. In the middle is an octagonal pool with axial water channels. Pleasure pavilions stand on the north side of the lake, one now serving as a small museum for antiquities.

Jaipur

At a ceremony held on 18 November 1727, an auspicious date determined by his court astrologer, Sawai Jai Singh founded a new royal city, named after him as Jaipur, some 11 kilometres (7 miles) south of the fort at Amber. On completion of the royal residence in 1733, the capital was transferred thence to the new site. The plan of Jaipur was based on a mandala, with the royal residence in the middle (see p. 12). Its regular grid plan is tilted at an angle of 12 degrees east of north to coincide with Leo, the astrological sign of the Kacchwaha dynasty. The city is provided with unusually wide streets, regularly intersecting to create square urban blocks, and surrounded by walls with monumental arched gateways. A central north-south route leads up to the main entrance of the **City Palace**, while the principal east-west thoroughfare is aligned with a shrine dedicated to Surya, the sun god, which is situated on a hill some distance away. The city is overlooked by two small forts, **Nahargarh** crowning the ridge to the north-west, and **Ambargarh** on the hill to the east.

The **Tripolia**, with its characteristic trio of arches, on the south side of the palace, serves as a ceremonial entrance; but public access, today as in the past, is from the east through the smaller **Sireha Deodhi**. This gateway is an ornate Mughal-style portal, the arched entrance surmounted by painted stalactite patterns and peacocks in foliage. It leads to the **Jaleb Chowk**, a spacious outer court surrounded on four sides by rooms for guards and attendants. Verandahs added to the rooms date from the 19th century when the chowk was used for municipal offices. To the south is the town hall, with its delicately painted classical façade, and the **Hawa Mahal**, or Palace of the Breezes, erected in 1799 by Sawai Pratap Singh (ruled 1778–1803) for courtly women to look out over the bazaar street. The latter has a remarkable façade with five diminishing tiers of shallow balconies, each with screened openings capped by miniature false vaults and domes; the skyline is a graceful curve of fanciful turrets.

17, 126

127

The **Jantar Mantar**, which occupies the open space in the south-east corner of the royal precinct, is the personal observatory of Sawai Jai Singh. His astronomical instruments are extraordinary constructions of sandstone and marble, each designed and oriented to observe the movement of the sun or the moon, or of a particular star or constellation. Angled and part-circular planes with calibrated scales etched onto stone strips create novel architectural shapes. By far the largest instrument is the Samrat Yantra, an impressive curved marble scale interrupted by a steep pyramid of steps with a chhatri at the summit. This was used to determine the time, declination and hourly angle of different heavenly bodies.

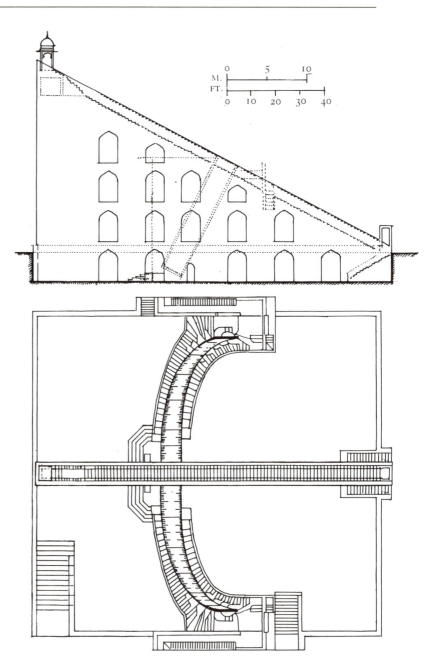

Sawai Jai Singh's observatory at Jaipur, the Jantar Mantar, is situated within the palace precincts. Masonry instruments, such as the Yantra Mantar, were architectural compositions with steep flights of steps from which to read the calibrations on the curving marble scales.

Two gateways lead into the **first inner court** of the palace complex. In the middle stands the **Mubarak Mahal**, a structure dating from the end of the 19th century designed by Samuel Swinton Jacob (see below, p. 217). It is a finely detailed pavilion with an arcaded balcony and an elaborate terrace at roof level. Arched openings of different shapes are combined with temple-like pediments over the lower doorways. The interior has a central double-height hall; the chambers around are now used for displays of costumes and textiles. The **Rajendra Pol** in the middle of the north side of the court is an elaborate gateway belonging to the same period. It is flanked by arcades on two levels, with lotus buds fringing the central archway.

Beyond lies the **second inner court**, surrounded by painted walls on three sides, with tiers of screens on the west. The structure in the middle is the **original Diwan-i Amm** of Sawai Jai Singh. It has triple arcades on each side, with paired marble columns supporting broad cusped arches; ornamental niches are outlined in white on a pink stucco background. An upper chamber rises from the middle of the roof. Gigantic silver vessels inside the hall served to store water brought from the Ganges River for royal rituals. The **later Diwan-i Amm**, which stands outside the court to the east, is now a museum housing a splendid collection of miniature paintings, carpets and palanquins. Added by Madho Singh (ruled 1750–62), the hall has impressive cusped arcades with a European chandelier suspended from the ceiling.

A **Ganesh Pol** to the west of the original Diwan-i Amm leads by way of a bent passageway into the **third inner court**. Ornate brass doors in the peripheral walls are surmounted by panels with brightly coloured peacocks or feather-like lotus patterns; the balconies above have vaulted roofs. On the north side of the court is the imposing multi-storeyed **Chandra Mahal**, or Moon Pavilion, the earliest and most important part of the complex. At ground level it consists of a low columned hall with cusped arches, beyond which is the broad verandah called the **Pritam Nivas**. A marble channel in the floor conducts water to a cascade that descends into the formal garden to the north. The first upper level of the Chandra Mahal consists of a double-height hall, the **Sukh Nivas**, extensively remodelled in the 19th century. At the fifth level is the **Chavi Nivas**, with three chambers richly decorated with inlaid mirrorwork. The top is crowned by a white marble pavilion with two small domes flanking a bangla roof. All of these storeys have projecting balconies which are arranged in a strictly symmetrical manner to create an impressive façade. The **Zenana**, built to accommodate a large number of women, adjoins the Chandra Mahal on the west.

The palace's formal garden, the **Jai Nivas**, extends northwards from the Chandra Mahal to occupy the site of the original hunting grounds on which the city was founded. Terraces and axial channels are laid out in squares in the Mughal manner with a central north-south waterway. The pavilion in the middle is the **Temple of Govind Deo** erected by Sawai Jai Singh. At the northern end stands the **Badal Mahal**; its central hall is overlooked by residential apartments at the upper level. From here

there are fine views of the Tal Katora reservoir and, on the summit of a hill beyond, a small Ganesha shrine.

Numerous buildings line the road running northwards from Jaipur to Amber. About halfway along, at Gaitor, is **Man Sagar**, a lake with a pleasure palace in the middle dating from about 1735; royal memorials of the Jaipur rulers overlook it from the west. About 3 kilometres (almost 2 miles) south-east of the city, in a wooded ravine through which the Agra road runs, is **Sisodia Rani-ki Bagh**, or Garden of the Sisodia Queen, built in 1710 by Sawai Jai Singh for his Mewari wife. This Mughal-style pavilion is of interest for the paintings on the outside walls depicting courtly women, hunting scenes and mythological stories. The apartments survey a formal garden, symmetrically laid out on descending levels, with pools and pavilions.

Dig

At the beginning of the 18th century the Jats seized control of a small territory in the vicinity of Bharatpur, midway between Agra and Jaipur. Having established their military prowess through a series of skirmishes with the Rajputs, they managed to achieve a certain degree of respectability by claiming kinship with their adversaries, with whom they eventually made peace. Badan Singh (ruled 1722–33) enjoyed the protection of the Amber Rajputs, and it was he who ordered the construction of a new residence at Dig, 30 kilometres (some 19 miles) north of Bharatpur. The palace was extended and elaborated by his successor, Suraj Mal (ruled 1733–63).

The complex clearly betrays the influence of Mughal practice in the use of formal garden layouts and regularly disposed pavilions with cusped arches, overhanging chhajjas, and large bangla roofs. The core, which dates from the end of Suraj Mal's reign, consists of four main *bhawans*, or pavilions, built in golden yellow sandstone. They overlook a spacious garden divided in the best Mughal manner into four main squares by raised walkways and axial water channels with fountains; the centre is marked by an octagonal pool. At either end are two reservoirs, Rup Sagar on the east and Gopal Sagar on the west.

At the northern and southern ends of the garden are two low buildings, each with a single central hall, the **Nand Bhawan** and the **Kishan Bhawan**, respectively. The flat-roofed **Gopal Bhawan** at the western end enjoys views of the Gopal Sagar; it is flanked by the **Sawan** and **Bhadon Bhawans**, named after the monsoon months. The lower arcades of these three pavilions are cantilevered out over the water so that they create perfect reflections. The Gopal Bhawan has arcades of cusped arches, doubled on the side wings, sheltered by a deep chhajja on decorated brackets. The central hall is divided by a transverse row of cusped arches supported on ornamented columns. A Mughal-style portico set in the rear wall was for the ruler when he held court; screened arcades for women overlook the hall at either end. The dining room is located at the upper level. The **Keshav Bhawan** at the eastern end of the garden is an open pavilion of simple design gazing over the Rup Sagar. Water could be conducted in pipes concealed in its columns and ceiling, and in the middle is a small seat, beneath which are stone balls that would be dislodged by this water to create thunder-like noises evocative of the monsoon season.

The **Purana Mahal**, or Old Palace, dating from the era of Badan Singh, is situated at the southern end of the garden. It contains two inner courts surrounded by apartments, now used as government offices, and is crowned by a small shish mahal with a bangla roof. In the south-west corner of the complex is the white marble **Suraj Bhawan**, facing south onto its own small four-square garden, with a central octagonal pool. It is distinguished by the finely carved ornamentation and coloured inlays of the surrounding porticoes.

132

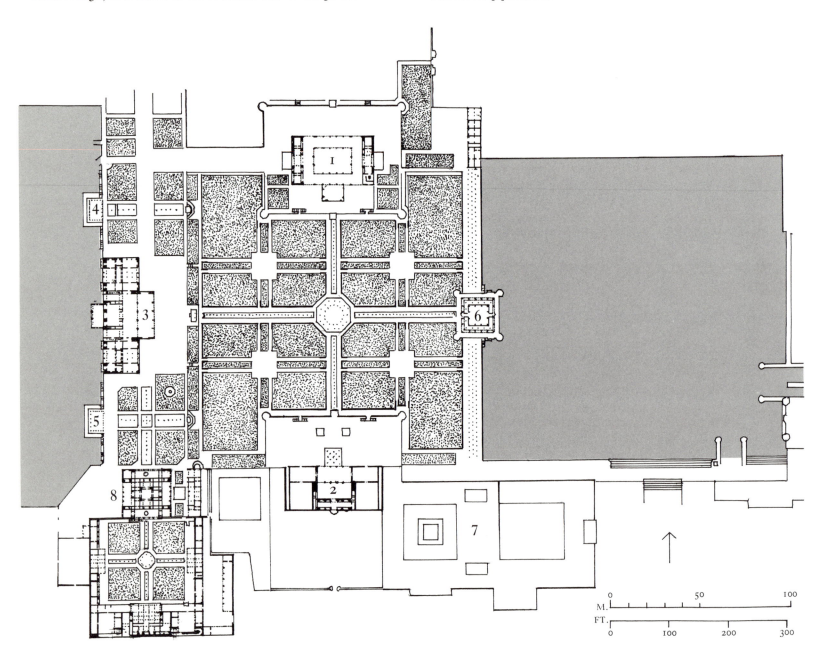

The garden palace at Dig. (1) Nand Bhawan, (2) Kishan Bhawan, (3) Gopal Bhawan, (4) Sawan Bhawan, (5) Bhadon Bhawan, (6) Keshav Badon, (7) Purana Mahal, (8) Suraj Mahal.

The citadel at Jodhpur.

Jodhpur

The capital of the arid Marwar kingdom in Western India, Jodhpur has been the residence of the Jodha Rajputs from the 15th century to the present day, and an independent state, except for the Mughal occupation of the town from 1678 to 1707. The town spreads out beneath **Meherangarh**, the citadel that occupies a long hill rising 125 metres (400 feet) above the plain, protected by high walls with massive bastions. The level top is divided into three areas: the palace to the north, the strongly fortified area to the south, and the long wide terrace to the east. Though construction work on the palace dates from the middle of the 15th century, most of the apartments belong to the period of Jaswant Singh (ruled 1638–78) and his son Ajit Singh (ruled 1707–24), the latter rising to power after the Mughal occupation came to an end.

The palace is approached by a steep zigzag path that ascends the east side of the cliff. It passes through seven arched gateways, the first of which is the **Fateh Pol**, or Victory Gate, and the last the **Loha Pol**, or Lion Gate, with hand-prints in relief on the stone blocks commemorating the ritual suicide, or *sati*, of fifteen royal wives. The royal complex consists of a sequence of interconnecting apartments that look down on irregularly shaped chowks. The façades of these apartments have tiers of shallow jharokas filled with stone screens; the balconies are supported on projecting brackets and capped with curved cornices. All of these elements are carved out of local pink sandstone, occasionally painted a pale yellow. The massive exterior of the palace, visible only from below, is relieved by cylindrical towers and heavy horizontal cornices.

The core of the palace is an upper-level court overlooked on three sides by zenana apartments. On the fourth – west – side is the **Moti Mahal**, added in the 18th century as a hall of public audience. It has arcades of cusped arches, flat ceilings with mirrorwork, and polished plaster walls. Immediately to the north is the **Khabka Mahal Chowk**, with apartments to east and west. The **Singar Choki Chowk** overlooks the ascending ramp on the east and is surrounded on three sides by zenana apartments one room deep, including the **Jhanki Mahal**, or Glimpse Pavilion. The court immediately to the north, the Daulat Khana Chowk, is overlooked by the **Umaid Vilas**, another 18th-century addition. It has a small shish mahal with coloured glass and mirror mosaics depicting mythological scenes and floral patterns; its vaulted ceiling is enlivened with glass inlays. The shish mahal gives access to a long balcony that overlooks the fort walls. Among the later extensions to the palace are the 18th-century **Phul Mahal** with its canopy-like vault covered with paintings, and the 19th-century **Takht Vilas** which has brightly coloured walls that include small niches and mythological panels.

The Jodhpur maharajas built subsidiary palaces in and around the town. The **Taleti Mahal**, intended for the royal concubines, is a 19th-century resort overlooking Lake Balsamand to the north. Its exterior is richly carved in the traditional Rajput manner, with jalis and bangla cornices; the interior, however, is purely European in style. At **Mandor**, some 8 kilometres (5 miles) north of the town, stand the memorial chhatris of the Jodhpur rulers. Here Ajit Singh erected a small pleasure palace consisting of apartments enclosing a formal garden, and here stands the **Ek Thamba**, a three-storeyed octagonal pavilion screened by jalis. The complex is entered through the impressive **Ajit Pol**, named after its builder, with a large cusped arch over the doorway.

Citadels of the South

Vijayanagara ❧ Chandragiri

Gingee ❧ Tanjore ❧ Madurai

Padmanabhapuram ❧ Cochin

Vijayanagara Southern Indian palace architecture begins at Vijayanagara, headquarters from the 14th century until 1565 of a powerful dynasty of rulers, known as rayas. The site, which is now mostly ruined, preserves a complete ensemble of royal monuments set in high-walled enclosures. The formal bath [*137*] may have been used by the rayas for their consecration rites. It is a spectacular feature fashioned entirely out of green chlorite. Steps and landings leading down to the water create complicated geometric patterns.

At the core of the palace at Vijayanagara is the Ramachandra Temple [138, 143], private chapel of the king. Courtly buildings are arranged all around. The queen's bath [139] has arcaded balconies projecting over a central water basin, now dry. Watchtowers, some with fanciful designs [140], guard the approaches to the royal enclosures. Inside stand pavilions, such as the Lotus Mahal [141], with cusped arcades and double-curved chajjas.

A solid masonry platform [142] was used by the rayas to view the parades of the Mahanavami festival. These processions – of elephants, horses, soldiers and dancing women – are portrayed on the nearby Ramachandra Temple [143]. Similar reliefs on the platform include depictions of royal activities such as hunting and reception.

138

140

139

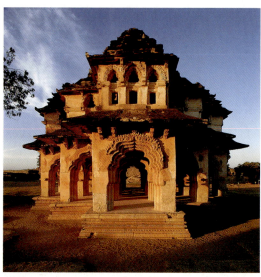

141

Chandragiri

After the sack of their capital in 1565, the Vijayanagara rayas were compelled to retreat southwards. They chose Chandragiri, a citadel in the forested hills of the Eastern Ghats, as their last capital. The palaces standing there are the biggest and most fully evolved of the Vijayanagara era [*145*]. The Raja Mahal, the larger of the two, successfully integrates Bahmani–derived arches, vaults and domes with indigenous pyramidal towers. The result is a symmetrical and imposing composition. Delicately worked plaster decoration adheres to the outer walls of the similar but simpler Rana Mahal [*144*].

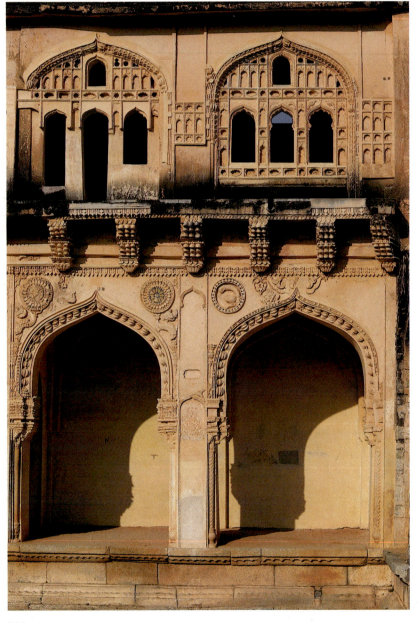

144

145

146

Gingee

As the Vijayanagara kingdom declined, the provincial governors, or nayakas, asserted their independence. By the 17th century they controlled much of Southern India, with Gingee being their greatest stronghold. Walls connecting a trio of hill citadels protect the royal complex in the middle of the site. Ramparts lined with steps scale the steep side of Krishnagiri [146], the northernmost citadel. The palace area below [148] is overlooked by a great six-storeyed tower; in the foreground is a tank surrounded by steps partly cut from the living granite rock. Supplies were kept safe in large vaulted granaries [147].

147

148

Tanjore

In the 17th century the Tanjore nayakas erected an arcaded tower [*149*] at the corner of their palace to oversee the inner courts. A pyramidal superstructure [*150*] with diminishing tiers of ornamental roof forms rises over the main residential block; balustrades and finials in European style were added later.

151

152

153

154

Madurai

Though Tirumala Nayaka of Madurai was an ambitious builder, only one court, the Darbar Hall, and the Dance Hall of his extensive 17th-century palace remain. The architecture demonstrates the final phase of the nayaka royal style. Ornate plasterwork cloaks the arcades of the court [152]. Off it the Darbar Hall opens [153–155]: here squat circular columns create long interior vistas, and cusped arches support vaults of different designs, as well as a large octagonal dome over the throne area [153]. The Dance Hall [151] is smaller, and has a lofty central space lit by a tall clearstorey.

155

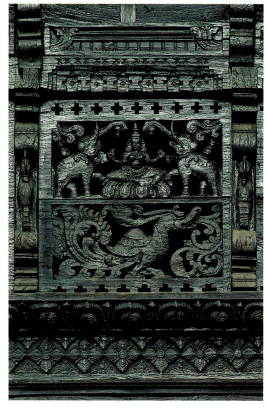

156

Padmanabhapuram

Palaces in the tropical Kerala zone of Southern India combine wooden framing with steeply sloping tiled roofs. The finest of them was the residence of Martanda Varma, king of Travancore in the 18th century. The first building [*157*] inside the royal compound has a reception hall below and an audience hall, the Pumukham, above [see *160*]. The tower to one side, the Upparika Malika, overlooks the whole complex. It houses the king's sleeping chamber and private prayer room [see *159*].

Delicate wood carving characterizes much of the palace decoration, especially screens and furnishings. Among the Hindu themes is the goddess Lakshmi bathed by elephants [*156*].

157

At Padmanabhapuram the king's private prayer room [*159*] at the top of the Upparika Malika contains a carved wooden bed intended for the god Vishnu under the name of Padmanabha, after whom the palace is named. A wall-painting in the same chamber shows this deity sleeping on the coils of the cosmic serpent [*158*].

158

A combination of slatted wooden screens and polished black plaster floor lends a gleaming quality to the palace interior. Wooden columns, ribbed rafters and outward-sloping screens in the Pumukham [*160*] filter the harsh external light as it enters the audience hall. Even the most private zone, including a privy in the women's quarters [*161*], is treated with distinction. The Dance Hall or Navaratri Mandapam [*162*] has, unusually, stone piers, whose complex carvings include figures of female attendants.

160

161

162

THE INVASION of Southern India by the armies of the Delhi sultans at the end of the 13th century marked the end of the older Hindu states, as one kingdom after another succumbed to the superior Muslim forces. The only warriors to assert themselves were the Sangama rulers of Vijayanagara – City of Victory – in the southern Deccan. By the end of the 14th century the Sangamas had won back many of the lost territories, checking any further advance of the Muslim armies and suppressing rebellions among competing rulers in the region. In the 15th and 16th centuries the Vijayanagara kings became *rayas*, or emperors, commanding an extensive and wealthy kingdom that extended from the Bay of Bengal to the Arabian Sea, and from the Deccan to the very tip of the peninsula. Italian and Portuguese traders testify to the brilliance of the capital and the ostentation of its Hindu court.

The rayas were contemporaries of the Deccan sultans with whom they were in constant conflict over the territories that lay between their capitals (see above, p. 86). In 1565 the Vijayanagara forces were overwhelmed by the armies of the sultans, who then ordered the sack of the capital. The city was never again occupied. Thereafter, the rayas were reduced to the status of lesser kings based in the hill forts at Penukonda and Chandragiri.

Already before that catastrophe the provincial governors of the empire, the *nayakas*, had become increasingly powerful; now they did not hesitate to proclaim their autonomy. Gingee, headquarters of one line of nayakas, was celebrated for its invincible fortress in the northern part of the Tamil country. Tanjore (Thanjavur), further south, was the seat of another group of nayakas, and one of the most cultured cities of its day. Madurai, the most southerly of these nayaka kingdoms, was also the wealthiest. European traders and missionaries at the Madurai court in the 17th century were attracted by its splendid textiles, ivories and jewels.

The west coast of Southern India bordering the Arabian Sea was relatively undisturbed by developments elsewhere in the peninsula, being more affected by international trading contacts. The Hindu rulers of Kerala, for instance, had longstanding relationships with Arab traders and, from the 16th century onwards, with the Dutch and Portuguese. The kingdom of Travancore reached the peak of its power in the 17th and 18th centuries, and survived into the present century. Malabar, further

to the north, was ruled by the zamorins, who benefited from the brisk trade with Europeans. In between these two kingdoms was Cochin; it, however, was virtually taken over by the Portuguese and Dutch in the 17th and 18th centuries.

Stylistic development

Nothing is preserved of royal architecture in Southern India before Vijayanagara, though some of the building types at the Hindu capital may have had a long history. Among the most archaic forms are the halls with evenly spaced wooden columns (cf. p. 68) and the residences with sequences of floor levels rising in steps and small chambers on top. Only the stone foundations and plaster floors of these structures survive; nothing is left of their elaborately carved columns and multi-storeyed towers.

Another, quite different, tradition also exists in Southern India, but this partly derives from the Muslim kingdoms of the Deccan and has no earlier precedents. Many of the courtly buildings at Vijayanagara are built entirely in solid masonry, generally of crudely cut stonework concealed by plaster. Windows and doors are arched or cusped, while domes and complicated vaults of different design roof the interior spaces. Plaster decoration makes frequent use of geometric and stylized foliage motifs. All of these techniques and forms imitate the courtly structures of the Bahmani sultans, such as those built at Gulbarga and Bidar from the late 14th century onwards. At Vijayanagara they are blended with indigenous features, such as double curved eaves, towers with pyramidal tiers of eaves, and pot-like and ribbed finials. The result is not merely a hybrid or eclectic building style, but an entirely novel synthesis that was closely identified with the rayas themselves, and, in time, was adopted as the official royal idiom in the palaces of all subsequent rulers of Southern India.

In the palaces of the later Vijayanagara rayas at Penukonda and Chandragiri this style is further developed. The Chandragiri residences, which date from the early 17th century, are symmetrical, monumental compositions. The palaces of the nayakas at Tanjore and Madurai were extensive complexes, with interconnecting halls, corridors and courts. Sequences of impressive interior spaces are punctuated by high vaulted chambers, exuberantly ornamented with plasterwork. Transverse arches with cusped profiles and curved vaults are repeatedly used, together with soaring pyramidal towers.

Other rulers in Southern India built palaces in their turn. The Wodeyars of Mysore, followed by the Muslim generals who displaced them in the middle of the 18th century, erected royal complexes at Bangalore, Shimoga and Seringapatam (Sriranga-pattinam) in a style that is partly affected by provincial Mughal practice. Their residences have large double-height reception halls with tall wooden columns; balconies at the rear give access to

137–143

138–141

35

144, 145

149–155

The vividly coloured paintings that cover the walls of Kerala palaces are executed in glowing ochres, reds and greens. Among the murals that adorn the inner chambers of the 18th-century palace at Cochin is a scene identified as the adoration of the Devi, or great goddess, in her supreme form [*163*]. The painting depicts two goddesses, the lower of whom – seemingly Mahalakshmi – is seated on a lotus pedestal and the upper one – Bhutamata – on a lotus flower. They are surrounded by adoring deities, bearded sages, and worshippers.

private chambers. The summer palace of Tipu Sultan, the Daria Daulat Bagh at Seringapatam, has Mughal-style cusped arches and decoration. Its verandah walls are entirely covered with murals illustrating glorious military campaigns. That paintings were considered an essential element in palace architecture of Southern India is seen in the 18th-century residence of the Setupatis at Ramnad, a small state in the south-east corner of the region. The darbar hall and sleeping chambers of this palace have murals showing gods and goddesses, as well as scenes of the ruler receiving foreign guests.

Royal architecture in Kerala is closely related to local architectural practice, with an emphasis on timber construction and sloping multi-tiered roofs covered with copper tiles. The palace at Padmanabhapuram, principal residence of the Travancore rulers in the 17th and 18th centuries, is the outstanding example of the Kerala royal style. The modest-size pavilions that stand within its compounds all have gabled roofs. Open timbered balconies and verandahs with slanting wooden screens filter the glaring tropical light. Teak columns, brackets, beams and ceilings are all elaborately carved. Paintings also form an important part of Kerala palaces. The plaster walls in the shrine room of the king are covered with brightly coloured murals, mostly mythological in content.

156–162

European architectural elements are also combined with indigenous traditions. The exterior of the palace at Cochin is typically Dutch in style, while the interior has carved wooden ceilings and painted walls in the typical Kerala manner.

163

Vijayanagara

The greatest of all Southern Indian royal cities was founded in the early 14th century on the bank of the Tungabhadra River as the headquarters of the newly established Sangama rulers. As Southern India came increasingly under their command, the capital at Vijayanagara was steadily built up to be a showpiece of imperial might, protected by massive granite walls and furnished with fine monuments. Both capital and empire flourished during the reigns of Krishnadevaraya (ruled 1510–30) and Achyutadevaraya (ruled 1530–42). But this glory was not to last, and after the defeat of the Vijayanagara forces in 1565 the capital was abandoned to the havoc of the Muslim armies.

Vijayanagara is laid out to the south of a rocky gorge. Its ruined structures, which are spread over an area of no less than 25 square kilometres (almost 10 square miles), are divided into two main groups: the temple complexes and shrines of the sacred centre overlooking the Tungabhadra, and the courtly structures of the royal centre, some 3 kilometres (1¾ miles) to the south. This latter zone functioned as the palace of the rayas as well as the residence of the royal household and the elite members of the court.

The fortifications of the **royal centre** enclose an almost circular area, about 1 kilometre across (just over half a mile). Gateways mark the principal roads that led into this zone from the surrounding city. Much of the royal centre is divided by high walls

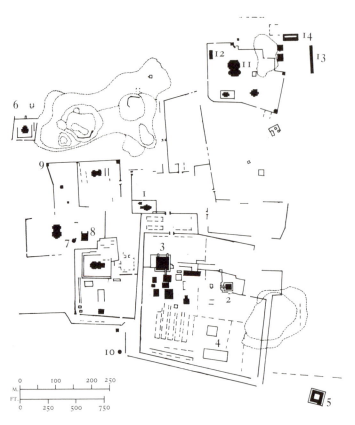

The royal centre at Vijayanagara. (1) Ramachandra Temple, (2) multi-storeyed platform, (3) hundred-columned hall, (4) bathing tanks, (5) queen's bath, (6) noblemen's quarters, (7) two-storeyed octagonal pavilion, (8) nine-domed pavilion, (9) multi-domed watchtower, (10) octagonal fountain, (11) Lotus Mahal, (12) rectangular vaulted pavilion, (13) elephant stables, (14) rectangular structure.

into irregular and interlocking enclosures. The walls are thin and tapering constructions with tightly fitted granite blocks. Courtly pavilions, watchtowers, bath-houses and other structures stand inside these enclosures, surrounded by the ruined remains of residential and administrative structures. Bathing tanks, wells and channels indicate a sophisticated system of water collection and disposal.

At the core of the royal centre is the **Ramachandra Temple**, the private chapel of the king, notable for the narrative sculptures inside illustrating the *Ramayana* story. These contrast with the reliefs on the outside walls depicting the Mahanavami festival (see p. 32), especially the processions of royal elephants, horses, soldiers and courtly women. The temple once served as a nodal point between the different enclosures: those to the east were connected with the public and ceremonial life of the king, while those to the west were associated with residential structures.

138
143

The largest compound of Vijayanagara's royal centre lies southeast of the temple in the public zone of the palace. It is dominated by the **multi-storeyed platform**, the granite sides of which are

142

covered with carvings that are exclusively royal in content: lines of soldiers, elephants and horses; hunting expeditions with lions, tigers and deer; scenes of wrestling and royal reception; rows of dancing girls, musicians and entertainers. Flights of steps ascend to the platform from which the rayas once viewed the parades of the Mahanavami. To the west of it is a large floor area, more than 40 metres (130 feet) square – all that survives of the **hundred-columned hall** (see p. 31). Stone steps indicate an upper storey, now vanished.

The remains of other smaller structures near the hundred-columned hall are built close together, sometimes even one upon the other at different levels, with courts in between, indicating a densely occupied area with successive phases of construction. The southern part of the enclosure is occupied by two large ritual *137* **bathing tanks**; one has finely worked chlorite steps in symmetrical formation descending to the water. Immediately outside the *139* compound, near to its south-east corner, stands the **queen's bath**, which displays many Bahmani-influenced elements. The pavilion consists of an arcade roofed with vaults and domes running around a square water basin. Balconies with arched windows project gracefully over the water. Steps ascend to the roof where there were once two towers.

Recent excavations within the enclosures of the western zone of the royal centre have exposed the foundations of numerous residences, some clustered together in a dense zone generally known as the **noblemen's quarters**. Each residence is laid out on ascending levels, symmetrically arranged around an open court, mostly in a U-shaped formation; small chambers surrounded by columned verandahs are situated at the topmost level. Among the courtly structures with Bahmani-influenced features that stand nearby is the **two-storeyed octagonal pavilion**. It has two chambers, one above the other, linked by a crudely constructed staircase tower. Walls and brackets are ornamented with foliage and bird motifs in delicately worked plaster; the roof is an octagonal pyramid with a ribbed finial. The adjacent **nine-domed pavilion** is enclosed on three sides, open to the north. Inside, it has pointed arcades and shallow domes. The **multi-domed watchtower** elevated on a corner of the surrounding enclosure walls has projecting balconies that survey the approach roads. To the south of these structures is the small **octagonal fountain**, open on either side, with a water basin in the middle. Fragments of terracotta water pipes are strewn all around.

The enclosure in the north-east quadrant of the royal centre may have accommodated the raya himself or his military *140* commander. It has three **watchtowers** built into the slightly tapering outer walls, each with a square or octagonal staircase and projecting balconies. An imaginative roof capped with a ribbed finial rises above the octagonal watchtower. The enclosure is *141* dominated by the two-storeyed pavilion known as the **Lotus Mahal**. This is laid out on a symmetrical plan, with double projections on each side, and a staircase tower in one corner. Both storeys have openings with cusped arches surrounded by birds, flowers and monster masks in thick plasterwork; there are also

traces of projecting brackets fashioned as rearing beasts, or *yalis*. Above the gracefully curved eaves rises a cluster of nine towers, each a tiered pyramid with a ribbed finial. The interior has shallow vaults; that over the central bay on the upper level rises up into the hollow interior of the highest tower.

A courtly residence stands in the middle of a small tank west of the Lotus Mahal. To the north are the remains of another residence, with numerous projections and the outlines of four square chambers. A **rectangular vaulted pavilion**, interpreted variously as a treasury, powder magazine, or exercise hall, occupies the north-west corner of the enclosure. Its unusual masonry gabled roof is partly concealed by an ornate parapet of pierced merlon motifs. Inside is a hall surrounded by colonnades and roofed with a vault supported on transverse arches, each with nine cusps.

The **elephant stables** located immediately outside the Lotus *8* Mahal enclosure on the east are the largest and most imposing of Vijayanagara's courtly monuments. They consist of a line of eleven square chambers roofed in symmetrical fashion with alternating domes and twelve-sided vaults; a ruined chamber, probably for drummers and musicians, rises over the central stable. The interior of the stables is enlivened by differently designed domes and vaults, some with miniature temple-like towers as decoration. The stables face westwards onto a large parade ground used for troops and animals; a ruined gateway provides access from the north-west. North of the parade ground is a **rectangular structure**, which was probably connected with military activities. It is distinguished by a lofty verandah with cusped arches that may have served as a reviewing stand. The interior arcaded court could have accommodated various martial sports.

Chandragiri

Having been forced to forsake Vijayanagara in 1565, the rayas settled at Chandragiri, some 250 kilometres (150 miles) to the south-east, from where they ruled over their dwindling kingdom for just under a century until their final extinction in 1659 by invading forces from Bijapur and Golconda. Chandragiri was chosen not only because it was safely hidden away in the wooded hills of the Eastern Ghats, but also because it was conveniently close to the flourishing town of Tirupati and the celebrated shrine of the god Venkateshvara located in the hills above.

Royal buildings are laid out on the southern flank of a massive granite rock, strongly fortified with walls that climb up its steep sides. Two palaces stand within a rectangular enclosure *145* approached from the east by a road lined with gateways. The Raja and Rana Mahals were probably erected by Venkata (ruled 1584–1614), the last of the truly powerful rayas, as formal places of reception and residences for the royal family.

The **Rana Mahal** or Queen's Palace, the smaller of the two, faces east towards an open court surrounded by an arcade, now mostly collapsed. The ground level of this two-storeyed building functions as a ceremonial entrance. The upper level, reached by

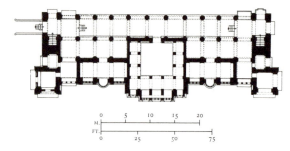

The Raja Mahal at Chandragiri.

144 staircases at either end crowned by towers, has a large reception hall opening off an arcaded corridor. The exterior is relieved by arched openings decorated with animal, bird and flower motifs in thick plasterwork. A stepped polygonal tower rises above the central chamber on the upper level. Archaeological investigations to the north have revealed the foundations of a royal residence similar to those excavated at Vijayanagara.

The **Raja Mahal** is a longer and much larger building facing north towards the hill. The exterior has tiers of arcaded openings and balconies arranged in a strictly symmetrical scheme. Staircase towers situated at both ends are topped by small pyramidal roofs. In the middle of the top storey is a square chamber crowned by a higher pyramidal tower, possibly a pleasure pavilion. The palace interior consists of three storeys of arcaded corridors with vaulted bays. At the core is a large double-height chamber overlooked by arcades at the upper level. Wall surfaces inside and out have lost their original decoration, but there are traces of beasts and lotus flowers in thickly worked plaster.

Gingee

The fort at Gingee was the headquarters of the northernmost group of nayakas during and after the period of Vijayanagara domination. Towards the end of the 17th century it was occupied in turn by the Golconda forces, the Maratha chief Shivaji, and the Mughal general Zulfiqar Khan; the French and British followed in the 18th century. Despite the tortuous history of the site, most of the surviving fortifications and courtly structures that still stand are associated with the reigns of Venkatappa, also known as Krishnappa (ruled 1570–1600), and Vardappa (1600–20), the most powerful of Gingee's nayakas.

148
146 The site is one of the most spectacular in Southern India, encompassing three rock citadels: **Krishnagiri** to the north, **Rajagiri** to the west and **Chandrayandurg** to the south. Each consists of a rugged granite hill strongly defended with encircling stone walls, interrupted only by gateways leading to precipitous flights of steps that ascend to the summits. Among the diverse structures perched on the tops are granaries with vaulted roofs, an oil press with two finely finished chambers, a ruined watchtower, and several small shrines. A partly demolished open structure on Krishnagiri has an upper chamber with balconies. The fanciful

style of its pointed arches and fluted dome suggests that it may have served as a pleasure pavilion.

Massive walls, with round towers and a protective moat, run across the level ground between the three citadels to enclose a vast triangular area, no less than 1 kilometre ($\frac{5}{8}$ mile) from north to south; interior walls divide this into outer and inner forts. In the **Outer Fort**, now mostly irrigated fields, stands the **Venkataramana Temple**, the largest religious monument at the site. The nayaka palace, which is situated within the **Inner Fort**, is entered through two heavily defended gateways with curved barbican walls, partly renovated during the French occupation. The royal complex is dominated by the **Kalyana Mahal**, or Marriage Hall, with apartments on four sides of a square water basin. On the north side is a six-storeyed tower, with arcades all around, topped by a chamber with a pyramidal roof.

A double line of small chambers, probably **stables** for horses and grooms, stretches westwards from the Kalyana Mahal to face onto a spacious parade ground. Foundations of a royal residence have been uncovered on the mound that rises to the west. Immediately below these ruins is a large polished granite slab and bolster, obviously a gigantic ceremonial seat from which the nayakas could inspect the troops and animals.

147 Two **granaries** with high pointed vaults stand to the southwest: one has four interconnecting chambers, while the other is single-chambered. Open pavilions nearby may have been places of reception and entertainment. Mounds of overgrown rubble indicate the presence of other buried structures connected with the court. To the south is a large tank, partly cut into the rock, 148 surrounded by a colonnade.

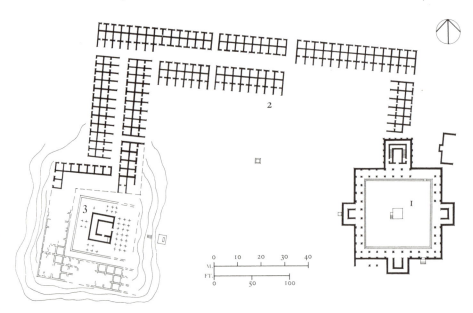

Gingee's main palace area. (1) Kalyana Mahal, (2) stables, (3) royal residence.

Tanjore

From the end of the 14th century onwards, Tanjore (Thanjavur) served as provincial seat of the Vijayanagara governors. Towards the middle of the 16th century, when the nayakas proclaimed their independence, it assumed the status of a capital. The city remained a nayaka headquarters, flourishing for more than a hundred years under such forceful personalities as Raghunatha (ruled 1600–1634). In 1674 it was overwhelmed by the invading Marathas led by Venkaji, one of the outstanding warriors of the period, who made it his own capital. Under rulers like Shahji (ruled 1684–1712), the Tanjore kingdom attained considerable economic importance. The Maratha line continued into the British period, coming to an end only in 1855.

The royal complex, which stands surrounded by walls in the middle of the city, is mostly dilapidated and abandoned; two sets of apartments have been renovated in recent times to provide accommodation for a sculpture gallery and a manuscript library. The **Nayaka Palace** consists of a sequence of open courts surrounded by open pavilions, colonnades and multi-storeyed structures. At the core is a square court with a domed entrance chamber on the north. The south side is overlooked by a two-storeyed structure divided into corridors and chambers, with pointed arches supporting shallow domes and vaults. In the middle of the roof rises a square chamber with a steep pyramidal tower. The diminishing eaves of the tower, which have balustrades in European classical style and fluted dome-like finials, are probably 18th-century additions. The darbar hall on the west side, which also faces onto the court, is now the sculpture gallery. Its massive circular piers support cusped arches and a pointed vault with ribbed and fluted surfaces. Plaster sculptures, including a large tableau depicting the coronation of Rama, adorn the walls. Animal brackets carry the overhanging eaves, while prominent lotus finials crowning domes and vaults protrude above the roof. A seven-storeyed tower with open arcades on all sides soars above the north-west corner of the complex.

The **Maratha Palace**, situated in the southern part of the complex, consists of a spacious court overlooked from the west by a darbar hall. It has slender timber columns supporting a flat timber roof. The walls are decorated with thick plaster ornamentation.

Madurai

Like Tanjore, Madurai was a provincial capital under Vijayanagara; its governors, too, declared independence towards the middle of the 16th century, and for the next hundred years ruled over a wealthy kingdom. The most famous of the Madurai nayakas, Tirumala (ruled 1623–59), is credited with the construction of the palace and the extensions to the great temple in the middle of the city. The Marathas, who had established themselves at Tanjore, put an end to this line of nayakas when they absorbed Madurai into their own kingdom towards the end of the 17th century.

150

149

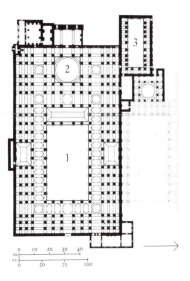

The 17th-century palace of the nayakas at Madurai. (1) Court, (2) Darbar Hall, (3) Dance Hall. It was no longer inhabited when portrayed by the Daniells at the end of the 18th century. Their exterior view shows the rising vault of the Darbar Hall on the left; the interior depicts the Dance Hall before its restoration in the 19th century (cp. plate 151).

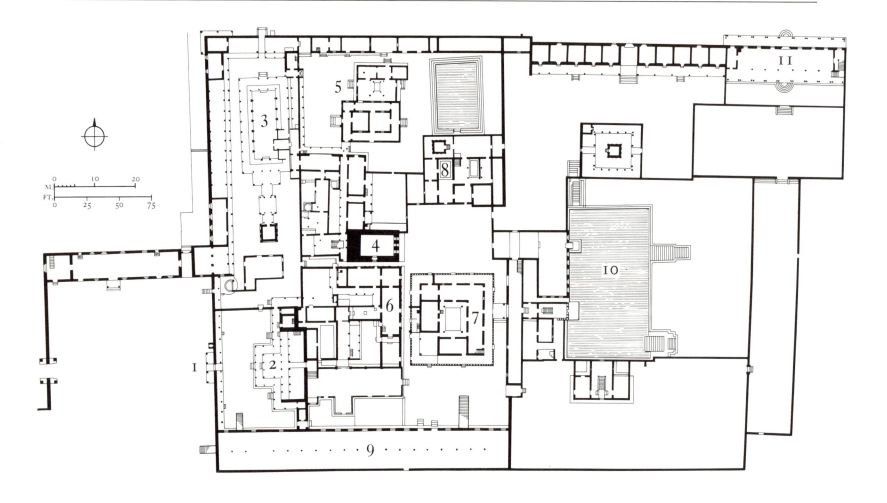

Large portions of the **Nayaka Palace** gradually collapsed or were dismantled by the British in the 19th century, while some parts were completely restored in 1871–82. The two remaining fragments, the Darbar Hall and Dance Hall, are impressive for the monumental scale of the interior spaces and the exuberance of the plaster ornamentation. A large **court** surrounded by colonnades leads to the **Darbar Hall**, of which the interior presents perspectives of solid circular piers that support broad arches with pointed and cusped profiles. It is roofed by alternating pyramidal domes and shallow vaults, some raised on clerestory walls with small windows to admit light, with a larger octagonal dome over the throne area. Plaster ornamentation smothers the arches and vaults with lotus and foliage motifs, elephants and mythical beasts. The exterior is relieved by animal brackets carrying the eaves, and lotus finials crowning the domes and vaults.

The **Nritya Sabha**, or Dance Hall, which adjoins the Darbar Hall at its north-west corner, has a double-height central space, flanked on two sides by an arcade below and chambers with arched windows above; the floor is raised slightly at the eastern end. Pilasters on the upper level are concealed by geese and winged beasts in high relief. Transverse arches support the pointed vault. The cusps of the arches are richly encrusted with plaster animals

Padmanabhapuram palace. (1) Padipura, (2) Pumukham, (3) Navaratri Mandapam, (4) Upparika Malika (with treasury, sleeping and fasting rooms of the king, and shrine room on successive levels), (5) Lakshmi Vilasam, (6) Pilamuttu Kottaram, (7) Thai Kottaram, (8) Homapura, (9) Uttupura, (10) Kalkulam, (11) Indra Vilasam.

and birds in scrollwork; flame-like motifs protrude from the fringes and there are monster heads at the apexes. Much of this plasterwork dates from the 19th-century refurbishment of the palace. A second court surrounded by colonnades with a domed chamber that once adjoined the Dance Hall on the east no longer stands.

Padmanabhapuram

Cut off from the rest of Southern India by the forested ridges of the Western Ghats, the Travancore maharajas enjoyed autonomous rule over the southern portion of Kerala. Their fortified headquarters were located near Cape Comorin (Kanyakumari), the southernmost point of the Indian peninsula. Under Martanda Varma (ruled 1729–58), the palace was rebuilt and renamed

Padmanabhapuram, City of the Lotus Born (Padmanabha, an aspect of Vishnu, tutelary deity of the ruling family). After 1790, when the capital was shifted to Trivandrum (Thiruvanantha-puram), Padmanabhapuram was used only as a summer residence.

The palace is laid out in a sequence of four adjoining walled compounds, providing a transition from public to private zones, connected by small and simple doorways. The complex displays no evidence of overall axial planning; rather, individual courtly structures are linked together by a maze of corridors, colonnades, verandahs and interconnecting courts. The principal entrance on the west is through an outer court reserved for public ceremonies. The **Padipura**, or main gate, is a traditional Southern Indian structure with an ornamented gabled roof. Facing it in the second court is an audience hall, the **Pumukham**, which occupies the upper level of a two-storeyed structure with large circular wooden columns. Delicately carved wooden screens adorn the entrance gable; angled timber screens filter light in the upper chamber. To the north stands the Dance Hall, known also as the **Navaratri Mandapam**, after the festival that was celebrated there. The blackened plaster floor reflects the carvings of female attendants on the rows of granite piers. A small shrine dedicated to the goddess Sarasvati opens off the south side.

The private zone begins with the third court. Here stands the tallest structure of the complex, the **Upparika Malika**, a masonry tower soaring above the sloping tiled roofs of the adjacent buildings erected in 1749 by Martanda Varma. It has four chambers arranged one above the other: treasury, sleeping room for the king, fasting room also for the king, and shrine room with an empty bed for Padmanabha. Narrow steep steps provide access to the upper levels, from which wooden balconies with angled screens project outwards. Shutters in the screens permitted the ruler to survey the court below, where warriors and courtiers assembled. The shrine room at the top has brightly painted compositions covering all four walls. Among the gods and goddesses depicted in these murals is the image of Padmanabha.

Residences of other members of the royal family are also situated within the third court. The **Lakshmi Vilasam** and **Pilamuttu Kottaram** are for courtly women. The residence of the queen mother, the **Thai Kottaram**, is one of the oldest buildings in the complex. Its chambers are arranged around a small square court with a shallow pool in the middle to collect rainwater. The building has a pyramidal tiled roof, with wooden screens at the upper level overlooking the inner court. Nearby structures include the **Homapura**, a building for ritual use provided with its own stepped tank, and the **Uttupura**, which consists of two exceedingly long dining halls, one above the other, with central lines of columns.

The fourth court occupies the easternmost part of the complex; here, additional dining rooms and residences are disposed around the **Kalkulam**, a reservoir reached down a flight of steps. The **Indra Vilasam** incorporates a residence and audience hall for European visitors, and is partly built in a Western classical style; it faces a garden, now sadly neglected. The offices for the palace are situated at the northern end of this compound, with access from the street that runs outside the palace walls.

Cochin

The busiest and best-appointed port on the Kerala coast, Cochin was the capital of an independent line of rulers in the 15th and 16th centuries. The Cochin rajas maintained profitable contacts with the international mercantile community, including Portuguese, Dutch and, later, British traders. There were, however, clashes of interests, and Europeans eventually gained control of the port and its profits; even so, the Cochin rulers continued to govern, at least in name. Their palace on Mattancherri, a narrow peninsula that separates the Arabian Sea from an archipelago, was originally erected for them in 1557 by the Portuguese, and renovated in 1663 by the Dutch; in its present state it is no earlier than the 18th century.

Despite the obvious European appearance of the exterior, with its round-headed windows and doors, the palace is typically Keralan in plan and interior scheme. It consists of a number of ceremonial and private chambers arranged around a square court, partly occupied by a small shrine. Sloping tiled roofs, projecting wooden balconies with screens, and carved timber ceiling panels are indigenous features.

Steps ascend to the main entrance in the middle of the south side. The principal chamber on the upper level is a long hall with a coffered wooden ceiling decorated with deeply carved lotus medallions. The king's sleeping chamber, situated at the south-west corner, has its walls entirely painted with scenes from the *Ramayana*. The crowded compositions are filled with deities and attendant figures in glowing yellows, reds and greens. Two superimposed rooms at the south-east corner of the complex, linked by narrow stairs, are adorned with paintings of other mythological subjects. Processions of courtiers are delicately drawn on the walls of another room at ground level.

A shrine with a circular sanctuary in traditional Keralan style, standing in a compound of its own immediately outside the palace, accommodates Krishna, the personal deity of the Cochin rulers.

Princely residences

Lucknow ❧ Hyderabad ❧ Gwalior

Baroda ❧ Indore ❧ Mysore ❧ Kapurthala

Jodhpur ❧ Morvi

Lucknow The adoption of European styles for Indian palaces was at first accompanied by considerable invention and improvisation, as can be seen in the courtly buildings of the nawabs of Lucknow in the 18th and 19th centuries. These rulers employed numerous Europeans, some of whom also acted as architects. The Sat Khande [164] was begun by Muhammad Ali Shah towards the middle of the 19th century; its designer is unknown. The four of its intended seven storeys present a diverse arrangement of arcaded openings, mixing European pediments with Indian cusped arches.

166

Hyderabad

The principal residence of the nizams was the Chau Mahalla in the heart of their capital, in use from the time of Asaf Jah I in the mid-18th century up until recently. In style, the palace looks back to the Qutb Shahi monuments at nearby Golconda. It is entered through a gateway marked by a clock tower [167]. Among the detached suites that make up the complex is the Khilwat Mahal, built to house a double-height darbar hall. Outside [166], rooftop apartments open on to a terrace with octagonal pavilions at the corners; the great hall inside [165] has a rich marble pavement and crystal chandeliers.

167

165

168

169

170

European styles were also in vogue at the court of the nizams of Hyderabad. The Falaknama, built for a rich nobleman in 1872, was purchased by the sixth nizam for his private use. Behind a Palladian façade [170] is a suite of elaborate rooms in a variety of styles.

The frescoed entrance hall [*168*] has a fountain and ornaments of Italian marble. Upstairs, a suite of rooms in a rich, dark French 17th-century mode includes a smoking room [*169*] with a sociable many-stemmed hookah.

171

Gwalior

Headquarters of the Scindia maharajas from the middle of the 19th century onwards, the Jai Vilas is one of the most ambitious of India's classically inspired residences. Built to celebrate the Prince of Wales's visit in 1876, to a design by Colonel Sir Michael Filose, it has three low ranges for services and minor apartments, and a grand towered range containing the state rooms. Of these the most notable is the Darbar Hall [*171*], glowing with gilt and golden curtains. Its gigantic crystal chandeliers have glass chimneys, a feature used in India to protect candles from the draughts caused by punkahs or, as here, Victorian ventilation systems.

172

173

Baroda

One of the greatest palaces in the Indo-Saracenic style is the Lakshmi Vilas, seat of the Gaekwad dynasty. Begun in 1878 by Charles Mant and completed by Robert Fellowes Chisholm, it stands in a vast park punctuated by sculptures. The interior is even more varied in style and materials than the exterior: a wooden gallery in the Darbar Hall rests on brackets with musicians [176]; an inner court provides the setting for a pool surveyed by statues [177]; and the entrance to the maharaja's private apartments [178] has an Italianate floor and fountain in a setting of 'Indian' cusped arches and rich foliage ornament.

200 · *Princely residences*

174

175

176

177

178

Indore

Lal Bagh, the residence of the Holkar family, a proud Maratha dynasty, was built at the turn of the century in a thoroughly European style. Yet while the arms on the entrance gate [181] appear Western at first glance, they incorporate the Indian royal emblems of umbrella [see 1] and sun [see 103, 104]; one of the supporters is a bull.

The sun theme is taken up again in the painted ceiling of the Darbar Hall [180]: here, above a throne room in 18th-century style furnished with imported fireplaces, carpets and chandeliers, the Greek sun-god Helios rides through the clouds in his chariot.

180   179

182

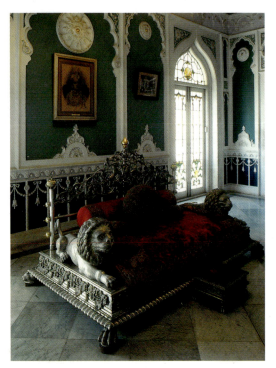

183

Mysore

A lively variation of the Indo-Saracenic style was chosen by the Wodeyar rulers for the rebuilding of their residence at the turn of the century. Their architect was Henry Irwin. The exterior is crowned by domed turrets that cluster around a central gilded tower – a silhouette further complicated by a distinctive ornate Hindu temple tower [184], and illuminated on special occasions [185]. The lavish interiors are basically Southern Indian in style, but with innovations: there is stained glass in the Kalyana Mandapa [186; see also 188], a hall made of cast iron, and the capitals in the Amba Vilasa [187; see also 189], another iron-roofed hall, are animated by painted plaster birds and miniature divinities. More traditional is the Darbar Hall [182]; here stood a throne of gold and silver. Another Wodeyar throne [183] is now in the palace museum.

184

185

186

187

188

The Mysore palace was the first in India to make use of cast-iron construction. Columns and roof frames were manufactured by Macfarlane's of Glasgow and then shipped to India. The octagonal Kalyana Mandapa [*188*] has a dome of stained glass with peacock motifs [see *186*] and a splendid tiled floor. In the Amba Vilasa [*189*], the hall of private audience, a stained-glass ceiling floats above a much more massive structure.

189

190

191

192

Kapurthala

The château style of Indian royal architecture is represented by a single example, the Jagatji, which was completed in 1908 for the maharaja of one of the Sikh states of the Punjab by a French architect, M. Marcel.

Everything about it is French – the formal garden in which it stands; its high pavilion roofs; its rich interiors [190] with their imported carpets and chandeliers and ornaments like the specially decorated Sèvres vase [191].

Jodhpur

Begun in 1929, the Umaid Bhavan is a
monumental complex dominated by a central
dome framed by bold towers of almost equal
height, set between widely spreading wings
[193, from the west]. Its British architects,
Lanchester and Lodge, skilfully balanced
contemporary European styles with
traditional Rajput elements. The central hall
[195] under the dome is framed by a circle of
piers with ornate brackets; stone screenwork
is used in balcony and openings. That the
royal founder of the palace, Umaid Singh,
wished to be permanently associated with the
building is revealed in one of the murals
[194] of the Darbar Hall, where the king is
shown in procession with the Umaid Bhavan
in the distance.

194

The private apartments in the Umaid Bhavan at Jodhpur reflect the profound impact of the Art Deco style. The Small Darbar Hall [196] has a curved golden ceiling and wall-paintings by the Polish artist Julius Stefan Norblin portraying legendary Rajput heroes, including Arjuna with his charioteer Krishna behind the throne. The bathroom [197] attached to the Maharani Badan Kanwar's bedroom has both tub and washbasin of onyx, with gilded fittings. The swimming pool [198] reflects the new fashion for such features in the West – but, like the lavish bathroom, it also belongs to the ancient tradition of palace hammams.

Morvi

The triumph of Art Deco in India is celebrated in the capital of a small state in the westernmost part of the country. Begun in 1931, the New Palace presents a streamlined exterior [199]. Inside, the marble entrance hall [203] has a ceiling painting by Norblin on the royal theme of the sun god in his chariot [cf. 180], and royal beasts flanking the door [cf. 2, 3]. Reminders of the cocktail era are two bars, both with murals by Norblin – one downstairs [200], and one on the upper level [202] with a circular marble fountain. The swimming pool [201] is itself fed from a monumental fountain.

199

200

201

202

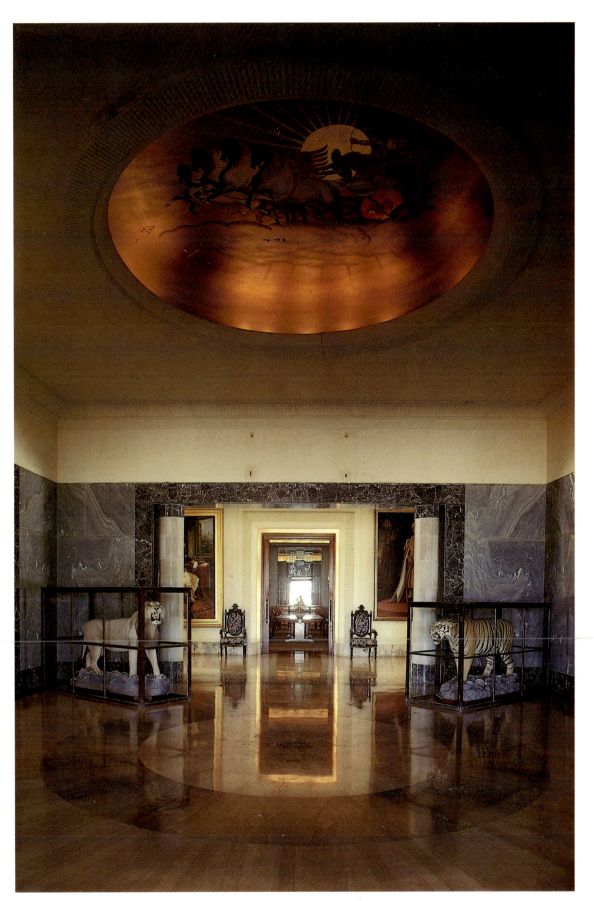

203

204

205

206

216 · *Princely residences*

WITH THE rise in the military and commercial power of the various East India Companies in the 18th century, Indian kings found it expedient to enter into commercial treaties with the Europeans. In 1772 the British Government took over the management of their East India Company, the most powerful of all, and the maharajas were compelled to acknowledge the supremacy of foreign rule. In the course of the 19th century the British took control of the subcontinent by defeating local rulers and forbidding them to maintain independent armies. In this way the maharajas were effectively subjugated, unable to dislodge the foreign forces or to engage in aggressive acts against one another. The era of India's 'great rulers' had come to an end; thereafter they were referred to and treated as princes. But Indian rulers were able to affirm their royal status in ambitious building projects. Large residences were erected throughout the country up until Independence in 1947, when all princely territories were absorbed into the modern states of India and Pakistan.

Stylistic development

The styles in which the princely residences are built attest to the prevailing influence of European culture on the Indian ruling classes. By the end of the 18th century Neoclassicism was in vogue, and the first palaces tended to imitate official buildings of the British, as in Madras and Calcutta. The independent governors of Bengal, the *nawabs*, for example, in their new capital at Murshidabad on the east bank of the Hooghly River, based the Aina Mahal of 1837 on Government House in Calcutta. Its imposing colonnaded portico leads to a suite of elegantly furnished rooms, formally appointed with mirrors, chandeliers and European furniture.

But there were also more inventive styles, some demonstrating the local builders' imperfect understanding of European architectural principles; some following the Western 19th-century passion for a diversity of historical styles; and some reflecting a growing taste for more fanciful and decorative designs that fused European models and indigenous traditions. Among the most exotic of these local variations are the palaces of Lucknow; sadly, most were demolished by the British after the Mutiny in 1857, or have since decayed. The Lucknow nawabs sponsored an architectural manner that juxtaposed pointed and cusped arches and domes drawn from Mughal architecture with European columns, pedi-

ments and round-headed openings. Many of these elements were ornamented with rich plasterwork which made repeated use of the fish motif, the nawabs' personal emblem.

Eventually, from Srinagar in the valley of Kashmir to Trivandrum in Kerala palaces sprang up with colonnaded entrance porticoes reached by flights of steps, imposing lobbies with lofty domes, and grand reception rooms lined with marble and adorned with crystal chandeliers and European furniture and oil paintings. The *nizams* of Hyderabad enthusiastically adopted the Palladian style. The Falaknama, which they acquired in 1897, *170* is one of India's finest classical compositions. Even more vast and elaborate is the sprawling Jai Vilas at Gwalior, which is set in *172* landscaped grounds – a growing fashion as the century progressed. In the remoter Eastern Indian states of Agartala and Cooch Bihar, *19,* impressive Baroque designs with imposing domes were chosen *20* at the turn of the present century. This preoccupation with European architecture was not exclusively based on the British experience: French royal styles were also imitated. The palace erected at Kapurthala in the early 20th century has an overall *190–* composition and tall pavilion roofs in the French manner, *192* providing the ruler of this small Sikh state in the Punjab with a setting in which to realize his dreams of being an Indian 'Sun King', surrounded with French furniture, porcelain and candelabras.

Simultaneously, some princes erected residences in indigenous architectural styles. The Rajput palaces at Jodhpur, Bikaner and Jaipur, for instance, were substantially enlarged during the 18th and 19th centuries. This resurgence of local patronage sustained builders and craftsmen who worked in a revived Rajput style, specializing in the reproduction of traditional features such as jalis, jharokas and chhatris, together with cusped arches and bangla roofs. British architects actively participated in this process. Samuel Swinton Jacob, the best-known, was employed for most of his career by the maharaja of Jaipur, for whom he built extensions *125* to the City Palace as well as a royal guest house outside the city, the Rambagh. In 1902, Jacob completed the Lal Garh for the maharaja of Bikaner. It was designed according to conventional Rajput patterns, with a set of chowks, or inner courts, surrounded by apartments with delicately worked red sandstone jalis and jharokas. Another traditional palace was erected by Jacob for the maharaja of Kota. To demonstrate his knowledge of Indian architecture, Jacob published a multi-volume work illustrated with detailed drawings entitled the *Jeypore Portfolio* which appeared from 1890 onward.

Rajput architecture seen in a less scholarly way had been a primary source for the 'Indo-Saracenic' style invented by the British for their own civic monuments, in which Indian elements are freely combined with European features, especially those drawn from Venetian Gothic architecture. The latter, which had

---

If the reception rooms at Morvi display a sophisticated elegance [*205*], royal luxury is fully manifest in the private apartments. The maharajah's bed [*204*] has a black marble podium and a built-in canopy. The massive marble tub in the maharani's bathroom [*206*], set in an alcove, extends from a carved shell.

become popular in Britain under the influence of John Ruskin after the mid-19th century, was particularly suitable, since it was a Western style with a distinct Oriental flavour. Indo-Saracenic architecture juxtaposes Rajput balconies, curved cornices, open pavilions and bulbous domes with Gothic pointed arches, arcades and towers. Though the results are a stylistic hybrid, they are consistently picturesque; more importantly, they were easily adapted to different uses. Innumerable Indo-Saracenic law courts, clock towers, railway stations, art galleries and government colleges sprang up all over the subcontinent in the second half of the 19th century.

By the turn of the present century many princes had chosen the Indo-Saracenic style for their new residences: it was acceptable to British taste, and at the same time it was more obviously Indian in spirit than classicism. Among British experts in this idiom who were employed by maharajas was Charles Mant. His projects at Kolhapur and Baroda (Vadodara), the latter completed by Robert Fellowes Chisholm, another specialist in the style, are among the finest of the series. The Baroda residence is the largest of all Indo-Saracenic palaces, its principal façade presenting an inspired synthesis of all the component elements. The success of the scheme may be judged by the fact that it served as a model for numerous smaller imitations, among them the early 20th-century palaces at Jamnagar and Wankaner. Another spectacular Indo-Saracenic royal monument was executed for the maharaja of Mysore to the design of Henry Irwin, whose mentor was Chisholm. A profusion of Indo-Saracenic elements graces the Mysore palace, especially the clusters of miniature domes and pinnacles rising above the roofline, and the dignified perspectives of cusped arches in the darbar hall. The complex also exploits the European fashion for stained glass and industrially manufactured cast iron structures, which were made to order in Glasgow and exported to India.

In the 20th century a wholly new mode, thoroughly Western but with no historical overtones, appeared, as European architects and artists schooled in the latest Modernist fashions came to India and found employment at the princely courts. Eckart Muthesius from Germany designed the Manik Bagh at Indore, and at Morvi, one of the princely states of Gujarat, a remarkable Art Deco palace was begun in 1931. The Polish-born painter Julius Stefan Norblin worked in India from 1941 to 1946; his murals grace the interiors of both the Morvi and Jodhpur palaces.

The climax of palace building before Independence put an end to it is seen at Jodhpur, where there is an effective fusion of imported and indigenous elements. The design of 1929, by Lanchester and Lodge, successfully combines the monumental trend that had developed by this time in British architecture with the symmetrical and picturesque schemes of the Rajputs and Mughals. Certainly it is the only princely structure to rival the architectural achievements of the British in their new capital at Delhi.

Lucknow

With the disintegration of the Mughal empire in the early decades of the 18th century, Saadat Khan, the nawab or provincial governor of Oudh (Awadh), a province in eastern Central India, founded a semi-independent kingdom with its capital at Faizabad. After the failure of the nawab's army to recapture Bengal from the British in 1764, a treaty was signed under which Oudh was restored to the nawab. A condition was that a representative of the East India Company supported by a contingent of British troops should be permanently stationed there. The capital was shifted to Lucknow in 1775 by Asaf-ud-Daula at the beginning of his rule, and the city grew rapidly in prosperity. Many fine palaces and gardens were erected on the south bank of the Gumti River, especially during the reign of Asaf-ud-Daula's successor, his brother Sadaat Ali Khan (ruled 1798–1814). The Lucknow court in the first half of the 19th century was one of the most brilliant in India, renowned for the refined (in some eyes decadent) tastes of its nawabs and courtiers, who included many Europeans employed in the military. Only after the Mutiny in 1857, when the city was badly damaged in fighting and subsequently annexed by the British, did its fortunes fade.

The impact of European architectural practice was profound at Lucknow, and classicism with a local flavour was the preferred style. Palaces were planned as sequences of large courts that led from public spaces to the private apartments of the nawab's household. Buildings within these courts were interspersed with gardens and tanks, sometimes in formal and symmetrical arrangements. Mansions in the city, too, were exuberant improvisations on European themes, the most remarkable being Constantia, built by Claude Martin, the French major-general employed by the Lucknow nawabs until his death in 1800.

Of the mid-18th-century **Macchi Bhavan**, or Fish Palace, only the Baoli Palace is preserved. It consists of a sunken reservoir surrounded on three sides by several storeys of arcaded rooms; steps lead down to the water on one side. The **Daulat Khana** was erected in the late 1780s by Asaf-ud-Daula, and is laid out in a somewhat haphazard manner with Neoclassical buildings standing freely among gardens and pools. Despite the demolition of most of this area, some fragments of the complex still stand, though in a ruinous condition. The Asafi Kothi has loggias on two storeys, with bays curving outwards from a central reception hall. The towerlike **Sat Khande** nearby was begun by Muhammad Ali Shah (ruled 1837–42); planned to have seven storeys, it displays four tiers of varied shape and design.

The chief residence of the nawabs until the middle of the 19th century centred on the **Farhad Bakhsh**, or 'Exhilarating Palace', which was once Claude Martin's own town house. Sold to Saadat Ali Khan in 1803, it was subsequently incorporated into his new palace, continued by his son Ghaziuddin Haidar (ruled 1814–27). It is distinguished by its open octagonal towers rising above a pedimented façade on the south. Extensive underground chambers were originally hot-weather retreats. Unlike earlier residences in Lucknow, this palace was a coordinated complex with a garden in the middle. Two separate ranges, both known as **Chhattar Manzil** from the umbrella-like finials or *chhattars* (chhatris) on their domes, stand nearby. Like the Sat Khande, they incorporate Indian cusped arches.

The last great building project of the nawabs in the heart of the city was the **Qaisar Bagh**, dating from the period of Wajid Ali Shah (ruled 1847–56). This most extensive of Lucknow's royal complexes is now reduced to a single rectangular court. One gateway is ornately embellished with fish and mermaid motifs over a cusped arch; above, a fanciful dome is formed from intersecting arches. In the middle of the court is a Mughal-style pavilion intended for formal receptions. Among the residences that open off the court is **Mahmudabad's House**. Its rooms have cusped arches rising above Italianate columns; doorways are adorned with coloured glass inserts and there are fanlights above the windows. The **Raushan-ud-daula Kachari**, an early 19th-century structure later incorporated into the Qaisar Bagh, is an elaborate classical palace with four stepped storeys. Towers with domes once rose above the corners, while a small pavilion with a pediment was positioned in the middle of the roof; these upper levels have been demolished.

Hyderabad

Founded in 1591 by the fifth ruler of Golconda, Muhammad Quli Qutb Shah, Hyderabad rapidly grew to become the leading centre of Muslim power and culture in the Deccan. Prosperity was not seriously affected by the Mughal occupation from 1687 onwards, but Hyderabad did not become a separate state again until 1724 when Nizam-al-Mulk, chief minister in Delhi, arrived and declared his independence, thereby initiating the Asafiya dynasty. During the course of the 19th century the Hyderabad rulers, who assumed the title of nizam, became allies of the British, concluding treaties by which they retained virtual automony, although a British Resident was appointed to the court. Some prime ministers and other citizens amassed considerable wealth and were able to build mansions that rivalled the palaces of the nizams; indeed, some were purchased by the nizams for their own personal use.

The city is laid out on a grid pattern on the south bank of the Musi River, with two main bazaar streets running north-south and east-west. At the intersection rises the **Char Minar**, or Four Minarets, a gigantic four-arched gateway with a mosque on top and lofty minarets at the corners. The first palaces erected by Muhammad Quli Qutb Shah were located nearby but they were destroyed during the Mughal conquest. Bazaars and parade grounds dating from this early period of the city's history, however, partly survive along the main streets of the old town.

The **Chau Mahalla**, or Four Halls, is the most impressive palace of the nizams. It is laid out in a vast walled compound south-west of the Char Minar, near to the largest mosque in Hyderabad, the Mecca Masjid. The Chau Mahalla comprises a linear arrangement of reception halls for state occasions added by

successive nizams from the time of Asaf Jah I (ruled 1724–48) up to the present century. The complex also contains offices and residential suites separated by formal gardens, disposed in strict linear fashion along a north-south axis. The main entrance is in the middle of the west side, through an arched gateway topped by a slender clock tower. A long garden with a central pool is flanked on the east and west by arcaded façades with cusped arches and balustraded parapets with domed finials. The most northerly building is the Khilwat Mahal, a double-height darbar hall, the upper level set well back to create a spacious roof terrace. Projecting corner wings have elaborate plaster ornamentation imitating earlier work at Golconda; corner chambers at the upper level are roofed with open octagonal pavilions surrounded by turrets and finials. Other buildings are more Neoclassical in design, generally with porticoes of giant columns on their north-facing fronts. Side wings reflect local architectural influence with the use of domed turrets and lively plasterwork.

The **Purani Haveli**, or Old Mansion, once the residence of the diwans, is also situated in the old city. Dilapidated portions of the complex are now used for colleges, libraries and offices. The central part consists of two long wings built in a severe Neoclassical style facing each other across a garden. Octagonal towers with octagonal domes and lotus finials mark the northernmost ends of the wings; they extend southwards with superimposed colonnades that make use of Ionic columns on both levels (a *faux-pas* in classical architecture). The main residence at the rear, which dates from the early years of the present century, is conceived as a European-style bungalow. Its verandahs, which give shelter to French and Italian marble statuary, are surmounted by balustraded parapets with corner vases. The entrance portico has a broken pediment on Corinthian columns.

Among the palaces that survive in the newer part of Hyderabad that grew up on the north bank of the Musi is **King Koti**, residence of the seventh nizam, Mir Osman Ali Khan Bahadur (ruled 1911–48). Its original owner was Kamal Khan, a wealthy citizen, who had his initials 'K.K.' incised on the walls and doors of his new palace in Neoclassical style erected at the turn of the century. After it was taken over by Mir Osman it was decided to retain these initials by renaming the palace 'King Koti'. It is distinguished by its purdah gate, an impressive arched entrance almost completely concealed by a hanging cloth, signifying the presence of the nizam. Part of the complex now serves as a hospital.

The **Falaknama**, or Mirror of the Sky, stands on Kohi-Tur Hill to the south of the city. The main block was built in 1872 for a rich nobleman, but in 1897 it was purchased by the sixth nizam, Mir Mahbub Ali Khan Bahadur (ruled 1869–1911), who used it as his private residence. The principal façade is Palladian in conception, with a rusticated basement storey pierced by arches supporting two open colonnades – Ionic below and Corinthian above. The terrace is reached by a majestic double flight of steps. The entrance hall is provided with an Italian white marble fountain and surrounding benches. Frescoes on the walls and ceiling have flowering garlands and flying cherubs on a vivid blue background. Apartments opening off on either side serve as studios, bedrooms and bathrooms. Doors at the rear lead to a sweeping staircase, with Italian marble figures holding candelabra; similar marble covers the floor and ceiling. The formal reception rooms on the upper level have French tapestries, ornate inlaid furniture from Kashmir and Victorian bric-a-brac. The darbar hall, with the throne at one end, is in French Baroque style, with heavily draped mirrors on the walls, extravagant chandeliers and a geometric parquet floor. A smoking room, billiard room and card room, connected by arched openings with curtains, lead to the banqueting hall where a long oval table is surrounded by 101 seats. The curved wings at the rear of the complex served as the zenana for the royal household, being separated from the front range by a large court. Nearby stands a separate pavilion, distinguished by its pinnacled roof, used for coronation anniversaries.

Gwalior

The Scindia Rajputs were permitted to continue to rule the Gwalior state in Central India as a reward for their loyalty to the British during the mutiny of the Rani of Jhansi in 1858. In the subsequent rebuilding of the city an entirely new palace was laid out. The **Jai Vilas**, or Victory Palace, was erected below the fort to mark the occasion of a visit by the Prince of Wales in 1876. It was designed by Colonel Sir Michael Filose, a member of a family of Italian origin with several generations' service in the Indian Army, who had long-standing ties with the local rulers. The complex is laid out as a vast square, with four long wings enclosing an inner court, reached through a ceremonial gate of finely detailed cast iron. The state rooms occupy the middle of the south wing; apartments and offices occupy the three other sides. Part of the palace is now a museum, while the remainder is the residence of the present maharaja.

The façades of the Jai Vilas are articulated by attached columns and pilasters, all painted brilliant white to simulate marble. Rooftop turrets signal the most important range, and confer a character that is both Indian and Elizabethan English. Inside, a double staircase with slender crystal balusters ascends to the Darbar Hall. This spectacularly decorated chamber, in a Victorian interpretation of a grand 18th-century classical style, is ablaze with gilded detail and golden curtains. Its lofty coved ceiling carries two gigantic crystal chandeliers, each with 248 candles, weighing no less than 4,000 kilograms (nearly 9,000 lbs); some of the furniture, too, is made of crystal. The carpet, reputed to be the largest in Asia, is usually covered with protective cloth. The banqueting hall on the floor below is celebrated for its solid silver table-top model railway that delivered after-dinner drinks and cigars.

A short distance to the north-west is another 19th-century building, the royal **guest house**. Suites of rooms here are enriched with coloured glass and painted scenes taken from Hindu mythology. The strictly symmetrical design of the building's main façade is emphasized by a central bow, enlivened with pilasters and

pinnacles and flanked by towers rising at either side; access is through projecting porticoes at both ends.

Baroda

The Gaekwad rulers rose to power in the wake of the Maratha expansion into Western India during the course of the 18th century. In the following century they concluded successful treaties with the British, maintaining control over their rich territories in the heartland of Gujarat. The Gaekwad capital (now also known as Vadodara) is notable for the many fine buildings erected by the maharajas, including several palaces, almost all of which conform to the prevailing Indo-Saracenic fashion.

The **Lakshmi Vilas** was begun in 1878 and finished some twelve years later as the city residence of Sayaji Rao III (ruled 1875–1939). In its general layout the complex retains the traditional division into three functionally specialized zones: the public reception rooms, including the Darbar Hall; accommodation for the maharaja and his immediate followers; and the zenana. Each of these is expressed as a distinct quadrangle, with its own entrance portico, arranged on a single north-south axis – the Darbar Hall on the north, the maharaja's private quarters in the middle, and the women's apartments on the south. Of the three courts, two are planted with trees, while the third is adorned with statuary surrounding a pool. The whole complex stands in a great park dotted with imposing marble sculptures and vases, and entered from the streets of the city through monumental arched gateways.

The exterior of the Lakshmi Vilas is a masterly exercise in the Indo-Saracenic style, exploiting the full range of architectural elements to create a picturesque composition. The west façade, more than 160 metres (525 feet) long, combines arched openings, projecting jharokas, domed chhatris and upper pavilions with bangla roofs. A pointed dome rises over the main entrance to the maharaja's wing; a tall, slender tower to the rear is capped with a miniature pavilion. The interior is equally eclectic. In the public zone, the Darbar Hall has crystal chandeliers, imported stained glass windows depicting mythological figures such as Rama and Krishna, and a geometric wooden ceiling in the Moorish manner. Jharokas project on wooden brackets in the form of winged musicians. The monumental entrance lobby leading to the maharaja's private apartments has an Italian marble floor with a central marble vase adorned with bronze figures; the surrounding arcades are in a lively Moorish style. Other rooms are decorated in a sumptuous but uniformly European manner, with wooden panelling, leather furniture and displays of armour and oil paintings.

A slightly later royal residence at Baroda is the **Pratap Vilas**, completed in 1914 as a residence for the crown prince (now the Railway Staff College). The two-storeyed centrepiece crowned by a dome is a sophisticated exercise in Edwardian Baroque.

Indore

Situated some 60 kilometres (40 miles) north-east of Mandu, the old capital of Malwa in Central India, Indore became the headquarters of the region under Malhar Rao, an 18th-century Maratha chief of the Holkar family. Under a successor, Yeshwant Rao, the armies of the Holkars spread havoc over much of Central India, only to be contained by the British with whom they signed treaties in 1806 and 1818. The British had repeated difficulties with the Holkars who did little to disguise their rebellious tendencies. Even so, when it came to designing a new palace at the end of the 19th century, Shivaji Rao (ruled 1886–1903) chose an uncompromising European idiom. The palace and its garden were given their final shape by Tukoji Rao III (ruled 1903–25). After his abdication in favour of Yeshwant Rao II, Tukoji Rao continued to reside there until his death in 1978.

The **Lal Bagh**, or Red Palace, is one of the finest Neoclassical designs in India. It stands in the middle of a vast formal garden, reached through commanding entrance gates adorned with the arms of the Holkar family in the manner of the gates of Buckingham Palace in London. The exterior is relatively severe, with shallow pilasters and, in the centre of each side, superimposed Doric, Ionic and Corinthian loggias. A circular porte cochère on the north leads to a circular entrance hall, which, in turn, gives access to a formal reception hall. The latter, flanked by arcades, is lavishly marbled and ornamented with gilded stucco on the walls and ceilings.

In the middle of the Lal Bagh is the Banqueting Room, overlooked by a colonnade, presumably for the female members of the royal household. It connects with smaller and more private dining rooms executed in different styles, including European and Rajput. The Darbar Hall, which projects eastwards from the main block of the palace, is distinguished by the French style of its decoration and the high quality of the workmanship. Purple silk covers the throne which stands between elaborate candelabras; gilded lamps and sculptures are separated by mirrored wall panels. Here as elsewhere there are imported marble fireplaces, crystal chandeliers and Aubusson carpets. The climax of the room is provided by the ceiling, which is painted in the Rococo manner with a panel showing the sun god, Helios, riding through the clouds in his chariot (a subject also chosen at Morvi). In contrast to these European-inspired chambers, the Dance Room, which is reserved for private performances, is in the Indian style: bare of furniture, it consists of an open space surrounded by a colonnade.

The young Yeshwant Rao benefited from a cosmopolitan education and was evidently interested in new developments in European architecture. In 1930–34 he ordered Muthesius to design for him the **Manik Bagh**, or Ruby Garden [Palace], in the latest Modernist manner. The result is one of the most remarkable royal residences in India, and indeed one of the best-preserved architectural projects of the period anywhere, complete with all its furniture and fittings. It is laid out in a U, with wings on three sides of a terraced garden with a central pool. The plain concrete exterior with unadorned colonnades and small windows protected by sun-shades gives little idea of the remarkable quality of the interior workmanship. The main entrance hall, like many rooms in the palace, is indirectly lit with concealed lamps; the staircase has a floating aluminium hand-rail. Many of the rooms are perfect re-creations of contemporary European settings, such as the Banqueting Room and Library, the latter with sliding glass doors. The furniture throughout is of ebony and chrome, with repeated use of curved forms; the carpets have bold geometric patterns in red and black. Muthesius carefully designed all the fittings down to the smallest details, including even bedside lamps and bathroom taps. (The same architect was commissioned by the maharaja to design the interior of a new royal railway carriage, which imitated on a smaller scale many of the Modernist details of the Manik Bagh.)

Mysore

One of the first projects of the Wodeyar rulers after their restoration by the British in 1799 was to transform their capital of Mysore in Southern India into a model royal city with a fortified residence in the middle. The palace that they erected at this time faced eastwards to overlook a vast parade ground next to which there were a number of small Hindu shrines, some dating back to the 17th century. Most of this complex was destroyed in a fire that occurred in 1897 during a marriage ceremony, and the queen mother, Vanivilasa Sannidhana, who was regent at the time, commissioned designs for a new palace. It was completed in 1912, during the period of Krishnaraja IV (ruled 1902–40), in an exuberant Indo-Saracenic style, and later extended in 1932. It is unique in making use of cast iron for its two great state rooms: the Amba Vilasa was proudly illustrated by its manufacturers, Walter Macfarlane and Co. of the Saracen Foundry, Glasgow, in their *Illustrated Examples of Macfarlane's Architectural Ironwork*.

The complex is approached through an imposing entrance on the east, the **Jaya Martanda Gate**, with a cusped archway some 20 metres (65 feet) high. The principal façade of the palace combines monumentality with fine detailing. It is dominated by a giant portico of polished granite columns supporting broad cusped arches. Above, arcades flank a centrepiece which has a bangla roof and domed chhatris. The twelve-sided tower behind, capped by a gilded dome with a miniature chhatri on top, rises over an inner chamber. Additional domes are clustered below. Towers grouped in pairs at the ends of each façade are also crowned by small domes. On special occasions, the entire composition is illuminated by no less than 50,000 light bulbs.

Inside, a ceremonial staircase ascends between walls faced with different coloured marbles; the intricate teak ceiling incorporates innumerable Hindu divinities, and figures of guards, carved in relief in white marble and set in oval frames, line the upper steps.

On the upper level lie a sequence of grand state rooms, first among them the **Darbar Hall**. Almost 50 metres (165 feet) long, it is divided into aisles by squat tapering columns in Southern Indian style ornamented with gilded leaves and lotus petals. Broad cusped arches support flat domes painted with lotuses and blue skies with stars. Together with the polished marble floor, the rich columns and arches create an impressive and spacious interior. A throne of gold and silver once stood in the middle, below a suspended royal umbrella of solid gold with a bird on top holding a garland of emeralds in its beak. On the rear walls are painted images of eight goddesses, including Chamundeshvari; the central panel depicts four generations of rulers.

22, 187, 189
Leading off the Darbar Hall on the south is the gorgeously decorated **Amba Vilasa**, serving as hall of private audience. Bulbous columns, again decorated in gold, screen a surrounding aisle, which is covered by a teak ceiling with inlaid and carved designs. The centre of the hall is completely roofed with glass, set in and supported by cast iron. Immense glass chandeliers cascade downwards from the top. Floor panels are inlaid with semi-precious stones in the Mughal style. The entrance, on the east, has silver doors ornamented with gods and goddesses. Other doors opening off the staircase are also in silver; one set leads to a Ganesha shrine for the private use of the royal family.

The middle of the complex is occupied by an **interior court** surrounded by colonnades. Stone carvings, some in ancient Indian style with full-breasted maidens and lotuses, ornament the brackets and upper pilasters. On the west side of the court are portions of the original **zenana** of the old palace, now a museum for displaying the maharaja's art collection; on the north side are the trophy room and armoury. To the south is the **Kalyana** Mandapa, or Marriage Pavilion, another cast-iron structure, with a remarkable octagonal dome of stained glass including peacock motifs, supported on triple groups of iron columns. The floor here is covered with dazzling multi-coloured Victorian tiles. The domed inner area is ringed by double aisles, the outermost two-storeyed, with a gallery above. The walls have murals depicting the Dasara processions in which the Mysore maharajas actively participated until 1970.

186, 188

The brilliantly whitewashed **Lalita Mahal**, or Palace of Pleasures, some 3 kilometres (2 miles) south-east of the city, is picturesquely sited at the foot of Chamundi Hill. It was designed by E. W. Fritchley in 1930 as a guest house for Krishnaraja's visitors, and is now a hotel. The long classical façade consists almost entirely of superimposed loggias fronted by paired columns, held between towers and emphasized in the centre by a porte cochère and a lofty dome. The interior is well maintained, with small stained glass domes over twin reception halls, fine ornamental plasterwork, and delightful suites of private rooms opening onto a spacious internal court.

Kapurthala

The capital of a former Sikh state on the Punjab plains in North-Western India, Kapurthala had been the chief residence of the Ahulwalia family since the conquest and consolidation of the region by Jasa Singh in the second half of the 18th century. During the Mutiny Randhir Singh (ruled 1853–70) remained unswervingly loyal to the British, and he was permitted to retain his kingdom. His grandson, Jagatjit Singh (ruled 1890–1947), was educated in London and Paris, becoming an ardent Francophile in the process. On his accession to the throne he invited three architects to submit designs for a new palace, awarding the commission to a Frenchman, M. Marcel.

190–192
The **Jagatjit**, or Elysées Palace as it is sometimes also known, is a spectacular French-style château completed in 1908. Like Versailles, it is set in a grandiose park populated with allegorical statuary. Immediately in front of the entrance is a circular marble fountain with figures riding seahorses and grasping a fish. Deer, panthers and other animals carved in stone are placed nearby.

The exterior of the palace is faced in pink stucco, with contrasting white ornamental details. Copper-clad mansard roofs stress the pavilions in the centre and at the ends of the entrance range on the north, and variations are played on the theme of superimposed porticoes. A central porte-cochère leads by way of a grand staircase to the double-height Darbar Hall on the main storey, now used as a library. It is decorated in a hybrid manner, with a parquet floor displaying the crest of Kapurthala, an upper gallery fronted by carved wooden screens, and a ceiling of stained glass. Doors on the east give access to the Dining Room, sumptuously decorated in a 17th-century style, with lapis-lazuli-blue marble columns and fireplaces, gilding on capitals, bases, walls and ceiling, and Gobelins tapestries. The corresponding apartment on the west side is the Louis XVI Drawing Room, now a museum. It, too, is in the French manner, with an abundance of gilded decoration and painted scenes on the walls and ceilings, and a fine selection of European furniture. A billiard room opens off to the rear.

On the outskirts of Kapurthala is the **Villa Buona Vista**, a private palace sometimes used as a state guest house. It was completed in 1894, with somewhat fanciful European-style arches and corner towers.

Jodhpur

Umaid Singh (ruled 1918–47) was one of the most prominent 20th-century Rajputs in Western India. In 1929 he embarked upon the construction of a new palace as part of a public works programme to relieve distress caused by famine. The site selected was some 3 kilometres (about 2 miles) south-east of the old citadel, well outside the city walls. Not completed until 1944, the palace was named after its founder as the **Umaid Bhavan**. It still partly functions as a royal residence.

For his architects, Umaid Singh chose the British firm of Lanchester and Lodge. H. V. Lanchester had risen to prominence at the turn of the century for his part in the design of Cardiff City Hall. He was one of the most brilliant planners of his time, and for the vast Umaid Bhavan, more than 200 metres (650 feet) in length, he produced a symmetrical plan worthy of a 17th-century palace or a 19th-century parliament building. Its disposition and details were carefully tailored to an Indian ruler's needs, with the zenana wing at one end, balanced symmetrically by a wing for guests and services. The stylistic details of the architecture – made of a beautiful golden sandstone – were deliberately based on indigenous models.

The public entrance is from the east, where a projecting block contains the grand state rooms. Behind it rises a huge dome braced by eight massive buttresses, each with its own pyramidal cap. The garden front, which faces west, has tiers of verandahs to shelter the interior from the sun. (Electric ventilation was provided as well.) The dome marks the position of a circular central hall, which lies on the entrance axis and marks the division of the palace into two zones – the maharaja's official and domestic quarters to the south, and staff and guest quarters to the north.

The entrance hall is flanked by the Banqueting Hall and the Ballroom, both with segmental vaults and mosaics and paintings depicting royal processions. Beyond the Banqueting Hall is a theatre, while beyond the Ballroom is the Darbar Hall. Moving further in, an oval staircase hall is reached, and then the circular central hall, which lies under the dome. To the left is the realm of the maharaja, terminating in the large zenana court. Between the hall and the court lie the maharaja's official rooms below, notably the Small Darbar Hall, which has a coved ceiling painted gold; a composition executed by the Polish artist Julius Stefan Norblin on the wall behind the elevated throne shows the traditional hero Arjuna with his charioteer Krishna. One corridor leading to these apartments has a fountain with crystal dishes. Above are the ruler's private rooms, communicating with the zenana. The maharaja's bedroom is in pink and black, complete with frescoes, mirrors and painted screens. A private bar and sitting room are attached. The bathroom has a black onyx tub and washbasin, both with gilded fittings. The leather and chrome furniture is Art Deco throughout. The maharani's bedroom and bathroom are in a similar style. To the north of the central hall, an area for less formal entertaining leads to the staff court, with accommodation for staff, officials and guests above a service basement. The swimming pool, which is located in the basement of an annexe, is painted entirely in blue and pink. Floor mosaics depict the signs of the zodiac.

Morvi

The small principality of Morvi, situated on the peninsula of Saurashtra in the westernmost part of Gujarat, enjoyed a period of prosperity from the middle of the 19th century onwards. At the beginning of the present century, Waghiji (ruled 1879–1922), the most influential of Morvi's rulers, embarked upon an extensive programme of modernization. One of his first acts was to equip his capital with an Indo-Saracenic palace, somewhat modified by classical details. His son, Lakhadiraj (ruled 1922–47), was responsible for one of the most remarkable 20th-century royal buildings in India, the Art Deco **New Palace**. Begun in 1931, it is laid out in a compact square around two interior courts surrounded by colonnades, each with a circular fountain. The exterior presents stretched streamlined façades in pink coloured plaster, emphasized by rounded extensions at the corners and punctuated by porticoed entrances in the middle of each side. The principal entrance on the north, with marble columns, is marked by an airport-like pyramidal tower. It leads to a hall entirely faced in marble, open on three sides, with a circular painting recessed into the ceiling showing the sun god in his chariot drawn by four horses. The artist responsible for this composition, Norblin (who also worked at Jodhpur), made a liberal use of gold paint which gleams in the concealed lighting. Formal reception and entertainment rooms together with quarters for guests occupy the ground floor. Among these are the dining hall located between the two interior courts, and the pink bar in the north-west corner. The latter has chrome trimming on benches and seats, and a mural of dancing girls by Norblin on the wall behind the bar. The offices in the south-west corner have wooden furniture and fittings. On the south side of the complex is a gymnasium, next to which is the monumental swimming pool, with grey marble on the floor and walls, and etched glass panels showing aquatic motifs. Water flows into the pool from a fountain at one end set into a dramatically illuminated semi-circular recess. A billiard room occupies the south-east corner.

The upper level is reached by a green marble staircase in the middle of the west side. Here are located the private quarters of the palace, including reception rooms, bars and bedrooms. The maharaja's bedroom has a black marble podium and built-in canopy for the bed, a fireplace with elaborate mantelpiece, and mirrored dressing tables, all in the Art Deco style. In the maharani's bathroom a massive marble tub is backed by a large shell. A second staircase, distinguished by illuminated painted panels, leads to a reception room with a circular marble floor that reflects the circular opening in the ceiling above. Opening off this room is a banqueting hall with blue carpet and blue wall decoration. The private bar situated at rooftop level, between the two courts, is surrounded by terraces. It has a circular rose pink marble fountain in the middle, with water dripping on to it from the ceiling. Side booths for dining recall the seating arrangements of luxury liners.

193
195
196
197
198
199
203
200
201
204
206
202

The palaces today

As PERMANENT and highly visible records of an era that has vanished, India's palaces have a role to play in the discovery and reshaping of the country's past. They endure as residences of the heirs of royal families, barracks for troops, offices for municipal authorities, museums thronged with visitors, and pleasure gardens filled with families on outings. Whatever their circumstances, the palaces evoke awe and respect for the splendour of their royal receptions and entertainments, possibly also horror at those times of war and repression. That the contemplation of history has become a major pastime is borne out by the substantial numbers of visitors, Indian as well as foreign, that crowd royal sites and residences all over the country.

Private and public occupants

Some palaces are still lived in by the descendants of the maharajas for whom they were originally built. This is particularly true for the 19th- and 20th-century residences that were erected to replace the no longer suitable accommodation in the fortified citadels of earlier rulers. Such 'replacement' palaces are comparatively well adapted to present-day living patterns, and indeed many have been converted successfully into comfortable and desirable habitations, with the addition of plumbing, electricity and other essential services. More recent palaces, such as those at Morvi and Indore, were erected in the years immediately prior to Independence in the latest European Modernist styles and were thus from the beginning adequately equipped for 20th-century living.

199– 206

More than any other group of royal families in India, it is the Rajputs who have successfully managed to maintain a presence in or near their original headquarters. The 18th-century palace at Jaipur continues to be privately occupied, with the consequence that several suites of formal reception rooms and much of the garden are inaccessible to the public. The Udaipur royal family inhabit the Shambhu Nivas, an early 20th-century annexe to the older Sisodia citadel. The inheritors of the Maratha rulers who rose to power in the 18th century have also been able to hold on to their palaces. Almost half of the vast Jai Nivas at Gwalior is occupied by the Scindia representatives; the Lakshmi Vilas at Baroda remains in the hands of the Gaekwad heirs; the Wodeyars possess a large part of the Mysore city palace.

124– 126

96

172

173

182– 189

Some palaces are used by the military, and are as a result strictly out of bounds. Following the earlier habits of the British, the Indian Army regrettably continues to inhabit portions of some of the most celebrated of the country's royal complexes. Ugly barracks erected in the 19th century to replace courtly pavilions in the Mughal forts at Delhi and Agra are still in use. The fort at Allahabad, which includes one of the most important examples of Mughal palace architecture, is beyond the reach of visitors due to the constant presence of troops.

Other palaces have been converted into offices for municipal authorities, thereby continuing to some extent the original administrative purposes of these buildings. The law courts at Bijapur occupy an arcaded court that dates back to the Adil Shahi period. Educational institutions have also made good use of palaces. The Kapurthala palace is now a military academy, the present descendant of its founding maharaja having moved to a more modest residence in the vicinity.

190– 192

Sites and museums

Fortunately, a good many of India's palaces are under the care of civic and archaeological authorities. The oldest are ruined and dilapidated; unoccupied except for their visitors and watchmen, they give only the barest idea of royal life in centuries past. The reception halls, zenana courts and stables at Tughluqabad and Firuzabad in Delhi, for instance, have altogether disappeared; only the fortification walls and entrance gateways stand relatively complete. Though the royal buildings at Chittor, Mandu, Daulatabad and Vijayanagara, to list only four of the most spectacular of India's royal citadels, have been cleared and restored, most structures there stand incomplete: their wooden columns, sumptuous plasterwork and coloured tiles have vanished forever.

90, 27– 32, 38

Other palaces are better preserved, and have benefited from elaborate programmes of restoration to become India's showcase royal sites, marked by ticket booths and signs, and thronged with tourists who are propelled through the empty halls by energetic guides. The Mughal complexes at Fatehpur Sikri, Agra and Delhi are among the greatest attractions of the country; despite their decay and vandalization over the centuries, they are still appreciated for the grandiose scale of their layouts and the exquisite quality of their craftsmanship, which evoke the formal majesty of the Mughal court. Fatehpur Sikri is the most completely preserved royal complex of the Mughal era, having been abandoned well before the Persian and British forces could wreak havoc; even so, many of its service structures are in ruins, and its sophisticated hydraulic system has long ago been abandoned. Together with the tomb of the Sufi saint buried in the adjacent Jami Masjid, the Fatehpur Sikri palace attracts multitudes of visitors who are the primary source of income for the inhabitants of the nearby villages.

41– 75

Rajput complexes such as those at Udaipur, Jodhpur and Bikaner give an even more vivid idea of Indian courtly life. Having been maintained right up to the present century, they were not permitted to fall entirely into ruin, even though some are now extremely run down. Unlike Mughal palaces, they often retain their carpets, furniture and lamps. Walls are covered with murals, inlays of coloured glass and even miniature paintings installed in protective frames. Assemblages of arms, armour, thrones,

96– 104, 135

1

umbrellas, standards, palanquins, costumes and other royal paraphernalia are permanently on display. Such collections effectively transform the palaces into museums, and they have come to function as such with the usual repertoire of glass cases, labels and guards. While the painting galleries at Udaipur and Jaipur are of artistic interest, most objects displayed in the royal apartments and darbar halls are more important for their role in satisfying visitors' curiosity and romantic nostalgia.

Gardens and parks

173 Royal pleasure gardens with reservoirs, pools and fountains overlooked by terraces and pavilions have not all succumbed to time. Gardens at Jaipur and Baroda, among others, have been transformed by city authorities into public parks for the enjoyment of the people who flock there for picnics, strolls and study retreats.
128– The garden residence at Dig, with its axial channels and fountains, 132 is in full operating order, its original system of storing and conducting water having survived virtually intact. On special occasions, visitors are treated to spectacular displays of coloured and illuminated fountains. However, few of India's royal gardens 21 are so fortunate. Most have fallen into disuse and little is left of their original planting except stone beds; their pools, channels and chutes are now empty of water. At Bidar and Golconda, and even 58 at Agra and Delhi, the barest skeletons of the gardens survive. Elsewhere, all traces of planting have disappeared, leaving only the walled compounds that once contained trees and plants.

Because of the continued attraction of Kashmir for visitors throughout the 19th and 20th centuries, the Mughal gardens in the Srinagar Valley have never been permitted to fall into disrepair. The garden palaces overlooking Lake Dal are maintained by the horticultural branch of the archaeological department which ensures that teams of gardeners are regularly at work, particularly in the spring. Even if the planting does not precisely conform to Mughal practice, the Kashmir gardens are alive with flowers that bloom in the shade of poplars and plane trees. Water flows through the channels and over the chutes, and fountains spray the royal pavilions. Here, better than in the Plains, visitors can recapture the Mughal ideal of courtly pleasure.

117 An important aspect of Indian royal life is the picnics and hunting expeditions that took place in vast wooded estates dotted with pleasure pavilions and shooting lodges. The parks at Udaipur 10 and Bundi, situated only a short distance from the palaces, can still be visited today. Hunting remained a favourite pastime for the maharajas and their guests throughout the course of the present century, with the result that many estates were regularly stocked with birds and game. In recent years such parks have fared less well; most are now being deforested and robbed of their wildlife. Pavilions and lodges, no longer visited by hunters and their retinues, are empty and dilapidated. Some royal parks survive in better condition, having been transformed into wildlife sanctuaries accessible to tourists. In the forested hills at Sariska and Ranthambore in Rajasthan, for instance, visitors stay in renovated and modernized royal lodges where their activities are restricted to viewing animals and birds, rather than trapping and shooting.

Luxury hotels

A significant development over the last twenty-five years has been the growth of tourism in India, on the part of both Indians and foreigners. This has given a new lease of life to some palaces, especially those originally designed as guest houses which have been transformed into luxury hotels. The great Rajput families of Jaipur, Jodhpur, Bikaner, Udaipur and Gwalior, together with the Wodeyars of Mysore, have had considerable success in creating elegant accommodation for paying tourists. Lavish services provided by hotel managements include elaborate musical and theatrical entertainments as well as sporting facilities with billiard rooms, tennis courts and swimming pools. Such leisure activities replicate those for which these palaces were first intended; in this sense, the hotels ensure their survival. Hotel incomes guarantee the maintenance of buildings and their gardens.

The grand scale of India's palace hotels is enhanced by the formal suites of sumptuously appointed reception rooms and apartments opening onto balconies and terraces. Pavilions overlook gardens, sometimes inhabited by peacocks; pools and fountains are filled with water. Such architectural opulence creates the illusion that courtly magnificence has somehow survived into the present day and that visitors are royal guests. The colourful uniforms of the large numbers of hotel staff, and the regal monograms on the door panels, tableware, stationery and even the bed linen, reinforce the impression that these hotels are private residences. Indeed, many are still managed by the heirs of the maharajas, or at least by the trusts set up by them. Suites in some palaces, as in the Umaid Bhavan at Jodhpur, are permanently reserved for princely families, members of which can occasionally be glimpsed disappearing down private corridors, barely distinguishable from the visitors themselves.

Inheritance disputes

Unhappily, not all the descendants of India's princely families have been able to safeguard their palaces. Disputes between family members, with decade-long litigation, have meant that some residences are constantly under threat. As the heirs of the once wealthy royal families squabble about ownership and rights, the palaces are stripped of their treasures and left to disintegrate; some are pulled down so as to sell off the increasingly valuable land on which they are built. Serving neither as private dwellings nor as public museums, these are the endangered palaces of India. A 165– particularly unfortunate case is the Chau Mahalla in Hyderabad, a 167 grandiose complex occupying a spacious and costly site in the middle of the old city. Closed now for years due to family disputes, it is protected neither by those who have inherited it nor by the local municipality, who cannot gain access to it. Its future, like that of so many other palaces in India, remains uncertain.

Glossary of Indian terms

abhisheka royal bathing ceremony

amir noble

apadana columned hall in ancient Persia

Arthashastra treatise on kingship

ashvamedha royal horse sacrifice

badgir ventilator tower

bagh garden

baithak sitting room

bakhshi paymaster-general

bala hisar upper fortress

bangla curved roof or vault derived from the Bengali thatched hut

baoli step-well

baradari ('twelve-doored') typical Mughal-style pavilion with triple arcades on four sides

bazaar market street

bhavan, bhawan hall

brahmin uppermost class of Hindu society to which priests belong

burj fortified tower

caravanserai shelter for travellers, merchants and mercenaries together with their animals

chahar suq open square with markets on four sides

chakra wheel, disc

charbagh ('four-gardens') walled garden of Persian origin

chauri fly-whisk, traditional royal emblem

chhajja angled eave

chhatri royal umbrella; roof-top pavilion with dome or vault; funerary monument

chhatta see *chhatri*

Chishti order of Muslim holy men

chitra mahal hall with paintings

chowk court; market street

dad mahal hall of justice

daftar khana records office

darbar royal audience

darshana auspicious visual contact with a god or king

darwaza entrance gate

Dasara ten-day festival in which the goddess Durga is worshipped

daulat khana ('house of wealth') treasury

deodhi doorway, terrace

Diwali Hindu festival of lamps in honour of the goddess Lakshmi

diwan-i amm hall or court of public audience

diwan-i khass hall of private audience

durg fort

gagan mahal sky pavilion

ganesh pol elephant gate

garh fort

ghat steps to bathing place; steep hill

giri hill

gumbad dome

hammam bath-house

harem residence of the women of the king's household

hathi pol elephant gate

hayat-bakhsh bagh life-bestowing garden

Holi spring festival

ibadat khana 'house of worship'

imam leader of public prayers in the mosque

imambara place of worship during the Muharram festival

jahaz mahal ship palace

jai mandir, jai mahal victory palace or pavilion

jali perforated stone screen

jami masjid congregational mosque, principal place of worship, especially on Friday

jas mandir palace of glory

Jataka birth story of the Buddha

jharoka projecting balcony roofed with a dome or vault

kalyana mandapa marriage hall; ceremonial hall

karkhana royal workshop, store

khass mahal private pavilion

Khushruz Muslim festival

khwabgah royal sleeping chamber

kitab khana library

kot, kotla fort

kshatriya warrior class of Hindu society to which many rulers belonged

kund pond

lal bagh ruby garden

lal qila red fort

madrasa Muslim theological college

Mahabharata one of India's great ancient mythological epics

mahal pavilion; apartment

Mahanavami ninth day of Dasara

maharaja great king

maidan open space; parade ground

makara aquatic monster

mandir palace; temple

manzil residence; tower

maqsura screen; gallery within a mosque

mardana men's quarters, fortified rectangular or square residence with a central court

masjid mosque

matbakh kitchen department

matha Hindu monastery

Mayamata treatise on architecture

minar light-tower; minaret

moti masjid pearl mosque

Muharram Shiite month of mourning

musamman burj octagonal tower

nahr-i bihisht ('stream of paradise') water channel in a palace

naqqar khana drum house

naubat khana guard house

nawab governor; ruler

Nawruz Muslim New Year festival

nayaka governor; ruler

nivas, niwas palace

nizam ruler

odi shooting tower

pan flavoured leaves for betel-nut

pol gate

purana qila old fort

qadi judge

qila fort

raja, rana, rao ruler

Ramayana the story of Rama, one of India's ancient mythological epics

rang mahal multi-coloured pavilion

raya emperor

sabha assembly hall

sagar ocean; lake

sarai see *caravanserai*

shah burj king's tower

shala, shali hall

shaykh Muslim holy man or saint

shikar hunting

shila khana armoury

shish mahal ('house of glass') mirrored room or pavilion

son mahal golden pavilion

stambha pillar

stupa hemispherical monument commemorating the death of Buddha

sufi Muslim mystic

sultan Muslim ruler

suq market street

suraj pol sun gate

taikhana underground vault; hot-weather retreat

takht seat; throne

talao pool; lake

tarkash mahal Turkish pavilion

tazia model of the tomb of the martyr Imam Husain, carried during the Muharram festival

tin darwaza triple gate

torana temple portal with decorated lintel

tripolia triple-arched ceremonial gate

Vastushastra manual on town-planning and building

vilas, vilasa palace

wazir chief minister

zamorin ruler of Malabar

zenana, zanana quarters for women

Bibliography

I. Courtly life

ALLAN, C. and DWIVEDI, S., *Lives of the Indian Princes*, repr. London 1984

ANSARI, M.A., 'Amusements and Games under the great Mughals', *Islamic Culture*, 35 (1961)

– 'Court Ceremonies of the Great Mughals', *Islamic Culture*, 35 (1961)

– *Social Life of the Mughal Emperors (1526–1707)*, New Delhi 1974

AUBOYER, T., *Le Trône et son symbolisme dans l'Inde ancienne*, Paris 1949

BASHAM, A.L., *The Wonder that was India*, London 1954

BEGLEY, W.E. and DESAI, Z.A., eds., *The Shah Jahan Name of Inayat Khan*, Delhi 1990

BEVERIDGE, A.S., trans., *The Babur Nama in English*, London 1921

BEVERIDGE, H., trans., *The Akbar Nama of Abul Fazl*, Calcutta 1903–39

BHAKARI, S.K., *Indian Warfare*, New Delhi 1981

BLAKE, S., *Shahjahanabad: The Sovereign City in Mughal India*, Cambridge 1991

BLOCHMAN, H. and JARRETT, H.S., trans., *Ain-i-Akbari of Abul Fazl*, Calcutta 1873–94

BUCK, W., trans., *Ramayana*, Berkeley and Los Angeles 1976

CHOPRA, P.N., *Some Aspects of Society and Culture during the Mughal Age (1526–1707)*, Agra 1963

CIMINO, R.M., ed. *Life at Court in Rajasthan*, Florence 1985

CONSTABLE, A., trans., *Travels in the Mogul Empire by François Bernier*, repr. Oxford 1914

CROOKE, W., trans., *Travels in India by Jean-Baptiste Tavernier*, London 1925

DESAI, V., ed., *Life at Court: Art for India's Rulers 16th–19th Centuries*, Boston 1985

DOWSON, J., ed., *The History of India as told by its own Historians: the Muhammedan Period*, IV, London 1872

FULLER, C.J., 'Rituals of Kingship', in *The Camphor Flame: Popular Hinduism and Society in India*, Princeton 1992

GASCOIGNE, B., *The Great Moghuls*, London 1971

GIBB, H.A.R., trans., *The Travels of Ibn Battuta*, III, Cambridge 1971

GONDA, J., *Ancient Indian Kingship from the Religious Point of View*, Leiden 1966

HASAN, A., *Palace Culture of Lucknow*, Delhi 1983

IRVINE, W., trans., *Storia do Mogor. Or Mughal India 1653–1708 by Niccolao Manucci*, London 1907–8

KANGLE, R.P., ed., *The Kautilya Arthasastra*, Bombay 1960–65

KNIGHTON, W., *The Private Life of an Eastern King*, Oxford 1921

LAL, K. S., *The Mughal Harem*, New Delhi 1988

LLEWELLYN-JONES, R., *A Fatal Friendship: the Nawabs, the British and the City of Lucknow*, Delhi 1985

LORD, J., *The Maharajahs*, London 1971

LUARD, C.E. and HOSTEN, E., trans., *The Travels of Sebastien Manrique*, Oxford 1927

MAHALINGAM, T.V., *South Indian Polity*, Madras 1955

MAYER, A.C., 'Rulership and Divinity: the case of the modern Hindu prince', *Modern Asian Studies*, 25/4 (1991)

PAL, P., LEOSHKO, J., DYE, J.M. and MARKEL, S., *Romance of the Taj Mahal*, Los Angeles and London 1989

PATNAIK, N., *A Desert Kingdom: the Rajputs of Bikaner*, London 1990

PRASAD, R.C., *Early English Travellers in India*, Delhi 1980

QURESHI, I.H., *The Administration of the Sultanate of Delhi*, Lahore 1942

– *The Administration of the Mughal Empire*, New Delhi 1979

RAMUSACK, B., *The Princes of India in the Twilight of Empire*, Wiesbaden 1980

RANGASVAMI SARASVATI, A., trans., 'Political Maxims of the Emperor-Poet Krishnadeva Raya', *Journal of Indian History*, IV (1926)

RAO BAHADUR and SRINIVASACHARI, C.S., *A History of Gingee and its rulers*, Annamalainagar 1943

RICHARDS, J., ed., *Kingship and Authority in South Asia*, Madison, Wis. 1978

RIZVI, S.A.A., *The Wonder That Was India*, II, London 1987

ROBINSON, A., *Maharaja: the Spectacular Heritage of Princely India*, New York and London 1988

ROE, SIR THOMAS, *The Embassy of Sir Thomas Roe to India, 1615–19*, ed. W. Foster, London 1926

ROGERS, A., trans., and BEVERIDGE, H., eds., *Tuzuk-i-Jahangiri or Memoirs of Jahangir*, London 1909–14

SAKAR, J., *Studies in Mughal India*, Calcutta 1919

– *Mughal Administration*, Calcutta 1924

SALETORE, B.A., *Social and Political Life in the Vijayanagara Empire*, Madras 1934

SATHYANATHA AIYAR, R., *History of the Nayaks of Madurai*, Oxford 1924

SEWELL, R., *A Forgotten Empire (Vijayanagara). A Contribution to the History of India*, London 1900

SHARMA, G. D., *Rajput Polity: a Study of Politics and Administration of the State of Marwar, 1638–1749*, Delhi 1977

SHARMA, G.N., *Social Life in Medieval Rajasthan*, Agra 1968

SHARMA, M.L., *History of the Jaipur State*, Jaipur 1969

SHERWANI, H.K. and JOSHI, P.M., eds., *History of Medieval Deccan (1295–1724)*, Hyderabad 1973

SRIDHARA BABU, D., *Kingship, State and Religion in South India According to Historical Biographies*, Göttingen 1975

STEIN, B., 'Mahanavami: medieval and modern kingly ritual in south India', in *Essays on Gupta Culture*, ed. B.L. Smith, New Delhi 1983

SUBRAHMANIYAN, K., trans., *Mahabharata*, Bombay 1971

SUBRAMANIAN, K.R., *The Maratha Rajas of Tanjore*, Madras 1928

TOD, J., *Annals and Antiquities of Rajast'han*, repr. London 1914

VRIDDHAGIRISAN, V., *The Nayaks of Tanjore*, Annamalainagar 1942

WAGHORNE, J.P., *The King's New Clothes*, University Park, Pa. 1993

WELCH, S.C. and PATNAIK, N., *A Second Paradise: Indian Courtly Life 1590–1947*, New York 1985

II. Palace architecture

ACHARYA, P.K., *Encyclopedia of Hindu Architecture*, London 1927–46

ASHER, C.B., *The New Cambridge History of India. I:4, Architecture of Mughal India*, Cambridge 1992

AUBOYER, J. and ENAULT, J.-F., *La Vie publique et privée dans l'Inde ancienne. Fasc. 1: l'architecture civile et religieuse*, Paris 1969

BAKHSH, N., 'Historical Notes of the Lahor Fort and its Buildings', *Annual Report of the Archaeological Survey of India, 1902–3*, Calcutta 1904

– 'The Agra Fort and its Buildings', *Annual Report of the Archaeological Survey of India, 1903–4*, Calcutta 1906

BATLEY, C., *Indian Architecture*, London 1934

BAUTZE, J., *Drei Bundi Ragamalas: ein Beitrag zur Geschichte der Rajputschen Wandmalerei*, Stuttgart 1987

BEGDE, P.V., *Forts and Palaces of India*, Delhi 1982

BLURTON, R.T., 'Palace Structures at Vijayanagara: the Archaeological Evidence', in *South Asian Archaeology 1985*, ed. K. Frifelt and P. Sorensen, London 1989

BRAND, M. and LOWRY, GLENN D., eds., *Fatehpur Sikri: A Sourcebook*, Aga Khan Program for Islamic Architecture, Cambridge 1985

BROWN, P., *Indian Architecture (Islamic Period)*, repr. Bombay 1968

BURTON-PAGE, J., 'Burdj', 'Chanderi', 'Daulatabad', 'Hind, vii-Architecture', 'Ma', 'Marasim', 'Matbakh', *Encyclopedia of Islam*, II, Leiden 1954–

– 'A Study of Fortification in the Indian Subcontinent from the Thirteenth to Eighteenth Centuries AD', *Bulletin of the School of Oriental and African Studies*, XXIII (1960)

– 'The Sitara-i Sulayman in Indian Muslim Art', in *The Islamic World: Essays in Honour of Bernard Lewis*, ed. C.E. Bosworth et al., Princeton, N.J. 1989

CHISHOLM, R.F., 'The Old Palace at Chandragiri', *Indian Antiquary*, 12 (1883)

COOMARASWAMY, A. K., *Early Indian Architecture: Palaces*, repr. Delhi 1975

COUSENS, H., *Bijapur and its Architectural Remains*, repr. New Delhi 1976

CROWE, S. and HAYWOOD, S., *The Gardens of Mughal India: a History and a Guide*, London 1972

DAGENS, B., trans., *Mayamata (an Indian treatise on housing, architecture and iconography)*, New Delhi 1985

DAVAR, S., 'Imperial Workshops at Fatehpur Sikri: the Royal Kitchen', *Art and Archaeology Research Papers*, 5 (June 1974)

DAVIES, P., *The Penguin Guide to the Monuments of India, II, Islamic, Rajput, European*, London 1989

DESAI, M., *Architektur in Gujarat, Indien*, Zurich 1990

DEVAKUNJARI, D., *Hampi*, Archaeological Survey of India, New Delhi 1970

– *Madurai through the Ages: from the Earliest Times to 1801 AD*, Madras 1979

EDWARDES, M., *Indian Temples and Palaces*, London 1970

FASS, V., *The Forts of India*, London 1986

FERGUSSON, J., *History of Indian and Eastern Architecture*, London 1876

FISCHER, K., *Dächer, Decken und Gewölbe Indischer Kultstatten und Nutzbauten*, Wiesbaden 1974

FRITZ, J.M., MICHELL, G. and NAGARAJA RAO, M. S., *Where Kings and Gods Meet: the Royal Centre at Vijayanagara*, Tucson, Ariz. 1985

GADRE, P.B., *Cultural Archaeology of Ahmadnagar during Nizam Shahi Period (1494–1632)*, Delhi 1986

GAEKWAD, F. and FASS, V., *The Palaces of India*, London 1980

GARRETT, A., *The Jaipur Observatory and its Builder*, Allahabad 1902

GHURYE, G.S., *Rajput Architecture*, Bombay 1968

GOETZ, H., *The Art and Architecture of Bikaner State*, London, 1950

– 'Indo-Islamic Figural Sculpture', *Ars Orientalis*, V (1963)

GOLLINGS, J., FRITZ, J.M. and MICHELL, G., *Vijayanagara: City of Victory, a South Indian Hindu Capital*, New York 1991

GOYAL, S., *Chittorgarh*, Udaipur 1983

HAMBLEY, G., *Cities of Mughal India*, London 1968

HAVELL, E.B., *Indian Architecture*, London 1927

HERAS, H., 'The City of Jinji at the End of the 16th Century', *Indian Antiquary*, 54 (1925)

HERDIG, K., *Formal Structure in Indian Architecture*, New York 1990

HESTON, M.B.C., 'The Palace Murals at Padmanabhapuram: the Politics of an Image', in *A Pot Pourri of Indian Art*, ed. P. Pal, Bombay 1988

ISSAR, J.P., *The Royal City: a Celebration of the Architectural Heritage and City Aesthetics of Mysore*, Bangalore 1991

JACOB, S.S., *The Jeypore Portfolio of Architectural Details*, London 1890–98

JAIN, J. and JAIN-NEUBAUER, J., eds., *Rajput Art and Architecture*, Wiesbaden 1966

JAIRAZBHOY, R.A., 'Early Fortifications and Encampments of the Mughals', *Islamic Culture*, XXXI (1957)

– 'Early Garden Palaces of the Great Mughals', *Oriental Art*, IV (1958)

JOSHI, M.C., *Dig*, Archaeological Survey of India, New Delhi 1982

– 'The Authorship of the Purana Qila and its Buildings', in *Indian Epigraphy: its Bearing on the History of Art*, ed. F.M. Asher and G.S. Gail, New Delhi 1985

KHAN, M.W.U., *Lahore and its Important Monuments*, Karachi 1961

KLINGELHOFER, W.G., 'The Jahangir Mahal of the Agra Fort: Expression and Experience in Early Mughal Architecture', *Muqarnas*, 5 (1988)

KOCH, E., *Shah Jahan and Orpheus: The Pietra Dura Decoration and the Programme of the Throne in the Hall of Public Audiences at the Red Fort of Delhi*, Graz 1988

– *Mughal Architecture: an Outline of its History and Development (1526–1858)*, Munich 1991

– 'Diwan-i Amm and Chehil Sutun: the audience halls of Shah Jahan', *Muqarnas*, 11 (1994, in press)

KRISHNA MURTHY, K., *Early Indian Secular Architecture*, Delhi 1987

LAL, B.B., 'Sisupalgarh 1948: an Early Historical Fort in Eastern India', *Ancient India*, 5 (1949)

LANCHESTER, H.V. and LODGE, T.A., 'The Maharajah's Palace, Jodhpur', *The Builder*, 178/1 (1950)

LATIF, S.M., *Lahore: its History, Architectural Remains and Antiquities*, Lahore 1892

LEHRMAN, J., *Earthly Paradise: Garden and Courtyard in Islam*, London 1980

LLEWELLYN-JONES, R., 'The City of Lucknow before 1856', in *The City in South Asia: Pre-Modern and Modern*, ed. K. Ballhatchet and J. Harrison, London 1980

LONGHURST, L., *Hampi Ruins Described and Illustrated*, Madras 1917

MATE, M.S., 'Daulatabad: Road to Islamic Archaeology in India', *World Archaeology*, XIV/3 (1983)

– and Pathy, T.V., eds., *Daulatabad: a Report*, Pune and Aurangabad 1991

MEHTA, R.N., 'Champaner: an Experiment in Medieval Archaeology', in *Madhu: Recent Research in Indian Archaeology and History*, ed. M.S. Nagaraja Rao, Delhi 1981

METCALF, T.R., *An Imperial Vision: Indian Architecture and Britain's Raj*, London 1989

MICHELL, G., ed., *Islamic Heritage of the Deccan*, Bombay 1986

– *The Vijayanagara Courtly Style: Incorporation and Synthesis in the Royal Architecture of Southern India, 15th–17th Centuries*, New Delhi 1991

– 'Courtly Architecture at Gingee under the Nayakas', *South Asian Studies*, 7 (1991)

– 'Royal Architecture and Imperial Style at Vijayanagara', in *The Powers of Art: Patronage in Indian Culture*, ed. B. Stoler Miller, New Delhi 1992

– and Eaton, R., *Firuzabad: Palace City of the Deccan*, Oxford Studies in Islamic Art, 8, Oxford 1992

– and Shah, S., eds., *Ahmadabad*, Bombay 1988

MOYNIHAN, E.B., *Paradise as a Garden in Persia and Mughal India*, New York 1979

– 'The Lotus Garden Palace of Zahir Al-Din Muhammad Babur', *Muqarnas*, 5 (1988)

MUHAMMAD, K.K., 'Hammams (Baths) in Medieval India', *Islamic Culture*, LXII/4 (1988)

– 'Bazars in Mughal India: an Essay in Architectural Study and Interpretation', *Islamic Culture*, LXIII/3 (1989)

– 'Excavation of a Catholic Church at Fatehpur Sikri', *Indica*, 28/1 (1991)

NAGARAJA RAO, M.S., *The Mysore Palace: a Visitor's Guide*, Mysore 1989

NATH, R., *Agra and Its Monumental Glory*, Bombay 1977

– *The Art of Chanderi*, Delhi 1979

– *History of Mughal Architecture*, Delhi 1985

– *History of Sultanate Architecture*, Delhi 1987

– *Colour Decoration in Mughal Architecture*, 2nd edn Jaipur 1989

NICHOLSON, L., *The Red Fort, Delhi*, London 1989

NILSSON, S., *European Architecture in India 1750–1850*, London 1968

– *Jaipur: In the Sign of Leo*, Lund 1987

PAGE, J.A., *A Guide to the Buildings and Gardens, Delhi Fort*, Delhi 1937

PATIL, C.S., 'Palace Architecture at Vijayanagara', in *Vijayanagara, Progress of Research 1983–84*, ed. M. S. Nagaraja Rao, Mysore 1985

PATIL, D.R., *Mandu*, Archaeological Survey of India, New Delhi 1972

PETRUCCIOLI, A., *La città del sole e delle acque: Fathpur Sikri*, Rome 1988

PICA, A., 'Eckart Muthesius in India 1930–34', *Domus*, 593 (April 1979)

PIEPER, J., 'Hyderabad: a Quranic Paradise in Architectural Metaphors', *Environmental Design* (1983)

– 'Hanging Gardens in the Princely Capitals of Rajasthan and in Renaissance Italy', *Marg*, XXXIX/1 (1987)

PIGGOTT, S., *Some Ancient Cities of India*, Oxford 1945

QAISAR, A.J., *Building Construction in Mughal India*, Delhi 1988

RANI, A., *Tuqhluq Architecture of Delhi*, Varanasi 1991

REUTHER, O., *Indische Paläste und Wohnhäuser*, Berlin 1925

RIZVI, S.A.A., *Fatehpur Sikri*, Archaeological Survey of India, New Delhi 1972

– and Flynn, V.J., *Fathpur-Sikri*, Bombay 1975

ROTZER, K., 'Bijapur: alimentation en eau d'une ville musulmane du Dekkan aux XIVe-XVIIe siècles', *Bulletin de l'Ecole Française d'Extrême-Orient*, LXXIII (1984)

ROY, A.K., *History of the Jaipur City*, New Delhi 1978

SANDERSON, G., 'Shah Jahan's Fort, Delhi', *Annual Report of the Archaeological Survey of India, 1911–12*, Calcutta 1915

– *A Guide to the Buildings and Gardens, Delhi Fort*, 4th edn, Delhi 1937

SANWAL, B.D., *Agra and its Monuments*, New Delhi 1968

SCHOTTEN MERKLINGER, E., *Indian Islamic Architecture: the Deccan 1347–1686*, Warminster, Wilts. 1981

SHARMA, Y.S., *Delhi and its Neighbourhood*, Archaeological Survey of India, New Delhi 1974

SHERWANI, H.K., 'Golconda', *Encyclopedia of Islam*, Leiden

SHOKOOHY, M. and SHOKOOHY N.H., *Hisar-i Firuza: Sultanate and Early Mughal Architecture in the District of Hisar, India*, London 1988

SHOREY, S.P., coordinator, *Conservation of Historical Buildings and Areas in Hyderabad City*, Hyderabad Development Authority 1984

SHUKLA, D.N., *Vastu Shastra*, Chandigarh 1960

SIDDIQI, W.H., *Fatehpur Sikri*, Archaeological Survey of India, New Delhi 1972

SINGH, A.P., *Defensive Art of India (with special reference to Bundelkhand)*, Delhi 1990

– and Singh, S.P., *Monuments of Orchha*, Delhi 1991

SINHA, B.P. and NAIN, L., *Patilaputra Excavation 1955–56*, Patna 1970

SKELTON, R., et al., *Facets of Indian Art: A Symposium held at the Victoria and Albert Museum . . .*, London 1986

SLESIN, S. and CLIFF, S., *Indian Style*, London 1990

SMITH, E.W., *The Moghul Architecture of Fatehpur Sikri*, repr. Delhi and Varanasi 1973

– *Moghul Colour Decoration of Agra*, Allahabad 1901

SOUNDARA RAJAN, K.V., *Islam Builds in India*, New Delhi 1983

SPEAR, T.G.P., *Delhi: its Monuments and History*, Oxford 1943

STAMP, G., 'Splendour at Jodhpur: the Jazz Age Palace of Maharaja Sir Umaid Singh', *Architectural Digest*, Jan.–Feb. 1980

TADGELL, C., *The History of Architecture in India*, London 1990

TILLOTSON, G.H.R., *The Rajput Palaces*, New Haven, Conn. and London 1987

– *The Tradition of Indian Architecture: Continuity, Controversy and Change since 1850*, New Haven, Conn. and London 1989

– *Architectural Guides for Travellers: Mughal India*, London 1990

TOY, S., *Strongholds of India*, London 1957

– *The Fortified Cities of India*, London 1965

VASUDEVA SASTRI, K., ed., *Visvakarma Vastusastram*, Tanjore 1958

VILLIERS-STUART, C.M., *Gardens of the Great Mughals*, London 1913

– 'Indian Water Gardens', *Journal of the Royal Society of Arts*, LXII (Apr. 1914)

VOLWAHSEN, A., *Living Architecture: Islamic Indian*, London 1970

WADDINGTON, H., 'Adilabad: a Part of the "Fourth" Delhi', *Ancient India*, I (1946)

WELSH, A. and CRANE, H., 'The Tughluqs: Master Builders of the Delhi Sultanate', *Muqarnas*, I (1983)

WESCOAT, J.L., 'Early Water Systems in Mughal India', *Environmental Design*, 2 (1985)

WHEELER, M., ed., *Splendours of the East: Temples, Tombs, Palaces and Fortresses of Asia*, London 1965

YAMAMOTO, T., ARA, M. and TSUKINOW, T., *Delhi: Architectural Remains of the Delhi Sultanate Period* (Japanese text), Tokyo 1967

YAZDANI, G., *Mandu: The City of Joy*, Oxford 1929

– *Bidar: its History and Monuments*, Oxford 1947

Index

Page numbers in *italic* refer to illustrations.

Acknowledgments for illustrations

All the colour plates and black-and-white photographs are by Antonio Martinelli, with two exceptions: plates 158 and 163, which are due to Riccardo Lazzeri. For the historical illustrations, acknowledgment is gratefully made to the Bodleian Library, University of Oxford, MS Ouseley Add. 173, No. 13 (p. 35); the British Library (India Office Library and Records), London (p. 6); by Courtesy of the Board of Trustees of the Victoria and Albert Museum, London (pp. 53, 160); Private Collection, Courtesy of the Arthur M. Sackler Museum, Harvard University Art Museums, Cambridge, Mass. (p. 59). The aquatints by Thomas and William Daniell are from their *Oriental Scenery*, I, London 1795 (p. 82) and II, London 1797 (p. 189). In preparing the line drawings, the following works were consulted: B. L. Dharma, *A Guide to the Jaipur Astronomical Observatory*, Jaipur 1974 (p. 164); R. Goghari, *The Role of Unbuilt Spaces in Clustered Organizations: A Study of Indian Palace Complexes*, Diploma Dissertation, School of Architecture, Ahmadabad, 1989 (p. 159); E. Koch, *Mughal Architecture*, Munich 1991 (p. 116); G. Michell, 'Courtly Architecture at Gingee Under the Nayakas', *South Asian Studies*, 7, 1991, (p. 188); G. Michell, *The Vijayanagara Courtly Style*, Delhi 1992 (p. 186); A. Petruccioli, *La città del sole e delle acque: Fathpur Sikri*, Rome 1988 (p. 119); O. Reuther, *Indische Paläste und Wohnhäuser*, Berlin 1925 (pp. 55, 68, 69, 86, 114–16, 154, 156, 157, 161, 163, 166, 188, 189); R. Rewal et al., eds., *Architecture in India*, Paris 1985 (pp. 83, 155); G. Yazdani, *Ajanta*, Oxford 1930 (p. 69); G. Yazdani, *Bidar*, Oxford 1947 (p. 85). Particular thanks are due to Ebba Koch and Attilio Petruccioli. Four of the plans were specially drawn by Graham Reed (pp. 12, 84, 167, 190).